CONCERNING HANDEL

GEORGE FREDERICK HANDEL.

ENGRAVING BY J. G. WOLFFGANG AFTER THE
PAINTING BY G. A. WOLFFGANG, c. 1737-9

From a copy in the possession of Wm. C. Smith

CONCERNING HANDEL

HIS LIFE AND WORKS

Essays by

WILLIAM C. SMITH

Hon. Freeman of the Worshipful Company of Musicians
Handel Medallist, Halle

WITH 15 HALF-TONE PLATES

CASSELL

AND COMPANY LTD.

LONDON, TORONTO, MELBOURNE

SYDNEY, WELLINGTON

First Published 1948

PRINTED IN GREAT BRITAIN
BY EBENEZER BAYLIS AND SON, LTD., THE
TRINITY PRESS, WORCESTER, AND LONDON
F.748

To my Wife

To my Wife

FOREWORD

To love the music of Handel so often provokes an interest in the man who composed it. An inquiring interest. Therefore one wishes to know something about this figure of genius—his method of work, his habits, his association with so many people of his time, both worthy and unworthy. This desire on the part of many has already been supplied by the several lives of the Master which have appeared.

But the author of this book has gone further. The biographer, in dealing with Handel's extensive life, finds it impossible to go into all the by-ways of that life. The author of this book has done so. He has given much which the biographers have not included. By his erudition he has discovered facts which the biographers did not know.

The author, in his ardour as a Handelian, a collector of Handeliana, as occupant of the post of Assistant Keeper of Printed Books in the British Museum for so many years, has delved deeper than many biographers into certain matters that concern Handel. His chapter on Handel's finances is the most complete summary of the subject. It could be presented only by infinite and long-time research. I doubt if the years in their passing can correct it at all. Again, his information on Handel's publishers—that jig-saw puzzle to Handel's biographers—he has spent years in sorting out. And he has sorted it out. His new letters of Handel, his chapter on the first editions of *Messiah*—these are all matters of first importance in searching into the inner life of Handel.

As a Handelian, I say that this book is most necessary to those who would study the measure of this man. Its erudition is brilliant. Its recordings must remain as an advance in our knowledge of Handel. Step by step we grow the closer to him as new discoveries are made. A finer shaping comes to the great figure; a greater humanism as every new fact is revealed.

This is not a book for Handelians alone. It is for those who, appreciating the music of Handel, wish to know something "behind the scenes" about him and his ventures.

To them all I commend it.

NEWMAN FLOWER.

CONTENTS

ILLUSTRATIONS

PREFACE

ALTHOUGH some of the essays included in this volume have appeared previously in musical periodicals, by far the greater part of the material has not been published before, and is not available elsewhere. This should be sufficient reason, if such is necessary, for another book on Handel. Three of the essays are entirely new, one is a very much enlarged edition of an earlier version, and the remaining four that have appeared elsewhere are presented here revised in accordance with the most recent research on the subjects.

The collection deals with various aspects of Handel's life, and raises a number of questions about his works and the period in which he lived that have not been dealt with in the existing biographies and other publications about the composer and his time.

The author's thanks and appreciation are due to the Editors of *Musical Opinion*, *The Musical Times* and *The Musical Quarterly* (G. Schirmer, Inc.) for permission to reprint and use articles previously appearing in those journals:—Nos. 1 and 6, in *Musical Opinion*, April, 1939; Dec., 1937-April, 1938; Nos. 3 and 5, in *The Musical Times*, Nov., 1925; Dec., 1941; July, 1936; No. 8 in *The Musical Quarterly*, Jan., 1939. Acknowledgments are also due to the authorities of the National Portrait Gallery for permission to use the F. Kyte and Van der Myn portraits; to the authorities of the British Museum for the drawing of Cuzzoni and the Schmidt portrait; to the Royal Musical Association for the extracts from the Thomas Coke papers; to His Grace the Duke of Devonshire and Francis Thompson his librarian for a transcription of and permission to include the Handel letter of 1719; to Gerald Coke for the use of the South Sea Stock document; to E. Croft-Murray for the Heidegger miniature; to C. T. Taphouse for the Waltz portrait; and to W. Harding for details of a manuscript of *Messiah* with a Handel address on the fly-leaf.

I

HANDEL THE MAN

HANDEL
THE
MAN

Written at the request of the Deutsch-Englischer Kul-
turaustausch of Halle, for publication in a Halle news-
paper DIE HALLISCHEN NACHRICHTEN *in connection*
with the Handel Birthday Celebrations in that city on
February 23, 1939.

HANDEL is appreciated to-day as a great composer more widely than ever before, thanks to the work of musicians and scholars in Germany and elsewhere. Although many of his works are still comparatively unknown or too rarely performed, there is little to be added to the existing knowledge of the outstanding qualities of his musical genius.

In his compositions he gave the truest portrait of himself. Some of his biographers, however, have drawn too freely on their imaginations in endeavouring to fill in the story of his life, and have presented inaccurate pictures of Handel, the man. In attempting to outline the main features of Handel's character, as they appear in the authenticated records of the composer's life, the present writer is aware of the fact that many of the less acceptable stories about the master can only be questioned and not emphatically contradicted.

A study of Handel's work in conjunction with an examination of the most reliable literary and historical material of the time leaves no doubt about the character of the man whose memory we are honouring to-day. If we do not exaggerate the few incidents in his life that seem to present his personal weak-

3

nesses, there rises up before us a figure, strong, calm, sure of himself, adventurous, heroic, and at the same time human and very lovable.

The first thing about him was the absence of pettiness. He was big in every way—in thought, purpose, fulfilment and in his heart. So far as we know, he never did anything mean. Although he accepted the patronage of royalty and nobility, he never bartered away his soul, or sacrificed his principles for profit or place. He has been presented as a rather difficult and irascible person, hard to get on with, impatient and tempestuous; yet his singers, as a rule, remained with him season after season, and his friends were usually his friends for ever.

Handel must have possessed qualities that made his greatness of personality obvious. The circles of literary, artistic, and social eminence in which he moved, were not accidental; they were those that expressed the greater minds of the day and that appreciated genius in others. Although the eighteenth century in London was a rather vicious age, there is no evidence that Handel, who lived and worked in a gay and artistic circle, ever indulged in vice or behaved even as loosely as the general manners of the time allowed. Attempts have been made to suggest that here and there some woman or another claimed his affections, but nothing has been discovered to prove that he ever gave his heart away. We do get glimpses, however, of loyal friendships with members of the opposite sex; but like many another great artist, nothing could come permanently between him and the purpose of his life.

Without doubt, Handel could show temper and anger; but genius must find it difficult at times to submit to stupidity, pride or ignorance. Living, as the composer did, in London society for nearly half a century, it is surprising that so little to his discredit, true or false, can be recorded against him. The popular story of his voracious appetite and coarse feeding has little to support it other than a fanciful report by Burney, the Goupy caricature, and later versions of it; the reasons for which may have been purely personal. If Handel had been a very gross liver, it is somewhat unlikely that he would have reached the age that he did, when the average length of life was so much shorter.

4

He is sometimes pictured as a bad business man—erratic, foolish and simple in dealing with his publishers, careless and slack in manner and method. There is little to justify this opinion. He would not have continued publishing through Walsh, father and son, as long as he did if he had not been satisfied with the association. When he died he left his manuscripts—autographs and copies—almost intact and in good order. If he did not preserve and arrange them himself, he was sensible enough to employ the right person to do so, a business which was simplified, no doubt, by his occupation of the same house for nearly forty years.

Fortunate in the receipt of considerable royal pensions, he could treat with comparative unconcern some of his failures, that would have otherwise embarrassed him, and perhaps spoiled and cheapened his work.

The picture of Handel as poor, bankrupt and alone, appears to be largely imaginary. He did not always succeed with his public, and at times found almost insurmountable difficulties in front of him. When a promised season of performances was failing because of lack of support, he offered the subscribers their money back; but at a word of encouragement from a few friends he determined to struggle on and if possible achieve success. Handel's letters to the London press of the year 1745 (see Chapter V) reveal the spirit of this truly great man.

Handel must have had an inner peace and calm that made his work what it was and his life as we know it to have been—solicitous for others, kind, thoughtful and generous. His association with, and the assistance he gave to, the Foundling Hospital and the Society of Musicians are two notable examples of his practical sympathy with suffering and distress. But there was something more than charity in the character of the man. While discounting the popular stories of his evangelical faith, and accepting his sacred oratorios as artistic rather than religious expressions, we can still say without any doubt that his life was truly religious, and the essence of his religion was to do good.

It would be out of place to attempt comparison between Handel and other great composers, but without question he is one of that select company of master musicians of all times and peoples who have contributed most to the development and

B

enjoyment of music, the oldest of the arts, and to the universal spirit of friendship which it engenders.

As an Englishman, I am proud and very pleased to be allowed to contribute this inadequate attempt at a portrait of one of Germany's greatest sons, who became an honoured British subject. It is to the lasting credit of the two nations that the country of his birth and the country of his adoption find in his work and life a bond of mutual friendship.

II
FINANCE AND PATRONAGE
IN HANDEL'S LIFE

FINANCE
AND
PATRONAGE
IN
HANDEL'S
LIFE

Handel is reputed to have left a fortune of £20,000 apart from personal effects. This is no small amount for anyone to accumulate, especially a musician about whom there are popular stories of failure, poverty, and distress, who is supposed to have been bankrupt twice, who had several periods of serious illness which incapacitated him from active work and brought him to a state of acute mental weakness, and who was never a place-seeker or parasite.

How did the composer live and make his money? What are the ascertainable facts behind the dramatic tale of the ups and downs of his public and private life? What was the secret of his long and active career, with its sure mastery of circumstances, and power of self-expression through the medium of his great gifts in spite of any temporary material difficulties or varying fortunes? Was he a business man as well as a great artist? What part did patronage play in placing him in a position of comparative security? What do we know of the financial conditions in the theatrical and musical world in which he lived?

9

In endeavouring to answer these, and some other incidental questions, it cannot be pretended that we have sufficient authoritative documentary evidence to present more than an imperfect account. But the record should serve as one more contribution towards understanding and justly estimating the life and character of the composer as seen against the background of his own day.

Handel did not start life with either of the handicaps of extreme poverty or of great wealth. His home and family circumstances were those of comfort, not luxury, and there was enough financial security to enable his parents to contemplate a professional career for him either in law or music, but not sufficient to encourage him to be a dilettante or an idler. His father, a barber surgeon and valet-de-chambre to Duke Augustus of Saxony and afterwards to his son Duke Johann Adolf of Saxe-Weissenfels, moved among people of wealth and influence, and the young Handel may have benefited in after life by introductions to helpful patrons which came to him from acquaintances of his father.

It may be as well to point out here, that the most valuable and original contribution to the study of Handel's early life was published at Halle, in 1935. It is entitled *Georg Friedrich Händel. Abstammung und Jugendwelt. Festschrift zur 250. Wiederkehr des Geburtstages Georg Friedrich Händels*, etc. This work deals exhaustively with the composer's family and its origins, his home life, the circle in which his parents lived, his education, musical training and associations, the musicians he came in contact with, the organs he played, etc. In spite however of all the local research that has gone to the making of the book, it still leaves unanswered some questions of interest, and gives little evidence for or against some of the popular anecdotes of the composer's youth as recorded in Mainwaring and elsewhere, although it provides a historical background against which they can be reassessed.

It is generally stated that Handel and his father differed as to the choice of a career, but that in the end a compromise was arrived at by which the composer agreed to continue his legal studies, while exercising at the same time his taste for music. From the existing records, including the work mentioned above, there seems little evidence that Handel ever studied seriously for the law, and if he did in answer to his father's wish, the impelling urge of his genius soon made him decide on a musical career. Without pressing the assumption too far, it can be suggested that if he did have any legal training, it may have helped him in later years in his business dealings which, in the opinion of the present writer and contrary to some popular ideas, show the composer to have been orderly, shrewd, and practical.

The foundation authority for many popular statements about Handel is Mainwaring's *Memoirs of the life of the late George Frederic Handel,* published anonymously in 1760. From the prefatory note to *Anecdotes of George Frederick Handel and John Christopher Smith* by W. Coxe, published anonymously in 1799, we learn that Mainwaring's work was "written under the inspection of Mr. Smith", that is John Christopher Smith the younger, Handel's amanuensis. In spite of that claim, however, and although the work gives us in main outline the facts of Handel's life, many of Mainwaring's statements are without corroboration from contemporary sources, and others are quite obviously inaccurate or fantastic. As later writers have selected or rejected passages from Mainwaring as it suited their purpose, very often an appearance of authenticity has been given to statements open to question, and, as will be seen later on, in some instances a passage in the original has been misquoted or misinterpreted when Mainwaring was right.

The English edition of the *Memoirs* is well-known and it is a pity that the German edition published in 1761 is not consulted more often. It was by Johann Mattheson, contemporary and friend of Handel, and is entitled *Georg Friderich Händels Lebensbeschreibung,* etc. Valuable critical notes were supplied by Mattheson, who prefaced his translation with the following quotation in English:

> Panegyricks are frequently ridiculous,
> let them be addressed where they will.
> *Tatler,* No. 92.

We shall have occasion to return to Mattheson later, when dealing with extracts from his well-known biographical dictionary *Grundlage einer Ehren-Pforte,* published in 1740, which contains most important material on Handel that must be read in conjunction with Mainwaring's biography and Mattheson's translation of it.

One of the most picturesque anecdotes told by Mainwaring is the story of how Handel, by running after the coach, forced himself upon the company of his father when the latter set out to visit a half-brother of George Frederick at the Court of the Duke of Saxe-Weissenfels, some twenty-five miles from Halle; and how at the Court the Duke urged upon the parent the need for letting young Handel follow his inclinations and become a musician. Mainwaring adds that: "At his departure from Weisenfels the Prince fill'd his [Handel's] pockets with money, and told him, with a smile, that if he minded his studies, no encouragements should be wanting."

The relative at the Court of Saxe-Weissenfels was not Handel's half-brother, but Georg Christian, a son of Handel's half-brother Karl.

This story is usually placed at the period when Handel was seven years old or a few years later. The expression "fill'd his pockets with money" may have meant at most some trifling gift—the first recorded encouragement to Handel, if he needed it, that music had some value in the world, and that there were people who were prepared to encourage it. The significance of the visit, if it took place as recorded, was that Handel's father was persuaded by the Duke to consent to engage a music-master for his son, and that on his return to Halle young Handel was placed under Friedrich Wilhelm Zachow, organist of the Liebfrauenkirche (Marienkirche) for his musical education, while at the same time he continued his general studies.

It is not intended to present here another chronological outline of Handel's life, but only to deal with those events that impinge on the subject in hand. As a contribution to a right assessment of the whole incident of the Weissenfels visit it must be pointed out that the latest researches (*G. F. Händel, Abstammung und Jugendwelt*; *Georg Friedrich Händel*, Müller-Blattau) show that Handel's father had a number of musical friends in his circle, that there is no evidence that he actually opposed his son's wishes, and that after the death of Duke Augustus of Saxony in 1680, his son Duke Johann Adolf held his court at

Weissenfels to which the elder Handel was a regular visitor as surgeon and valet-de-chambre.

For some three or four years from about 1692 Handel studied under Zachow, and at times deputized for him, while also learning the harpsichord, violin and possibly the oboe. His musical education in addition to his general schooling must have cost his parents something, even if not a great deal, and the strain on the family resources must have been increased when the composer's father died in February, 1697. However, Handel continued his general education and eventually entered Halle University in 1702.

Mainwaring says, that after three or four years with Zachow, Handel "was impatient for another situation. . . . After some consultations, Berlin was the place agreed on. He had a friend and relation at that court, on whose care and kindness his parents could rely. It was in the year 1698 that he went to Berlin. The Opera there was in a flourishing condition under the direction of the King of Prussia." At that time, however, it was the Elector of Brandenburg, afterwards Frederick I of Prussia, and his wife the Electress Sophia Charlotte, who ruled over a court where the arts were freely encouraged. Mainwaring tells us how Handel met Attilio (Ariosti) and (G.B.) Bononcini at Berlin, the former welcoming and encouraging the young musician, while the latter treated him with "distance and reserve". Continuing, Mainwaring says: "Thus much is certain, that the little stranger had not been long at court before his abilities became known to the King, who frequently sent for him, and made him large presents. Indeed his Majesty, convinc'd of his singular endowments, and unwilling to lose the opportunity of patronizing so rare a genius, had conceived a design of cultivating it at his own expence. His intention was to send him to Italy, where he might be formed under the best masters, and have opportunities of hearing and seeing all that was excellent in the kind. As soon as it was intimated to Handel's friends (for he was yet too young to determine for himself) they deliberated what answer it would be proper to return, in case this scheme should be proposed in form. It was the opinion of many that his fortune was already made, and that his relations would certainly embrace such an offer with the utmost alacrity. Others, who better understood the temper

13

and spirit of the court at Berlin, thought this a matter of nice speculation, and cautious debate. For they well knew, that if he once engag'd in the King's service, he must remain in it, whether he liked it, or not; that if he continued to please, it would be a reason for not parting with him; and that if he happened to displease, his ruin would be the certain consequence. To accept an offer of this nature, was the same thing as to enter into a formal engagement, but how to refuse it was still the difficulty. At length it was resolved that some excuse must be found. It was not long before the King caused his intentions to be signified, and the answer was, that the Doctor would always retain the profoundest sense of the honour done to him by the notice which his Majesty had been graciously pleased to take of his son; but as he himself was now grown old and could not expect to have him long with him, he humbly hoped the King would forgive his desire to decline the offer which had been made him by order of his Majesty.

"I am not able to inform the reader how this answer was relished by the King, whom we may suppose not much accustomed to refusals, especially of this sort. Such an incident made it improper for Handel to stay much longer at the court of Berlin, where the more his abilities should be known and commended, the more some persons would be apt to sift and scrutinize the motives of his father's conduct.

"Many and great were the compliments and civilities which he received on his leaving Berlin."

This pretty little story, as given by Mainwaring, is very much to be questioned when it is remembered that if the visit took place before Handel's father's death it must have been before February, 1697, and before the Elector became King of Prussia; moreover there is no reason for thinking that Ariosti was in Berlin before the spring of 1697 or that Bononcini was there before 1702. While it is not improbable that Handel may have visited Berlin in 1702–3, as Percy Robinson and others have suggested, when the Elector had become King of Prussia and the composer could have met Ariosti and Bononcini, there is no historical evidence elsewhere of such a visit. In questioning the accuracy of Mainwaring's statement in general we are compelled to query the gift of "large presents" to the composer and the offers of the King's patronage. If the account of Mainwaring is, however, substantially true except for date, it was a good thing for the musical life of England in the eighteenth century that Handel did not agree to remain permanently attached to the Prussian court.

The first recorded paid professional engagement of Handel was as Organist of the Domkirche (Cathedral) Halle; an appointment he took up on March 13, 1702, in succession to Johann Christoph Leporin. The congregation was of the Reformed (Calvinist) Faith, but that did not prevent the appointment being given to Handel, a Lutheran. The salary was fifty thalers a year, and a free lodging in the Moritzburg which was sublet for sixteen thalers a year, Handel not requiring the official residence as he was living with his mother. The total income from salary and rent has been estimated to have been about £10.

Handel had something else to do besides play the organ on Sundays, festivals and other occasions. He had to see that the instrument was kept in proper repair, and had to provide cantatas, psalm tunes, etc. for performance at the services. Handel held the appointment only for the probationary period of one year. During that time, occupied as he was in addition as a student at the University, he could have had little opportunity for making money in other ways, so he must have been largely dependent on his mother, who may have been living on capital she had acquired from the sale of her late husband's business. This year's experience as organist and composer, coupled with the limitations of the family income, probably convinced Handel that the time had come for him to leave Halle and seek wider and more profitable fields of opportunity for developing his gifts, in order to support himself and to assist his mother. Throughout his life the composer showed his spirit, independence and generosity, and his first step out into the world from his own home and associations, as a young man of eighteen, was an expression of the character and purpose which were so unfailingly exemplified during the whole of his career.

Curiously enough, the well-authenticated appointment as organist at the Domkirche is entirely omitted by Mainwaring, although this important incident in the composer's early life could hardly have been overlooked by Handel if he ever recounted to J. C. Smith or others the biographical details on which Mainwaring and Coxe are said to have written their works.

Having been entered as a student at Halle University, in February, 1702, and continuing his studies concurrently with his appointment as organist for a year, the composer left Halle for Hamburg in the spring of 1703.

Mainwaring tells us that Handel's "thoughts ran much on a journey" to Italy. "But this project required a longer purse than he was as yet provided with, and was therefore suspended till such time as it could be compassed without hazard or inconvenience. In the mean while, as his fortune was to depend on his skill in his profession, it was necessary to consider of some place less distant, where he might employ his time to advantage, and be still improving in knowledge and experience. Next to the Opera of Berlin, that of Hamburgh was in the highest request. It was resolved to send him thither on his own bottom, and chiefly with a view to improvement. It was a wise resolution not to engage him too early with a view to profit. How many parents have murdered the fine talents of their children by weakly sacrificing that liberty and independency, which are essential to their exertion!"

Mainwaring here suggests that Handel went to Hamburg at the instigation of, and supported by, his parents, but from the evidence already given above, it is more reasonable to suppose that he went on his own initiative, although not necessarily without friendly introductions from the Halle circle. The fact remains, that he went to Hamburg for employment, and, apart from the experience that he gained there, the step was one of the most significant of his career, as it introduced him to Johann Mattheson and an important set of influential and professional people.

Mainwaring says, that "his father's death happened not long after his return from Berlin. This event produced a considerable change for the worse in the income of his mother. That he might not add to her expences, the first thing which he did on his arrival at Hamburgh, was to procure scholars, and obtain some employment in the orchestra. Such was his

16

industry and success in setting out, that the first remittance which his mother sent him he generously returned her, accompanied with a small present of his own."

Where did this story come from? Hardly from Handel himself. It was not in the nature of the man to mention his own generosity.

Speaking of the opera at Hamburg, Mainwaring says: "The principal singers were Conratini and Mathyson. The latter was Secretary to Sir Cyril Wych, who was resident for the English court, had Handel for his music-master, and was himself a fine player on the harpsichord."

Before dealing further with Mattheson and his relations with Handel, it is worth while endeavouring to clear up once for all the confusion that has arisen from Mainwaring's statement about Sir Cyril Wych. Rockstro, Flower, Dent (*Handel. Great Lives*), Abdy Williams and others are wrong in their allusions to the person concerned, while Mattheson (*Ehren-Pforte* 1740; *Lebensbeschreibung*, 1761), Chrysander, Percy Robinson, Streatfeild and Dent (*Händel in England*) are correct in stating that John Wych (Wich) was the English resident to whom Mattheson first became secretary, and that his son Cyril, afterwards Sir Cyril Wyche, Bt., was the one who had Handel and afterwards Mattheson for his music-teacher, and for whom Mattheson also acted in an official capacity.

The correct details of the family as obtained from trustworthy English sources are as follows. John Wyche was the son of Sir Peter Wyche, formerly envoy at the Court of Muscovy and Resident at Hamburg. John became Her Majesty's Resident at Hamburg about 1702 and held the appointment until his death in 1713, a few years before which date the office had been extended to include "the Courts of Holstein and Mecklenburgh and the Hans-Towns".

Cyril Wyche, the son of John, succeeded his father, probably in 1714, and he was described as "Resident" or "Envoy Extraordinary to the Hans Towns of Lubeck, Bremen and Hamburg". In 1729 he was created a baronet, and held the appointment at Hamburg until as late as 1743, afterwards becoming "Envoy Extraordinary to the Court of Russia", and died in 1756, when the baronetcy became extinct. Sir Cyril married Anne, daughter of Magnus von Wedderkopp, first minister to

the Duke of Holstein; and it is interesting to note that Wedderkopp was the person who, as Mattheson tells us, invited him to
Lübeck in 1703 as applicant for the post of organist in succession
to Dieterich Buxtehude, and that Mattheson took Handel with
him as a fellow-competitor. (*Ehren-Pforte.*)

It is obvious that the Wyche (Wych) (Wich) family with its
official court appointments as far back as the early half of the
seventeenth century, and its long-standing associations with
Hamburg and other parts of the Continent, must have had
considerable social influence. Professor Dent in his illuminating
sketch *Händel in England* (Halle, 1936) says that Wyche was
related to the Granville family, and the Granville's were most
loyal friends of Handel in England right up to the time of his
death. We shall have occasion later on to speak of the composer's association with Bernard and Mary Granville (Mrs.
Delany) and their circle. It is sufficient to add here that the
Wyches were also related by marriage to the Carterets and
other families of importance and social standing in England,
and although we have no actual details of Handel's introduction to that circle it can be assumed, with little doubt, that the
composer's acquaintance with John and Cyril Wyche in Hamburg must have been helpful to him in making contacts with
influential people in England.

It is interesting to note that Mattheson (*Ehren-Pforte*) tells us
that "My Lord Carteret" [i.e. John Carteret, afterwards Earl
Granville, Ambassador to Sweden, 1719, Lord Lieutenant of
Ireland, 1724] travelled to England in 1720 with his relative
"Herrn von Wich."

John Carteret's grandfather married a daughter of the Earl
of Sandwich, a relative of the Earl of Manchester who is
supposed to have met Handel in Venice.

Mattheson gives us the most reliable accounts of Handel's
association with the Wyche family, and there is no reason to
doubt the general accuracy of his statements, although at times
he is prejudiced and inaccurate, and occasionally contradicts
himself.

It is possible to give only a summary here of such details as
affect our subject. Mattheson says that Handel came to
Hamburg in the summer of 1703, "rich in ability and good
will," made early acquaintance with Mattheson, who took him

18

round to organs, choirs, concerts and operas, and introduced
him to a certain house which was devoted to music, this
obviously referring to the house of John Wyche. Handel also
frequently took his meals at Mattheson's father's house and
gave Mattheson help in counterpoint while the latter assisted
him in developing a "dramatic style", so "one hand washed
the other". Mattheson refers to Handel as having given lessons
to Cyril Wyche, but contrary to the generally accepted impression, dismisses the instruction as "a few trifling lessons
which were not very effectual".—"Der junge Herr Wich hatte
zwar vorher ein Paar sehr geringe Lectionen von Händel
genommen; sie wollten aber nicht anschlagen." (*Lebensbeschreibung.*) Mattheson who, in 1704, took over the general
instruction of Cyril Wyche, also undertook his musical education and, according to Mattheson, the young man acquired
great perfection from the tuition. In January, 1706, Mattheson
became secretary to John Wyche, and when the son, Cyril,
succeeded his father as Resident Minister, continued as
Secretary and acted at times as the Resident Minister when
Wyche was away on other duties.

It seems clearly established that Handel had some employment in the Opera Orchestra at Hamburg both as a violinist
and a harpsichord player, but the statements of Mattheson and
Mainwaring are at variance on the point. The latter writer
tells us about the quarrel that arose through Handel demand-
ing to play the "first harpsichord" in the orchestra, adding, "he
had played a violin in the orchestra, he had a good command
on this instrument, and was known to have a better on the
other" (i.e. harpsichord); and how Handel was appointed to
the first harpsichord, and soon afterwards "from conducting
the performance, he became Composer to the Opera". It is
unnecessary to detail here the whole story as given by
Mattheson. The significant points in his account are, that
Handel was nearly twenty years old, not as Mainwaring
indicates, about fourteen, that there never were two harpsi-
chords in the orchestra, and the dispute was as to whether
Handel should vacate his place at the harpsichord for
Mattheson to take over and conduct the remaining portion of
his opera *Cleopatra* after he had finished his part as a singer on
the stage. With regard to Handel's performances as a violinist,

in one place (*Ehren-Pforte*) Mattheson says, "Anfangs spielte er
die andre Violine im Opern-Orchester, und stellte sich als ob
er nicht auf fünfe zählen könnte," etc. Rockstro translates this
passage: "At first he played the second Violin in the Opera
Orchestra, and behaved as if he did not know how to count
five; for he was by nature, full of dry humour. But once, when
the Harpsichord-player was absent, he yielded to persuasion,
and supplied his place, acquitting himself like a man, though
no one but myself supposed him capable of doing so." Rockstro
also says that he was "admitted at once into the Opera
Orchestra in the capacity of *ripieno* second Violin".

In commenting on Mainwaring's reference to Handel's
violin-playing Mattheson (*Lebensbeschreibung*) gives a rather
fuller description which explains the different statements in
various later writers, some referring to "ripieno second violin"
and others simply to "second violinist": "Händel hat nur
anfänglich die andre oder zwote, doppeltbesetzte Violin im
Orchester gespielt, und war auf solchem Instrument, wie leicht
zu erachten, nicht stärker, als ein Ripienist."

Chrysander adds to this passage: "Er setzte sich so zu sagen
auf die unterste Bank."

It seems that "second ripieno violin" rightly describes
Handel's humble place in the orchestra.

In addition to his performances in the opera orchestra and
the composition and production of his own works, mentioned
later on, it is reasonable to accept the statements that Handel
had a number of pupils in Hamburg, and probably played at
concerts and elsewhere. Of these activities we have no details
nor any accounts of his earnings from these sources, although
Mattheson tells us (*Ehren-Pforte*) that he himself received from
three to six thalers (nine to eighteen shillings) a month for his
pupils, or as Chrysander points out, on the average half a
thaler a lesson.

Handel probably composed a number of works at Hamburg
that have been lost. The important ones of which we have
knowledge are the *St. John Passion* (1704); and the Operas
Almira (1705), *Nero* (1705), *Florindo und Daphne* (1706).

The *Passion* is presumed to have been performed in Passion
Week, 1704, but whether Handel was commissioned to write
it or was paid for it we do not know. *Almira*, produced on

January 8, 1705, was apparently a great success, and ran until February 25. Mainwaring and others have said for thirty nights, which is an exaggeration, some twenty performances or less being nearer the truth. This latter number must be considered as very satisfactory for an original production. In Handel's most successful years rarely did a new work run for more than thirteen or fourteen performances, although one must bear in mind the different conditions of opera production on the Continent and in London.

What part the composer had in the mounting and control of the work and the kind of payment he received is not known. It is certain, however, that the success of *Almira* must have greatly enhanced his reputation, and it can be assumed that it was financially advantageous to him.

His next opera, *Nero*, the music of which is lost but of which the libretto survives, was apparently a failure. Produced on February 25, 1705, it had only three performances at the most, and the production may have swallowed up what profits or payments Handel had received from *Almira*. If so, it would only be in keeping with the experience of the composer in after years in England.

Handel's third Hamburg opera, *Florindo und Daphne*, composed 1706, was produced as two separate works in 1708, after Handel had left Hamburg, so it may be assumed that he was commissioned to write the work, as Chrysander tells us, for Saurbrey the opera-manager, and was paid for it. The score is lost.

Mainwaring, after quite inaccurately dealing with the above-mentioned operas, says of the composer: "It never was his intention to settle at Hamburgh: he told the Manager, on his first application to him, that he came thither only as a traveller, and with a view to improvement: that till the Composer should be at liberty, or till some other successor or substitute could be found, he was willing to be employed, but was resolved to see more of the world before he entered into any engagements, which would confine him long to any particular place. The Manager left that matter for him and his friends to determine; but so long as he thought proper to be concerned in the Opera, he promised him advantages at least as great as any Composer that had gone before him."

This all seems too trite, and hardly fits in with the facts that after *Nero*, in 1705, Handel produced no opera in Hamburg, although he appears to have remained there until late in 1706. Presumably during this period he was busy with teaching and composing. (Mattheson, Mainwaring, Burney, etc.)

Mainwaring tells us that, "at the time that *Almeria* and *Florinda* were performed, there were many persons of note at Hamburgh, among whom was the Prince of Tuscany, brother to John Gaston de Medicis, Grand Duke", who discussed with Handel the merits of Italian music, and suggested that the composer should return with him to Florence, and "Handel without intending to accept of the favour designed him, expressed his sense of the honour done him. For he resolved to go to Italy on his own bottom, as soon as he could make a purse for that occasion."

This reported meeting of Handel with the Prince of Tuscany, which could not have taken place when *Florindo* was performed, has given rise to confusion, misquotation, and misstatement. First of all, it must be noted that Mainwaring says the "Prince of Tuscany, brother to John Gaston de Medicis, Grand Duke". Now the writer may have been wrong in his identification of the Prince, but he certainly did not say, as so many writers have done, that Handel met John Gaston de' Medici who invited the composer to Italy. It may help to clarify the position to state that Cosimo III, Grand Duke of Tuscany, had issue (a) Ferdinando, 1663–1713; (b) Anna Lodovica, *b.* 1667; (c) Giovanni Gastone (Giangastone) 1671–1737. Ferdinando, the Prince of Tuscany, to whom it appears Mainwaring was referring, never became Grand Duke as he predeceased his father. The latter died in 1723, and it was not till then that Giangastone (John Gaston) became Grand Duke, although he never took formal possession of the state or had a coronation. He would probably have been known historically to Mainwaring as "Grand Duke". Ferdinando and Giangastone were both patrons of the arts and either could, conceivably, have been interested in Handel as a musician. There appears to be no corroboration elsewhere of Mainwaring's account of Handel's meeting in Hamburg with either Ferdinando or Giangastone. How can it be explained that Giangastone has been so written up as the person in question. The present writer's suggestion is that the confusion has arisen first of all because Mattheson in *Lebensbeschreibung* ambiguously translates Mainwaring thus: "Prinz von Toskanien, Bruder des Grossherzogs von Florenz, Johann Gaston de Medicis", the last four words being given in heavier type. Secondly, it is known that Giangastone was in Hamburg in the winter of 1703–04 and, in consequence, an unjustified correction of Mainwaring has been made in keeping with the movements of this Prince, and to fit it with certain statements about Handel's subsequent Italian visit. Rockstro gives the same person as Mainwaring, but in the form "the Prince of Tuscany, brother to the Grand Duke Giovanni Gaston de' Medici". Amongst modern writers Streatfeild, usually so careful, can be largely credited with spreading the belief that it was Giangastone who made the acquaintance of Handel, and exercised an important influence upon his career. Streatfeild writes at length about the Prince, his culture, refinement, and deplorable morals.

Without accepting Streatfeild's identification in preference to Mainwaring's, we can agree with the former writer that Giangastone "never offered to pay Handel's expenses on a trip to Italy. Gian Gastone wanted all the money he could lay hands upon for himself, and never was a man in a worse position for playing Mæcenas to a promising young musician. He was always in debt. . . . But if Gian Gastone was not in a position to play the princely patron, he could promise Handel a warm and kindly reception at his father's court whenever he was able to make the journey south."

Of Handel's Italian visit we will speak later, but it may be pointed out here, that as Giangastone surrounded himself with a numerous band of young men and women of the most depraved tastes and practices, Handel was probably very lucky in not accompanying the Prince to Italy. From all we know of the composer, throughout the whole of his life there was never a suggestion of vice or even of what might have been considered in the world in which he lived, pardonable laxity.

The best authorities are agreed that Handel left Hamburg for Italy in the latter part of 1706, and we can only assume that he went of his own accord. Mattheson (*Ehren-Pforte*) says that "he remained four or five years at the opera and had

23

many scholars. He produced *Florindo* and *Daphne* in 1708, which did not come up to *Almira*. In 1709 he did nothing and after that took the opportunity of undertaking a free journey to Italy with von Binitz." The identity of this generous travelling companion has not been traced, and Chrysander does not accept Mattheson on this point. The latter is also wrong in dating Handel's journey to Italy 1709 or after.

Mainwaring's account says: "Four or five years had elapsed from the time of his coming to Hamburgh, to that of his leaving it. It has already been observed, that instead of being chargeable to his mother, he began to be serviceable to her before he was well settled in his new situation. Tho' he had continued to send her remittances from time to time, yet, clear of his own expences, he had made up of purse of 200 ducats. On the strength of this fund he resolved to set out for Italy."

Abdy Williams estimates that the 200 ducats were equal to about £96. Whatever the amount in Handel's purse—and the 200 may be just an approximate round figure—it is hardly likely that the composer from this time forward failed to maintain himself, either by direct earnings, or by pensions and patronage which were on account of services rendered and therefore justifiably acceptable. Throughout his subsequent career it appears, from the limited knowledge we have of some of his personal affairs, that Handel always had something in his pocket, and even if at times financial demands on him were heavy there is not the slightest evidence that he experienced periods of extreme and continued poverty.

The itinerary and circumstances of Handel's Italian tour have been the subject of much research and speculation, and it is only necessary to concern ourselves here with the questions of how far this very formative period in his life found him patrons and influential friends, and provided him with funds. It seems certain that he visited Florence, Rome, Venice and Naples, although the dates of arriving at and leaving these cities are uncertain, and the extent to which he moved about from one place to another, or lived in other cities, is unknown. This can be said without dispute, that in the prime of young manhood, with some reputation and enough experience to give him confidence, he found himself moving in the most magnificent and artistic circles of the time, many members of which were very wealthy, and those who were not lived as though they were. The arts were sumptuously supported and sustained by a society in which there was much profligacy and vice.

Mainwaring says: "We left him just on the point of his removal to Italy; where he arrived soon after the Prince of Tuscany. Florence, as it is natural to suppose, was his first destination; for he was too well known to his Highness to need any other recommendations at the court of the Grand Duke, to whose palace he had free access at all seasons, and whose kindness he experienced on all occasions. The fame of his abilities had raised the curiosity of the Duke and his court, and rendered them very impatient to have some performance of his composing. . . . At the age of eighteen he made the Opera of *Rodrigo*, for which he was presented with 100 sequins, and a service of plate. This may serve for a sufficient testimony of its favourable reception."

It will be noticed, that in this passage Mainwaring is consistent with his former reference to the Prince of Tuscany. According to Streatfeild, Giangastone, who was in Florence from June, 1705, to November, 1706, introduced Handel to Ferdinand, who was a great patron of musical performances in the private theatre at his famous villa at Pratolino, some few miles out of Florence.

All sorts of attempts have been made, without success, to fix definitely the date and place of the production of *Rodrigo*. Whether it was sponsored by Prince Ferdinand (the Prince of Tuscany) and produced at Pratolino, or as Mainwaring suggests for the Grand Duke (John Gaston de Medicis as he calls him previously) and his court, or for the reigning Grand Duke, Cosimo III, father of Ferdinando and Giangastone, or under what other circumstances or patrons, we do not know. It can only be assumed that the place was Florence or the district, and the time, probably the autumn of 1707 or 1708.

What about the present of "100 sequins and a service of plate" recorded by Mainwaring? In the same paragraph he is wrong about Handel's age, and is open to question in his reference to a singer, Vittoria, and her affection for Handel.

Why should we accept the story of the present. According to Puliti's *Cenni storici della vita del serenissimo Ferdinando dei Medici*, Prince Ferdinand gave Handel a hundred sequins, together with a porcelain service, in return for his Opera, although Puliti knows nothing of the details of its production.

A service, or dinner-service as it is described by some later writers, either in silver or porcelain, was surely a strange gift to a young man of twenty-two or so, who had no establishment of his own, at least, so it can be presumed, and who was likely to be moving about. However, there the statement is for what it is worth. Probably the Medici family would have had less difficulty in finding a service or two they could dispense with than the 100 sequins, estimated to be about £50. (Abdy Williams.) We shall have occasion to refer to another similar gift later on. At any rate *Rodrigo* must have put something into Handel's pocket as well as increasing his reputation.

In addition to his association with members of the Medici family during his Italian tour, Handel met and received the support and patronage of a number of other famous wealthy, artistic and influential people. Fuller details can be read elsewhere; it is only necessary to refer briefly here to some of the generally accepted statements.

In Rome.—Cardinal Ottoboni, great-nephew of Pope Alexander VIII; Cardinal Benedetto Pamfili who provided the text of the cantatas *Il Trionfo del Tempo e del Disinganno*, *Apollo e Dafne*, etc.; and Prince Ruspoli at whose palace Handel stayed in March and April, 1708. (Flower.)

In Venice.—Prince Ernest Augustus of Hanover (youngest brother of the Elector of Hanover, afterwards George I of England), who is reported to have asked Handel to pay a visit to Hanover when he left Italy; Charles 4th Earl (afterwards 1st Duke) of Manchester, Ambassador to the Republic of Venice, a keen patron of music and of the Italian opera in particular, who helped Vanbrugh to obtain singers for the Opera House in the Haymarket, and who is supposed to have invited Handel to London; Baron Kielmansegg, the Elector of Hanover's Master of the Horse, who is said to have made friends with Handel and supported Steffani's suggestion that Handel should succeed Steffani as Kapellmeister at the Court of the Elector, and who may have taken Handel to Hanover when he left Italy.

In Naples.—Cardinal Vincenzo Grimani who wrote the libretto of *Agrippina,* and whom Handel had probably met in Venice; The Duke of Alvito for whose marriage Handel is said to have composed *Aci, Galatea e Polifemo.*

We know very little of the actual terms and conditions of Handel's service or employment with these and other members of the nobility and governing classes. That he found himself in the courts of the wealthy and powerful patrons of the arts was in keeping with the practice of the time, but we can be perfectly certain that his service was never servitude, neither did he prostitute his art for material advantage. The composer must have made many other personal contacts of which we know nothing, but which may have vitally influenced him in his art and career; and at the same time he must have met many musicians, singers, and instrumentalists, some of whom, as we know, were employed afterwards at the Italian Opera in London.

Steffani, musician and diplomatist, who was in Italy from October, 1708, to June, 1709 (Streatfeild), is supposed to have made the acquaintance of Handel there, and to have suggested to Handel that he should succeed him as Kapellmeister at the Court of the Elector of Hanover, and Handel promised to take advantage of the offer. From a statement of Handel, recorded by Hawkins, the composer as a young man under twenty met Steffani at Hanover where he had the favour and patronage of the Princess Sophia and the Elector's son; but Handel's age must have been incorrectly reported by Hawkins, whose references to Princess Sophia and the Elector's son are open to question. The Elector, afterwards George I of England, had a daughter Sophia, his mother was named Sophia, and his divorced wife Sophia. The Elector's son may have been a reference to Ernest Augustus, the brother of the Elector, already referred to. Hawkins's statement, if it has any value at all, may be accepted as an inaccurate version of Handel's visit to Hanover in 1710, when he was made Kapellmeister in June of that year. Mainwaring says that Handel had met Steffani in Venice, and renewed acquaintance with him at Hanover.

In addition to smaller works (*Dixit Dominus, Laudate pueri,*

27

Gloria Patri, cantatas, etc.) the Italian tour also produced the following larger works:

The oratorio *La Resurrezione*, given at the expense of Prince Ruspoli at the Palazzo Bonelli, Rome, on April 8, 1708. (Flower.)

Il Trionfo del Tempo e del Disinganno, produced under the patronage of Cardinal Ottoboni at his Palace, in Rome, in 1708, Cardinal Pamfili writing the libretto. This same cardinal wrote the poem in honour of Handel, "Hendel, non può mia Musa" which the composer set to music. The original manuscript of this work was recently discovered by Prof. Dent in the University Library at Münster, and copies of it are at the Fitzwilliam Library and in the Granville MSS. at the British Museum beginning 'Handel' not 'Hendel'.

The pastoral *Aci, Galatea e Polifemo*, written for the marriage of the Duke of Alvito, at Naples, on July 19, 1708. (Flower, Dent.) Mainwaring says "it was composed at the request of Donna Laura, whether a Portugueze or a Spanish Princess, I will not be certain. But the pomp and magnificence of this lady should seem to speak her of Spanish extraction."

The opera *Agrippina*, libretto by Cardinal Grimani, produced December 26, 1709, at the Teatro di San Giovanni Crisostomo (Grisostomo) in Venice. An outstanding success, having, according to Mainwaring, twenty-seven performances, and including in the cast Boschi, his wife Signora Boschi, and Margherita Durastanti, all of whom sang for Handel in London —Boschi and his wife in *Rinaldo* on its production and Durastanti in *Radamisto* (1720), etc.

Merely to recite this list of works commissioned or produced by such influential people, some of whom collaborated with the composer and one of whom wrote a poem in his honour, is enough to show that Handel must have been well recompensed in kind or money according to the payments of the day, and it was certainly not because he failed to support himself that he left the country in 1710, but ostensibly to take up his appointment in Hanover (June 16, 1710) and with a modest security in funds to try his luck ultimately in England.

Before leaving this part of our inquiry, it may be as well to give a few more relevant quotations from Mainwaring: "From Rome he removed to Naples, where, as at most other places, he had a palazzo at command, and was provided with table, coach, and all other accommodations. . . . While he was at Naples he received invitations from most of the principal persons who lived within reach of that capital; and lucky was he esteemed, who could engage him soonest, and detain him longest."

After Handel left Italy he first stopped at Hanover, where he renewed his acquaintance with Steffani and with "a Nobleman who had taken great notice of Handel in Italy, and who did him great service (as will appear soon) when he came to England for the second time. This person was Baron Kilmanseck. He introduced him at Court, and so well recommended him to his Electoral Highness, that he immediately offered him a pension of 1500 Crowns per annum as an inducement to stay."

Chrysander suggests that Mainwaring's statement of the sum offered was merely an English way of saying a good salary, which Chrysander estimated at not more than a 1000 thalers, i.e., 600 crowns, and as indicated later on his guess was correct.

Continuing the story, Mainwaring goes on to say that Handel while expressing his gratitude to the Baron for the recommendation and to the Elector for his goodness and generosity stated that "the favour intended him would hardly be consistent either with the promise he had actually made to visit the court of the Elector Palatine [at Düsseldorf], or with the resolution he had long taken to pass over into England, for the sake of seeing that of London.[1] Upon this objection, the Baron consulted his Highness's pleasure, and Handel was then acquainted, that neither his promise nor his resolution should be superseded by his acceptance of the pension proposed. He had leave to be absent for a twelve-month or more, if he chose it; and to go whithersoever he pleased. On these easy conditions he thankfully accepted it.

"To this handsome pension the place of Chapel-master was soon after added, on the voluntary resignation of Steffani. . . . Notwithstanding the new favour conferred upon him, he was still in possession of the privilege before allowed him, to perform his engagements, and pursue his travels. He considered it as

---

[1]It seems he had received strong invitations to England from the Duke of Manchester.

his first and principal engagement to pay a visit to his Mother at Hall [i.e. Halle]. . . . When he had paid his respects to his relations and friends . . . he set out for Dusseldorp. The Elector Palatine was much pleased with the punctual performance of his promise, but as much disappointed to find that he was engaged elsewhere. At parting he made him a present of a fine set of wrought plate for a desert, and in such a manner as added greatly to its value."

Subsequent writers, with one or two exceptions, have generally accepted Handel's visits to Hanover, Halle and Düsseldorf, modifying and varying some of the details without much evidence of research. The parts played by Steffani and Baron Kielmansegg are not clear, neither does there appear to be any corroboration from contemporary sources of the visit to Düsseldorf in 1710, and the gift of plate, described by Abdy Williams as "a silver table-service". It is not unlikely, however, that Handel visited Johann Wilhelm, Elector Palatine, at Düsseldorf, as his wife Anna Lodovica (or as Streatfeild calls her, Anna Maria) was the daughter of Cosimo III and sister of Prince Ferdinand and Giangastone de' Medici; and we know for certain that Handel was known to Johann Wilhelm and his wife and that he stayed with them for a few days in 1711. As Streatfeild points out, there is definite evidence that Handel was appointed Kapellmeister at Hanover, 16th June, 1710, at an annual salary of 1,000 thalers (Fischer, *Opern und Concerte im Hoftheater zu Hannover*, 1899), which Schœlcher, Abdy Williams, etc. give as 1,500 ducats, about £300.

In the same passage where Mainwaring tells us of Handel's visit to his mother at Halle, he speaks of "her extreme old-age and total blindness". There is no reason for supposing that Handel did not visit his mother on his return from Italy, but Mainwaring's account of her age and blindness at that time is misplaced and actually describes her condition when Handel visited her for the last time in 1729, eighteen months or so before her death. The point is mentioned here as an evidence of Mainwaring's inaccuracy, in consequence of which we can question the Düsseldorf visit and the gift of plate. If Handel was by this time moving about with two sets of plate, this one and that supposed to have been presented to him at Florence, he must have found travelling expensive and rather trouble-

30

some. A reasonable question is—What did he do with the services? We know nothing about them afterwards.

Towards the end of 1710 Handel arrived in London, and if we do not know the details of his circumstances, we can be perfectly certain that he brought with him some money, that the experience and reputation derived from his German and Italian productions must have helped him, and that in addition to introductions and references to English circles, he had securely in his possession the original manuscripts of *Aci, Galatea e Polifemo, Agrippina, La Resurrezione, Rodrigo, Laudate pueri, Dixit Dominus,* etc.—early evidence of the care with which throughout his life he retained and preserved the personal copies of his works.

Just how and when he made contact with the English professional and society circles we do not know. The following accounts contain more or less plausible statements.

Mainwaring says: "The report of his uncommon abilities had been conveyed to England before his arrival, and through various channels. Some persons here had seen him in Italy, and others during his residence at Hanover. He was soon introduced at Court, and honoured with marks of the Queen's favour. Many of the nobility were impatient for an Opera of his composing. To gratify this eagerness, *Rinaldo,* the first he made in England, was finished in a fortnight's time."

This reference to the Queen and Court has been expanded by some writers to mean that Handel was well received at court by the Queen because she played the clavier well and Handel's playing was of particular interest to her; not an unlikely conclusion, but without corroborative evidence. Romain Rolland, for example, makes the much too definite statement: "Having been presented to the Queen Anne, who loved music, and played the clavier well, Handel was received with open arms by the Director of the Opera, Aaron Hill." This appears to be an amplification of a suggestion by Chrysander. Thus the legends about the master grow.

A letter from the Duchess of Marlborough to the Earl of Manchester, April 13, 1708, gives a different picture of the Queen's interest in music by stating that "The queen has so little time that she never heard any of her own music, among which she has some that is very good, and, I believe, she will not care to take any new." (Duke of Manchester, *Court and Society*.)

Burney (*History of Music*) says Handel came to England "on a visit of curiosity, and in compliance with an invitation from several English noblemen, with whom he had made acquaintance at the court of Hanover, but without any design of remaining in England. . . . Aaron Hill was now in the direction of the theatre in the Haymarket, and hearing of the arrival of a master, the fame of whose abilities had already penetrated into this country, he applied to him to compose an opera."

Dent (*Händel in England*) says that Handel was indebted to Lady Burlington (mother of the young Lord Burlington) for the favour of the Queen.

Mary Granville, afterwards Mrs. Delany, has left on record the following account of her first meeting with Handel at the house of her uncle Sir John Stanley, and the importance of the composer's association with the Granville family has been referred to already: "In the year 10 I first saw Mr. Handel, who was introduced to my uncle Stanley by Mr. Heidegger, the famous manager of the opera, and the most ugly man that ever was formed. We had no better instrument in the house than a little spinnet of mine, on which that great musician performed wonders. I was much struck with his playing, but struck as a child, not a judge, for the moment he was gone, I seated myself to my instrument, and played the best lesson I had then learnt; my uncle archly asked me whether I thought I should ever play as well as Mr. Handel. 'If I did not think I should,' cried I, 'I would burn my instrument!' such was the innocent presumption of childish ignorance."

Commenting on this passage the following note appears in the published *Autobiography and Correspondence of Mary Granville, Mrs. Delany*: "Here ends this fragment, which was probably written by Mrs. Delany in her latter years."

The present writer suggests that it is reasonable to suppose that the incident happened in Mrs. Delany's eleventh year, i.e. in the early part of 1711, when Handel had produced *Rinaldo* and was known to Heidegger at the Opera House. The preceding passage in the autobiography refers to an undated incident, which is known to have taken place in March, 1711, and as it was customary at that time under the old calendar to end the legal year with March 24th, March, 1711, N.S. would be referred to as March, 1710.

Dent suggests that it was through Boschi the singer that Aaron Hill, of the Queen's Theatre, invited Handel to compose *Rinaldo*, but whatever the facts are about the employment of Handel, we know that he was soon busy on the writing and production of the work, the story of which need not be repeated here. Produced February 24, it had fifteen performances during the season. Hawkins says, "The success of this opera was greater than can be imagined; Walsh got fifteen hundred pounds by the printing it." In Coxe's *Anecdotes* the statement is given in this form, "Walsh, the music-seller, is reputed to have gained fifteen hundred pounds by printing the scores", and this has been repeated in one way or another by many writers. It is quite obviously an absurd exaggeration. Opera scores, containing, as they usually did, the overture, songs and final chorus only, were sold by Walsh, as a rule, at not more than half a guinea a copy, *Rinaldo* being advertised at 9s., and if the publisher made £1,500 out of one work the number of copies sold must have been in the nature of 3,000–4,000. From what we know of the number of subscribers to certain works, the comparative rarity of copies to-day, and the reluctance of even the most music-loving public to indulge in the purchase of the vocal scores of the operas they patronize, we can safely deduce that Hawkins, or whoever gave him the information, was speaking without knowledge. According to Schœlcher, Hawkins also tells us that it was in connection with this fantastic story of £1,500 profit that Handel said to Walsh: "My dear sir, it is only right that we should be upon an equal footing, *you* shall compose the next opera, and *I* will sell it." As Chrysander points out, there is no reliable authority for this remark. It doesn't appear to be in Hawkins and is an invention of Schœlcher, or taken over from some other source.

Cluer, and his successors, who published Handel's operas for a few years from 1724 onwards, issued them at various prices: *Giulio Cesare* (1724) at 15s.; *Tamerlano* (1724) at 16s., then at £1 1s.; *Rodelinda* (1725) at 15s. to subscribers in two payments of 7s. 6d.; *Scipione* (1726) at 18s.

The financial terms under which Handel produced *Rinaldo* and most of his subsequent operas are quite unknown. Existing documents or statements on the subject are not clear, and at best only provide details of some payments. In 1711 the composer was probably prepared to accept anything in order to get before the public, and nothing in the nature of a long contract could have been made. Amongst important records of the period is the collection of papers that Dr. Cummings brought to public notice in the *Proceedings of The Musical Association*, 1914—a most valuable contribution to London stage history in the early days of the eighteenth century. The collection formerly belonged to Thomas Coke, Vice-Chamberlain at the time, and consists of upwards of eighty papers connected with the Opera House (Queen's Theatre), Covent Garden and Drury Lane Theatres. From these genuine records we get definite information on some aspects of theatrical finance, but it is only necessary to quote here those details that are relevant to our subject. In a general way, it is clear that anything from about £80 to £240 per night were taken at the Opera House apart from subscriptions; that seat prices were as a rule: stage boxes 10s. 6d., boxes 8s., pit 5s., lower gallery 2s. 6d., upper gallery 1s. 6d.; that gallery receipts were about £20-£30 per night, that principal singers' payments ranged from about £300 to £600 or so per season—some stars, as we know from other records, received £2,000 or more—and instrumentalists as a rule anything from about 8s. per night upwards to £1 or more.

The papers include some references to *Rinaldo* and to Handel. One statement in Heidegger's hand reads: "May the 5, 1711. Mr. Collier agrees to pay Mr. Lunican for the copy of *Rinaldo* this day the sum of eight pounds, and three pounds every day *Rinaldo* is play'd till Six and twenty pounds are pay'd, and he gives him leave to take the said Opera in his custody after every day of acting it, till the Whole six and twenty pounds are pay'd." Cummings adds: "Mr. Lunican was a viola-player in the opera orchestra and received payment according to these documents of 8s. per performance. The £26 was, of course, for writing the vocal and orchestral parts." But this explanation does not seem to fit the case. The work had been playing from February 24, 1711, and only had three more

34

performances that season after May 5, the last performance being on June 2. Players' copies must have been in existence before May 5. It might be assumed that the copy was for the publisher Walsh to prepare his first edition from, but that had already appeared, on April 24. If we knew more about Mr. Collier and Mr. Lunican, the problem could probably be solved. Perhaps Mr. Lunican acted as Handel's agent and Collier represented the Opera House management. It is clear that payment depended on the run of the work for the last four performances of the season only. Whether similar payments were made for the previous eleven performances we do not know.

Cummings continues: "There are several memoranda of payments in which Handel's name occurs. One written by Heidegger, probably in 1711:

	£	s.	d.
M. Long . .	150	0	0
M. Potter . .	72	0	0
Mr. Hendel . .	50	0	0
Sig. Nicolini . .	50	0	0
Pilotti . .	50	0	0
The Instruments .	50	0	0
Sig. Valentini .	38	0	0
	£460	0	0
Mr. Hendel . .	761	0	0
	50	0	0
	£811	0	0

	£	s.	d.
Siga. Margaritta in the first division .	80	0	0
In the second . . .	25	0	0
Her benifit	76	5	8
Remains due to her . . .	218	14	4
	£400	0	0

Mrs. Barbier has received:			£	s.	d.
In the first division	.	.	60	0	0
In the second	.	.	18	15	0
Her benifitt	.	.	15	0	0
Remains due to her	.	.	206	5	0
			£300	0	0

Mr. Hendel has received:			£	s.	d.
In the first division	.	.	86	0	0
In the second	.	.	26	17	0
His benifitt day	.	.	73	10	11
Remains due	.	.	243	12	1
			£430	0	0

Signr. Valeriano has received:			£	s.	d.
In the first division	.	.	129	0	0
In the second	.	.	40	6	0
His benifitt day	.	.	73	19	0
Remains due to him	.	.	401	15	0
			£645	0	0

Signora Pilotti has received:			£	s.	d.
In the first division	.	.	89	5	0
In the second	.	.	27	14	0
From Mr. Swiney	.	.	53	15	0
Her benifitt day	.	.	75	7	3
Remains due to her	.	.	255	18	9
			[1] £500	0	0

[1]This is as given in the MS.

36

Signr. Valentini has received:	£	s.	d.
Of Mr. Swiney . . .	107	10	0
In the first division . .	86	0	0
In the second . . .	26	17	0
His benifitt day . .	75	8	5
Remains due to him .	241	14	7
	£537	10	0

Signora Manina received:	£	s.	d.
In the first division . .	20	0	0
In the second . . .	6	5	0
Remains due to her . .	73	15	0
	£100	0	0

Cummings is not quite correct in assigning these lists to 1711. From what we know of the singers mentioned, the details of payments appear to refer to the years 1711–13. The first list almost certainly refers to the early 1711 performances of *Rinaldo*, and the payment of £811 to Handel was presumably for his work during that season. The other lists refer to the 1711–12 or 1712–13 seasons, and probably cover the production of *Il Pastor Fido*.

It will be noticed that Handel is stated to have received a total of £1,291, and if we conclude that the one payment of £811 is for one season, even if he had to pay his instrumentalists out of this (say an approximate total of £200–£300) he didn't do so badly for a new-comer to the London Opera. Other interesting points are that the benefit night proceeds were apparently considered as a contribution towards the agreed salary of the individual concerned for the season, not as an addition, and that first and second payments were made on some agreed share-out of takings or profits. It is admitted that some of the suggestions offered here might have to be modified if the original documents were available for examination.

The prices of seats was generally as quoted in the Coke

D

documents, but on special occasions they were increased—stage boxes to 15s. or more, pit and other boxes 10s. 6d., gallery 2s. 6d.—and when a new subscription was opened the sale of tickets was sometimes restricted to not more than 400 at half a guinea each.

For certain later performances of oratorios, etc., prices were raised to as much as one and a half guineas, and there also appears to have been in existence unofficial trafficking in tickets, which forced the price up to as much as £5 5s. (*Ottone*—Cummings, *Handel*.)

Before presenting the evidence that exists with regard to Handel's financial dealings with his publishers, particularly Walsh, father and son, it is as well to point out that Schœlcher is largely responsible for the story that the firm were mean and parsimonious. He says that he met "John Caulfield, who had been an engraver of music, and whose father, who had followed the same business, was apprenticed to Walsh", and that Caulfield, then eighty-three years old, told Schœlcher that "Walsh, who was extremely rich, very parsimonious, and so suspicious that he would sometimes leave pieces of gold upon his desk in order to test the honesty of his clerks and workmen, gave twenty guineas to the great composer for each oratorio which he printed." In another place Schœlcher, quoting Caulfield, says, that "according to what he remembers of his father's conversation . . . after the performance of *The Messiah*, Walsh demanded the MS., sending at the same time, the usual *honorarium* of twenty guineas, which was the stipulated price of every oratorio which he printed. But the composer would not accept them, saying, that rather than receive such a sum he would not publish the oratorio."

The history of the Walsh firm has still to be written, and these statements of Caulfield cannot be checked, but from the following evidence it seems that the figure of twenty guineas per work has some foundation in fact, although it may only have represented a first payment.

Sir George Macfarren, in his *Sketch of the Life of Handel*, 1859, says: "A very interesting document, illustrative of this subject, was forwarded to me, as Secretary of the Handel Society in 1844 by Mr. Nottingham. This was a leaf from the cash-book of Walsh the music-seller, which there has hitherto been no opportunity to print. The following is a faithful transcript of it:

Money paid to Mr. Handel for copy:

			£	s	d
1722	Opera	Otho . . .	£42	0	0
1721	,,	Floridan . .	£72	0	0
1723	,,	Flavio . . .	£26	5	0
1729	,,	Parthenope . .	£26	5	0
1730	,,	Porus . . .	£26	5	0
1736	,,	Armenius . .	£26	5	0
1736	,,	Atalanta . .	£26	5	0
1737	,,	Berenice . .	£26	5	0
1737	,,	Justin . . .	£26	5	0
1732	,,	Orlando . .	£26	5	0
1732	,,	Aetius . . .	£26	5	0
1737	,,	Faramondo . .	£26	5	0
1737	,,	Alexander's Feast .	£105	0	0
1738	,,	Xerxes . .	£26	5	0
1738 Sept. 28th, six organ concertos		in p. . .	£26	5	0
1738. Oct. 7th, six new sonatas		. .	£26	5	0

Returning to Handel's movements immediately after the season of *Rinaldo*, Mainwaring says: "He had now been a full twelve-month in England, and it was time for him to think of returning to Hanover. When he took leave of the Queen at her court, and expressed his sense of the favours conferred on him, her Majesty was pleased to add to them by large presents, and to intimate her desire of seeing him again. Not a little flattered with such marks of approbation from so illustrious a personage, he promised to return, the moment he could obtain permission from the Prince, in whose service he was retained."

Hawkins and Coxe take over this account from Mainwaring; and Burney, (*Sketch of the Life of Handel*) omitting mention of the Queen, says that Handel, "returned to Hanover, on a promise made to his most powerful English friends to revisit this kingdom again, as soon as he could obtain permission of his Electoral Highness and patron". There seems to be no contemporary corroboration of Mainwaring's statement about Handel meeting the Queen during his first visit to England.

As we know, Handel returned to his duties at the Hanoverian
Court after the *Rinaldo* season in 1711, stopping on the way for
a few days at Düsseldorf with the Elector Palatine. (Einstein.
Zeitschrift der Internationalen Musikgesellschaft. Bd. VIII, pp. 277–
8.) According to Mainwaring, "Towards the end of the year
1712, he obtained leave of the Elector [of Hanover] to make a
second visit to England, on condition that he engaged to return
within a reasonable time. . . . The great character of the
Operas which Handel had made in Italy and Germany, and
the remembrance of *Rinaldo* joined with the poor proceedings
at the Haymarket, made the nobility very desirous that he
might again be employed in composing for that theatre. To
their applications her Majesty was pleased to add the weight
of her own authority; and as a testimony of her regard to his
merit, settled upon him a pension for life of 200*l. per Annum.*
This act of the royal bounty was the more extraordinary, as
his foreign engagements were not unknown."

Hawkins, Burney and Coxe, all record the granting of this
pension, although Burney mentions it after the composition of
the *Utrecht Te Deum* and *Jubilate,* and Schœlcher as if it were
a reward for those works. Professor Dent speaks of the pension
as a practical result of the *Birthday Ode* for Queen Anne, first
performed February 6, 1713. Abdy Williams puts out the
purely imaginary explanation of Queen Anne's pension as
follows:

"She did not love the Hanoverian Court, and it was perhaps
for this reason rather than because of any great appreciation
of art that she rewarded the Hanoverian *Capellmeister* with a
salary of £200 for life. It was a means of keeping him away
from his German patron. As he was already in receipt of £300
a year from the court of Hanover, and was at no expense for
board and lodging, he must have been in very comfortable
circumstances for a bachelor."

For the latter statement about board and lodging there is
no authority whatever. It is a great pity that we have no
contemporary documents regarding the pension that Handel
is supposed to have received from Queen Anne. Mainwaring,
it will be noticed, considered the pension as rather extraordinary in view of Handel's engagement at the Hanoverian
Court; and if the composer was only on a visit it does seem

strange that a pension should have been conferred for life. Presumably, Handel had some pay from Hanover, but as he never returned to that Court after 1712, and only renewed his contact with the Elector after the latter came to England following the death of Queen Anne in 1714, it is not unlikely that Handel's salary from Hanover was stopped during the early days of his second visit to England. At any rate, we hear nothing more of it, and the pension which the Elector, as George I, is recorded to have given Handel in addition to that conferred by Queen Anne could hardly have been while Handel was still drawing another £300 as *Capellmeister*, which would have made a total of £700 per annum. It is worth noting, that the libretto of *Teseo*, published in 1713, describes Handel as "Maestro di Capella di S.A.E. di Hannover". This question of royal pensions will be referred to again, for the moment it is only necessary to say that the present writer is inclined to the opinion that while it seems clear that Handel did enjoy a royal pension until his death, it was probably less than the £600 (made up of the three pensions of £200 each) which it is generally stated that the composer received.

In Edward Chamberlayne's authoritative work, *Angliæ Notitia*, continued by his son John as *Magnæ Britanniæ Notitia*, which includes lists of the Officers of the court and state, pensioners, etc., there is no mention of any paid or unpaid official appointment being held by Handel until 1727, a matter that will be dealt with later on.

From a letter which Handel wrote in June, 1725, to Michaelsen, his brother-in-law, it is clear that the composer expected to travel to Hanover in attendance on the King, and in a letter written to Jennens from Ireland, December 29, 1741, he says, in reference to a proposal for more subscription performances, that the Lord Lieutenant "will easily obtain a longer Permission for me by His Majesty, so that I shall be obliged to make my stay here longer than I thought." Clearly Handel was in service both to George I and George II.

Mainwaring is responsible for the popular story that Handel was reconciled to George I by a performance of music for a water party, Handel being presented to His Majesty by Baron Kielmansegg as the composer, and "as one that was too conscious of his fault to attempt an excuse for it; but sincerely

41

desirous to atone for the same by all possible demonstrations of duty, submission, and gratitude, could he but hope that his Majesty, in his great goodness, would be pleased to accept them. This intercession was accepted without any difficulty. Handel was restored to favour, and his Music honoured with the highest expressions of the royal approbation. As a token of it, the King was pleased to add a pension for life of 200*l*. a year to that which Queen Anne had before given him. Some years after, when he was employed to teach the young Princesses, another pension of the same value was added to the former by her late Majesty." [Caroline of Anspach, wife of George II.] This story, accepted and elaborated by Hawkins, Burney, Coxe and most subsequent writers, is now known to be another of Mainwaring's questionable statements. The facts about the *Water Music* are given in Flower's *George Frideric Handel* and in Chapter VIII of this work. As the *Water Music* story, as told by Mainwaring, is open to question, the granting of the pension by the King may be equally in dispute, although the reference to the pension for teaching the young Princesses has some foundation in fact, as will be seen later.

Before dealing with Mainwaring's references to the Earl of Burlington, it is necessary to mention another patron of Handel, referred to by Hawkins:

"Being now determined to make England the country of his residence, Handel began to yield to the invitations of such persons of rank and fortune as were desirous of his acquaintance, and accepted an invitation from one Mr. Andrews, of Barn-Elms, in Surrey, but who had also a town residence, to apartments in his house. After some months' stay with Mr. Andrews, Handel received a pressing invitation from the Earl of Burlington . . . to make his house in Piccadilly the place of his abode."

Nothing else appears to be known about "Mr. Andrews".

We now come to the period 1715–20, when the composer is generally believed to have spent three years or so in the household of the Earl of Burlington and two years or more with the Duke of Chandos.

Mainwaring's actual words about this period are: "During the first three years of it, he was chiefly, if not constantly, at the

42

Earl of Burlington's. . . . The remaining two years he spent at Cannons. . . . Whether Handel was *provided* as a mere implement of grandeur, or *chosen* from motives of a superior kind, it is not for us to determine."

What other evidence is there that the patronage of these two noble persons was bestowed on Handel? Although there is no definite proof that he lived for continuous periods with either of them, it can be accepted without question, that he had close associations with both, but the extent to which he was indebted to them financially or for his maintenance is quite unknown.

The third Earl of Burlington, born in 1695, was, as we know, a wealthy and interested patron of the arts, whose mother the Dowager Countess, one of the Queen's Ladies of the Bed-chamber, may have invited Handel to the family mansion, according to some writers. The libretto of Handel's *Teseo* (1713) was dedicated to the Earl of Burlington by Haym, and in the dedication of *Amadigi* (1715) Heidegger speaks of the Earl's generous support of "theatrical musick" and adds, "but this Opera more immediately claims Your Protection, as it is compos'd in Your own Family." The poet Gay, who with Pope and others are generally mentioned as having lived under the patronage of the Earl, says in his descriptive poem *Trivia* [1716]:

> Yet *Burlington's* fair Palace still remains;
> Beauty within, without Proportion reigns.
> Beneath his Eye declining Art revives,
> The Wall with animated Picture lives;
> There *Hendel* strikes the Strings, the melting Strain
> Transports the Soul, and thrills through ev'ry Vein;
> There oft' I enter (but with cleaner Shoes)
> For *Burlington's* belov'd by ev'ry Muse.

The above-mentioned details are the only evidence for the more fuller statements of Hawkins and subsequent writers, although recently a letter written by Handel to the Earl of Burlington in 1719 has come to light at Chatsworth (Devonshire MSS.) which shows that the composer was very much indebted to the Earl. This letter is quoted later on.

There is some reason for thinking that Handel went to Germany during the years 1715–18, although the various writers are not in agreement, neither are the facts very clear. Coxe (*Anecdotes of John Christopher Smith*) says that he arrived at Anspach in 1716. Percy Robinson says that he was unable "to discover any substantial evidence that Handel was in Germany in 1716". (*Music and Letters*, January, 1939.) Mattheson mentions him as being in Hanover about 1717. The possibility of these journeys having taken place must be kept in mind before accepting the conclusion of those writers who assert that Handel lived for three years at Burlington House.

The continued residence for two years or so (1718–20) with the Duke of Chandos is similarly without much documentary evidence. It is impossible here to go over the whole question, which has been dealt with more fully by the present writer in Chapter VII. That Handel was employed as musical director or in some such capacity by the noble Duke, and received some financial or material assistance from him, is hardly to be questioned. Mainwaring mentions the *Chandos Anthems* and *Acis and Galatea*, and Hawkins *Esther*, as having been made for the Duke, although the details of production of the last two works are uncertain and do not rest on very definite documentary evidence. We know that Handel was in Germany in 1719 and corresponding with the Earl of Burlington, and that during the years 1718–19 he was busy in several ways, so it is reasonable to suppose that he was not continuously in residence with the Duke of Chandos either at Cannons[1] or at his London residence. We have no evidence of any payment made to Handel by the Duke of Burlington or by the Duke of Chandos, except the unsubstantiated statement that the latter paid Handel £1,000 for *Esther*. This information is quoted by Schœlcher as from *A Journey through England*, but it really comes from a footnote to Miss E. I. Spence's story *How to be rid of a Wife* (1823).

Handel had started to save money in England as early as 1714 or 1715. There is in the British Museum, a note dated June 29, 1716, in which the composer gives instructions for the payment of dividend on his £500 of South Sea Stock. This note is generally known and has been reproduced elsewhere, but an earlier instruction in the possession of Gerald Coke reads as follows:

[1]The forms 'Canons' and 'Cannons' appear in early references. 'Cannons' has been used throughout this work, except in quotations giving 'Canons'.

44

The 13 March 1715

Pray pay Mr. Phillip Cooke my Dividend being Fifteen pounds on Five hundred pounds wch. is all my Stock in the South Sea Company books & for half a year due at Christmas last & this shall be your Sufficcient Warraant from

Sr Your very humb Servt.

George Frideric Handel.

This note, which bears no address, is signed by Handel, but otherwise is not in his hand, except perhaps "13" in the date. If 1715 was the actual year and not Old Style calendar for 1716, Handel must have held his stock as early as 1714.

After a few years of uncertain success, the Italian Opera at the King's Theatre closed down in 1717. Up to this time Handel had produced four of his own works, *Rinaldo, Il Pastor Fido, Teseo* and *Amadigi.* What he earned from these performances can only be surmised from the details already quoted, and whether he was personally employed in any capacity in connection with works of other composers we don't know. Only *Rinaldo* was published and thereby brought him in something.

In 1719 a new attempt was made to start Italian Opera again, this time under entirely new auspices—in short a body of the nobility interested in this form of entertainment, who formed themselves into The Royal Academy of Music. The Duke of Newcastle was Governor and Lord Bingley Deputy Governor, and the Earl of Burlington was one of the Directors, according to the list in Burney, but the libretto of *Numitore,* the first work to be performed, gives a different list, with the Duke of Manchester as Deputy Governor with Heidegger among the Directors, and Paolo Rolli as Italian Secretary. A guarantee of £50,000 was promised or privately subscribed; the King, according to Mainwaring, giving £1,000. From the Treasury Papers of the period it is possible to give authentic evidence of the King's financial interest in the venture. From an entry February 16, 1722, it is clear that the King had promised £1,000 annually for seven years (presumably 1721–1727), and this is confirmed by entries in June, 1722, and 1723. Heidegger was manager as well as being a governor, and Handel was principal composer from the inception of the concern; G. B. Bononcini and Ariosti joining later on. It is unnecessary to recapitulate here the story of the institution, which lasted until 1728. Burney and many other writers provide fuller details. Under the auspices of the Academy over 240 performances of operas by Handel were given (out of a total of nearly 500); the composer producing fourteen new works of his own during the period. The early negotiations for the establishment of the Academy took place, evidently in 1719, and by that time it is reasonable to suppose that Handel had no fixed engagement with the Duke of Chandos. In fact, from the letter in the possession of the Duke of Devonshire at Chatsworth (here published by kind permission of his Grace), it seems that the composer was still very much in the service of and indebted to the Earl of Burlington, who appears to have had an authoritative voice in the establishment of the Academy and the employment of Handel as composer and musical director. Mainwaring tells us that it was during Handel's last year at Cannons that the Academy was projected and that Handel "after he quitted his employment at Cannons was advised to go over to Dresden in quest of Singers. Here he engaged Senesino and Duristanti, whom he brought over with him to England."

Mainwaring needs correction here, as Senesino did not come over to England until late in 1720, but Durastanti was here for the opening of the season in April of the same year. From other sources it has been known that Handel went abroad for singers during 1719, calling at Düsseldorf, Dresden, Hanover and Halle, but very little contemporary evidence about times and places has been forthcoming. The transcript of the letter in the possession of the Duke of Devonshire which follows, clearly establishes for the first time that Handel was in Dresden in July, 1719, and what his business was; also that the Earl of Burlington was personally concerned in the composer's movements and affairs.

My Lord,
    C'est toujours autant par une vive reconnoissance, que par devoir, que je me donne l'honneur de Vous dire le

zele et l'attachement que j'ay pour Vôtre personne. Je Vous dois de plus un Conte exact de ce que j'ay entrepris, et de la reussite du sujet de mon long voyage.

Je suis icy à attendre que les engagements de Sinesino, Berselli, et Guizzardi, soyent finis, et que ces Messieurs d'ailleurs bien disposés, s'engagent avec moy pour la Grand Bretagne. tout sera decidé en quelques jours; j'ay des bonnes esperances, et dés que j'auray conclû quelque chose de réel, je Vous l'ecrirai My Lord, comme a mon bienfacteur, à mon Protecteur. Conservez moy, My Lord, Vos graces, elles me seront pretieuses, et ce sera toujours avec ardeur et fidelité que je suivray Vôtre service, et Vôs nobles volontés. C'est avec une soumission egalement sincere et profonde que je serai à jamais.

My lord
Vôtre
tres humble tres obeissant, et tres devoue
Serviteur
à Dresde   George Frideric Handel
ce 26/15 de Juillet
1719.

NOTE
To the Earl of Burlington. Devonshire MSS., 1st Series, 150.0. The letter has no address but is endorsed in the hand of the 6th Duke of Devonshire: Mr. Handel to Ld. Bn.

While in Dresden (1719) Handel played the harpsichord before the Elector and Electoral Prince of Saxony, and received in February, 1720, one hundred ducats, presumably a delayed present for his earlier performance (Fürstenau, *Zur Geschichte der Musik und des Theaters am Hofe zu Dresden*, Chrysander, Dent), although this late payment is difficult to understand unless Handel was in Dresden until then, or the money was forwarded to him.

We have no information as to the terms of Handel's engagement with the Academy, but it is reasonable to suppose that it was at a salary which may or may not have included payment for any works of his own that he produced, and we can assume that the amount was substantial, in view of the reports of salaries of £2,000 or so having been paid to several of the principal singers. (Cuzzoni, Faustina.)

Handel's first work for the Academy was *Radamisto*, generally considered a fine opera, that promised well for the success of the institution, and the composer must have felt that his future was assured for some time, as he published the score of *Radamisto* himself in a most sumptuous way. The work was engraved by T. Cross, and printed and sold by Richard Meares and Christopher Smith under Handel's own royal licence, dated June 14th, 1720. The style, size, and engraving of the work place it among the finest specimens of music-publishing of the period.

Although not bearing on our subject, it may be of interest to mention here the confusion that has arisen in some writers about the cast of *Radamisto* and the arrival of Senesino and Durastanti in England, and that the whole position is made clear in the two libretti of *Radamisto*, one issued in April, 1720, and the other in December of the same year. Durastanti was in the first cast as *Radamisto*, the role which Senesino took in the following December when Durastanti played Zenobia, the wife of Radamisto; a change of parts by one singer probably unique in Italian opera history. Senesino was not in the first cast, as he did not arrive in England until the end of the year.

The two libretti of *Radamisto* have a dedicatory preface "To the King's Most Excellent Majesty", signed: "Sir, Your Majesty's Most Devoted, Most Obedient, And Most Faithful Subject and Servant, George Frederic Handel."

To return to the question of Handel as publisher of his own works: he may have intended to issue other operas in the manner of *Radamisto*, but unless the Academy had some responsibility for its publication, the composer may have lost money over it which compelled him to change his ideas about publishing other works. At any rate, only some songs in *Muzio Scævola* were issued by Meares, quite attractively engraved by Cross, but in a less ambitious way than that of *Radamisto*; and Walsh with John and Joseph Hare put out a rival edition of *Muzio Scævola* which may have been without Handel's authority. The next three Handel operas *Floridante*, *Ottone* and *Flavio*, were published by the composer himself, under his licence, through Walsh and John and Joseph Hare, in fine large folios far superior in style and workmanship to much of Walsh's work. Why Handel employed Walsh for these works is not known, but for some reason, probably cost and personal

48

dealings with Walsh, he again broke with his old publisher, and the next eight Handel operas produced for the 'Academy' were done by Cluer. The first of these *Julius Cæsar*, was issued July 24, 1724, as an octavo volume with a beautifully designed illustrated title-page (see Plate No. 2), engraved in a style superior to the next seven operas by the same publisher, spurious editions of the songs in *Julius Cæsar* being issued probably by Walsh and John and Joseph Hare. The songs in *Tolomeo* by Walsh and Joseph Hare appeared in September, 1728, then *Lotario* by Cluer in February, 1730, and after that until Handel's death, the firm of Walsh acted as his publishers. Probably the directors of the Academy had some say in the method and manner of publication of the works produced for them, which may explain the changes of publishers. We do not know, but it seems clear that Handel was at times interested enough to see that his works were well published. Perhaps the financial question, or the fact that he was an employee of the Academy, prevented him from doing as he would have liked.

In 1725, or perhaps a few years earlier, Handel settled in the commodious house at Brook Street, which he occupied until his death. It was unnumbered in Handel's time, but became No. 57 and from 1857 No. 25. There is no doubt about his occupation of the house as early as 1725, because it is recorded in the rate-books of St. George's, Hanover Square for that year that he was rated at £35 per annum for a house in Brook Street, being then the fourth house rated in that street. This evidence given by Schœlcher was followed up by Cummings who visited the house just prior to December, 1893, and discovered there "a fine cast-lead cistern, on the front of which in bold relief I read '1721. G. F. H.' " Cummings suggested that this was probably the cistern scheduled in the "Inventory of goods". Can this be accepted as evidence that Handel was living in the Brook Street house as early as 1721? It is true that the Inventory of Handel's furniture sold after his death to John Du Burk (du Bourk, de Bourke, etc.) and now in the British Museum (Egerton MSS. 3009) includes, "In the Area & Vault a Large Lead Cistern & Brass Cock & beer stylion". As a piece of furniture this can hardly have been part of the

49

house, and if Cummings's statement of date is correct it is quite likely that Handel brought the cistern with him when he took possession of the house in 1725 or earlier. Schœlcher could find nothing in the house to remind him of Handel, and it seems strange, that a movable piece with Handel's initials on it should have remained unnoticed in the house for about 130 years. Would the composer have had his initials put on the cistern; was it usual to do such things? Was Cummings mistaken? Where is the cistern now? These speculations do not get us very far beyond the fact that by 1725, at the latest, Handel's financial position had become sufficiently assured to enable him to purchase a house, and set up his own establishment in a fashionable part of London. Probably a search among the rate-books of St. Martin-in-the-Fields, from which parish St. George's was separated in 1725, might provide further information.

Before leaving the question of Handel's house, it may be pointed out that John O'Keeffe, the actor and dramatist, stated in his *Recollections*, London, 1826:

"About half a mile from my house at Acton-Wells, lived Handel; and that place thus became the grand rendezvous of the court and all the lovers of sublime music of his day. Mr. and Mrs. Mattocks (about my time) lived there."

No evidence supporting this statement has been traced. Doctor Thomas Morell, author of the libretti of *Judas Maccabæus* and of other works set to music by Handel, who was on intimate terms with the composer, lived at Turnham Green, and it is quite possible that Handel visited him, and stayed from time to time at his house. This may have given rise to a local tradition some sixty years later that Handel had lived there.

There is an eighteenth century manuscript of "Songs In the Oratorio Call'd The Messiah", with the strange, and at present unexplained entry on the fly-leaf: "Mr. Handel, 22 Aye Street, Bryanstone Square", and also the signature 'M. Viney'. Aye Street may refer to Aybrook Street of the present day, but Handel could hardly have had any connection with it, as the district of Bryanstone Square was developed after his time. Mrs. Anne Viney is mentioned in Mrs. Delany's *Autobiography and Correspondence*.

The pension of £200 per annum paid to Handel by Caroline of Anspach, wife of George II, when the composer was "employed to teach the young Princesses", as recorded by Mainwaring and modified by other writers, has been mentioned earlier. What corroborative evidence is there? George II had five daughters, Anne, Amelia Sophia, Caroline Elizabeth, Mary, and Louisa, the first born in 1709 and the last in 1724. Handel, assuming that he was employed as music-master to the eldest, could hardly have started his duties before about 1720, the time when the first volume of his *Suites* was issued, a work frequently stated, without any evidence, to contain lessons for his young royal pupils. The earliest mention in Chamberlayne's *Magnæ Britanniæ Notitia* of any such appointment is in the year 1728, when under the Establishment of the Princess Royal (Anne), Princess Amelia and Princess Caroline, is listed "Musick Master Mr. George Frederick Handell £200". This appointment, which must have involved only nominal duties as time went on, appears in Chamberlayne 1729, and in the subsequent issues from 1735-55 as applying to Princess Amelia (d. 1786) and Princess Caroline (d. 1757) only. The Princess Royal married the Prince of Orange in 1734, Princess Mary married in 1740 Frederick of Hesse-Cassel, and Princess Louisa married the King of Denmark in 1743. Mary and Louisa had a joint establishment with their brother the Duke of Cumberland from 1735 onwards, but there is no mention of a music-master. On August 29, 1724, there are newspaper reports of Princess Anne and Princess Caroline attending St. Paul's on August 24 and hearing "Mr. Handel (their master) perform upon the Organ". It is not unreasonable, therefore, to suppose that Handel was appointed about 1720, his name not appearing in Chamberlayne until the Princesses had their own establishment. The Treasury Papers contain one or two references that throw new light on this question of payment for services to the Princesses. In 1727 we find a statement of what is due to the Countess of Portland "for the expense of their Royal Highnesses officers and servants under her government, Mich. 1726 to Mich. 1727, when the new establishment commenced". Among the payments made was one "To Mr. Handell [£]195". There are later references (1730 etc.) to the Establishment of the Princess Royal, Princess

Amelia and Princess Caroline. After the marriage of the Princess Royal, in 1734, the establishment was for the Princesses Amelia and Caroline only. On September 27, 1736 there is a reference to the

> Royal Warrant by the Queen as Guardian of the Kingdom, countersigned by the Lords of the Treasury establishing a yearly payment of 200*l*. to George Frederick Handel as music master, and 73*l*. 10*s*. to Paoli Antonio Rolli as Italian master to the Princesses Amelia and Caroline, same to date from 1734, Lady day the date from which the salaries payable under the establishment of 1734, July 2, for the said Princesses commenced; the above two sums having been omitted to be inserted in said establishment.

From these extracts it seems clear, that whereas in the early years of the Princesses Handel received definite payments as their music-teacher, Queen Caroline in the absence of the King abroad in 1736, either with or without his consent fixed by royal warrant an annual payment of £200 to Handel as music-master, an appointment to the two Princesses, which he held until the death of Caroline in 1757, and afterwards to Amelia only until his death (Rider's *British Merlin*, 1759). In his later years the appointment could not have involved any instruction by the composer, but probably entailed the performance and provision of music for the Princesses' pleasure. One other interesting detail is worth noting—the existence in the King's Music Library of an eighteenth century manuscript copy of two harpsichord suites labelled "Lessons composed for the Princess Louisa". (R.M. 19. d. 11.) These two suites consist of (1) Allemande, Courante, Sarabande and Gigue (H.G. II, pp. 125–127) and (2) Allemande, Courante, Sarabande and Gigue (H.G. II, pp. 128–130). If they were written as lessons for Princess Louisa they must date from about 1730–34.

It is significant that the only other reference to Handel in Chamberlayne is in 1727—"Composer of Music for the Chapel Royal Mr. George Handel", no salary being mentioned. In the next two issues of Chamberlayne, 1728 and 1729, which have similar lists of royal appointments on p. 63, "The Composer of the Musick for the Chapel Royal" is left blank, but on p. 253 under the head of 'Royal Chapels' Green [i.e. Maurice Greene]

JOHN JAMES HEIDEGGER

MINIATURE BY NATHANIEL HONE AFTER THE
PAINTING BY J. B. VANLOO

From the original in the possession of Edward Croft-Murray

TITLE-PAGE OF THE FIRST EDITION

OF "JULIUS CÆSAR," 1724

From a copy in the possession of Wm. C. Smith

PLATE NO. 2

appears as "Organist" and "Composer". From 1735 onwards his name appears in each place, in the lists, i.e., as "Organist" and "Composer", and also as "Composer of the Music of the Chapel Royal". Presumably Handel's appointment was as "composer" for the coronation year only.

There doesn't appear to be any contemporary evidence that George II "continued" to pay to Handel any of the pensions granted by his predecessors, although it is generally assumed that he did.

In June, 1728 the Royal Academy of Music came to an inglorious end, and it is generally said that Heidegger, as lessee of the King's Theatre, with Handel as his partner responsible for the musical arrangements, revived the idea of a new Academy. According to Mainwaring "The agreement was for the short term of three years, and so settled as to subsist only from year to year". Streatfeild quotes the following details: "He joined forces with his old friend Heidegger, and took the King's Theatre. A partnership of five years was agreed upon, and the first season was to include fifty performances at a subscription of fifteen guineas a ticket. The enterprise was under the special patronage of Handel's old pupil the Princess Royal."

(Shaftesbury, *Biographical Sketch.*)

In January, 1729, Handel left London for Italy in order to obtain singers for the new Academy; Heidegger having made a similar journey to the Continent a little earlier, without much success. The details of the composer's itinerary and of the people he met are not clear, but he was in Venice in March, 1729, and on his way home visited Halle in June, where he saw his mother for the last time. She was paralysed and blind, and died in December, 1730. Handel reached London by July 1, 1729, and the new season of opera at the King's Theatre opened with *Lotario* on December 2.

Under one management or another Handel continued the composition and production of Italian operas and other works at the King's Theatre and Covent Garden until 1737, when he broke down physically, and according to most reports, financially.

It is impossible to give here in detail the history of the

Italian Opera after the collapse of the first Academy, but it seems clear that an attempt was made to recommence something of the sort again immediately, and that the King, Court and some of the nobility were interested. The Treasury Papers again furnish important reliable evidence that this later undertaking was also known as The Academy of Music or The Royal Academy of Music and that the King's subscription of £1,000 was paid in 1730, 1731, 1732, 1733, 1735, 1736, 1737 and 1738 either to Heidegger or to the "Undertakers of the Opera", but in 1734 to Handel himself, a matter to which we will refer again later.

From letters of Handel sent to Francis Colman in Italy, in June and October, 1730, it is clear that the composer was concerned about pleasing the Court in the arrangements he was making for the ensuing season, and in a letter to Mattheson in July, 1735, he regrets that it is impossible for him to supply his correspondent with some personal details which he requires because of his "continual attention to the service of the Court and Nobility".

Prior to the year of Handel's physical and financial collapse (1737) there are records of one or two financial statements that need consideration. From an anonymous scurrilous pamphlet *See and seem blind*, Flower quotes the writer as saying, after referring to the success of Thomas Arne's English performances at the Haymarket Theatre in 1732, in contrast to the Italian Opera: "This alarm'd H——l, and out he brings an Oratorio, or Religious Farce, for the deuce take me if I can make any other Construction of the word, but he has made a very good *Farce* of it, and put near £4,000 in his pocket, of which I am very glad for I love the man for his Musick's sake." From the rest of the quotation it is clear that it refers to the six highly successful performances of *Esther* which Handel gave under the patronage of the King at the King's Theatre in 1732; but such performances could hardly have made a net profit of £4,000. If such was the case Handel need never have been financially embarrassed for very long.

Mainwaring says of the Oxford tour in 1733, when *Athalia* was performed there, "By this journey the damages he had suffered in his fortune were somewhat repaired, and his reputation more firmly established". But as a matter of fact, his most precarious years from a financial point of view appear to have been a little later. In connection with the Oxford visit, Flower quotes a long passage from a manuscript, *Compendio della vita di G. F. Händel*, in the library of the Liceo Musicale at Bologna, in which the writer states that he was present at the Public Act, and that "the University of Oxford invited Handel to come and give a performance of an Oratorio or some solemn music on that occasion for a very generous fee though not pretending to say generally what it should be. . . . The success of the Oratorio matched completely the work of the virtuosi and the splendour of the performance, and it was said that Handel took back to London £4,000 clear of all expense."

Although the Oxford performances appear to have been very successful, there is nothing in the English records to confirm the obviously fantastic sum which Handel is reported to have made out of the visit as recorded in the document quoted by Flower, which inaccurately gives the date as about the year 1738, and may be unreliable in other respects. Hearne gives Handel's Oxford earnings at upwards of £2,000. (*Remarks and Collections of Thomas Hearne*, 1885–1921.)

In January, 1735, Handel produced *Ariodante* at Covent Garden and *The London Daily Post* of November 4, 1734, stated: "We are informed that when Mr. Handel waited on their Majesties with his new Opera of *Arisdante*, his Majesty express'd great Satisfaction with the Composition, and was graciously pleased to subscribe £1,000 towards carrying on the Operas this season at Covent Garden." From the notices in the Treasury Papers October 23 and 29, 1734, it is clear that for some unknown reason the King personally gave his £1,000 to Handel and not to the Academy of Music. The entry on October 23, 1734, reads: "Mr. Chancellor [of the Exchequer] says the King intends that the £1,000 for the undertakers of the Opera shall be paid to Mr. Händel ('Hendell') and not to the Academy of Music, as the last £1,000 was," and the notice of the warrant for the same dated October 29, says for "George Frederick Handel, Esq. £1,000. Royal Bounty towards enabling the undertakers of the Opera to discharge their debts". This personal payment may be that referred to by Burney and in the newspaper notices as the King's gift of £1,000 as an expression of his satisfaction with

Ariodante, which was completed in October, 1734. It is, more-over, of interest to record that Handel's personally signed receipt for this payment is still in existence, having been sold at Sotheby's July 22, 1936. It was in 1734 that Handel changed over from the King's Theatre to Covent Garden, but he joined Heidegger at the former theatre again in 1737–38 for a brief period. Speaking of the season 1734–35, Malcolm (*Anecdotes*, etc.) says that "The King gave his annual £1,000 to the Managers of the Opera-house [that is to Handel's rivals] on this occasion, and added £500 as a subscription to Mr. Handel, who had Operas at Covent-garden Theatre, [adding, ambiguously] in consequence of a dispute with the latter, which caused an expenditure of £12,000 at the Haymarket and £9,000 to Handel."

As pointed out later on, other writers estimated that Handel lost about £10,000 prior to his collapse in 1737, and con-temporary evidence that his affairs were going badly in 1734–1735, is given in "A Letter to a Friend in the Country" (*The Old Whig*, No. 2, Mar. 20, 1734–35): "Handel, whose excellent Compositions have often pleased our Ears, and touched our Hearts, has this Winter sometimes performed to an almost empty Pitt. He has lately reviv'd his fine *Oratorio* of *Esther*, in which he has introduced two Concerto's on the Organ, that are inimitable. But so strong is the Disgust taken against him, that even this has been far from bringing him crowded Audiences; tho' there were no other publick Entertainments on those Evenings. His Loss is computed for these two Seasons at a great Sum."

On February 19, 1736, Handel produced at Covent Garden one of his most famous choral works, *Alexander's Feast*, which was an immediate success. According to *The London Daily Post* (February 20) there were at least 1,300 persons present and the receipts of the house not less than £450. The pit and boxes were laid together at half a guinea each person, and the first gallery was 4s. and the second 2s. 6d.

W. H. Husk, in his *Account of the Musical Celebrations on St. Cecilia's Day* (1857), records the following entry of charges made to Handel for the theatre which appear in the Account of the Treasurer of Lincoln's Inn Fields and Covent Garden Theatres:

Mr. Handel's Music

Dr. 1735-6	Charge	£	s.	d.
Thursday Feb. 19	Alexander's Feast	52	5	8
Wed. 25	Alexander's Feast	52	5	8
Mar. 3d	Alexander's Feast	52	5	8
Friday 12	Alexander's Feast	19	5	8
Wed. 17	Alexander's Feast	19	5	8
Wed. 24	Acis & Galatea	19	5	8
Wed. 31	Acis & Galatea	19	5	8
Wed. Apl. 7	Esther	19	5	8
Wed. „ 14	Esther	19	5	8
Wed. May 5th	Ariodante	52	5	8
Fri. „ 7	Ariodante	52	5	8
Wed. „ 12	Atalanta	52	5	8
Sat. „ 15	Atalanta	52	5	8
Wed. „ 19	Atalanta	52	5	8
Sat. „ 22	Atalanta	52	5	8
Wed. „ 26	Atalanta	52	5	8
Sat. „ 29	Atalanta	52	5	8
Wed. June 2	Atalante	52	5	8
Wed. „ 9	Atalante	33	13	8
In all 19.				

Received 1735-6	Nights paid for	£	s.	d.
Feb. 27 } Mar. 3 }	For Rent & Actors Servants pr. list	90 14	0 11	0 4
„ 12	Received in full	52	5	8
„ 17	Received in full	19	5	8
„ 24	Received in full	19	5	8
„ 31	Received in full	19	5	8
Apl. 7	Received in full	19	5	8
„ 14	Received in full	19	5	8
May 5	Received in full	19	5	8
„ 7	Received in full	19	5	8
„ 12	Received in full	52	5	8
„ 15	Received in full	52	5	8
„ 19	Received in full	52	5	8
„ 22	Received in full	52	5	8
„ 26	Received in full	52	5	8
„ 29	Received in full	52	5	8
June 2	Received in full	52	5	8
„ 19	Recd.	33	13	8

Husk comments on the above statement as follows:
"The charges in this account may be thus explained:

	£	s.	d.
"The rent of the theatre per night amounted to	12	0	0
The charge for Servants, i.e. Doorkeepers, etc.	7	5	8
Making together	19	5	8

To which was added the amount of the nightly salaries which the actors were entitled to receive from the manager for every night on which the theatre was open during the season, and on which dramatic performances could have been given   33   0   0

Making a total of   £52   5   8

The reduction of the charge to £19 5s. 8d. for each of the six nights commencing 12th March and ending 14th April is owing to those nights being the Wednesdays and Fridays in Lent, when (as the theatre could not be opened for dramatic performances) the actors were not entitled to be paid their salaries. The reduction of the charge of £33 to £14 8s. on the 9th June cannot be accounted for."

The fine score of *Alexander's Feast*, one of the best of Walsh's productions, was published in March, 1738, at two guineas, after a year's advertisement for subscribers who only numbered 124 (for 146 copies) to the first issue. Schœlcher says that Handel gained by this subscription nearly two hundred guineas.

Handel's failure is described by all of the early writers, but wrongly placed and dated by some. It is certain that it was in 1737 that his health failed and that he went to Aix-la-Chapelle for a cure; and although during the two or three preceding years he was finding opera production difficult at times, it seems that 1737 was the worst year. Extracts from several authorities follow. Mainwaring places the collapse and the visit abroad before *Alexander's Feast* and says: "instead of having acquired such an addition to his fortune, as from his care, industry, and abilities, he had reason to expect, he was obliged to draw out of the funds almost all that he was worth, in order to answer the demands upon him. This upshot put an end for the present to all musical entertainments at Convent-garden, and almost put an end to the author of them. The violence of his passions made such a disaster operate the more terribly."

Burney (*Sketch of the Life of Handel*) tells us that "Handel had been so unfortunate in all his attempts to carry on Operas at the three several theatres of the Haymarket, Lincoln's-Inn-Fields, and Covent-garden, in opposition to his former protectors, the members of the Royal Academy, that he was reduced to the necessity of drawing out of the funds ten thousand pounds, which he had lodged there in his more prosperous days; and still Strada, Montagnana, and other singers employed in his last Operas were unpaid, and obliged to quit this country with promissory notes instead of cash."

As a matter of fact, Montagnana did not sing in opera for Handel for a few years prior to 1737, but returned to the composer in *Faramondo* and *Serse* (1738).

Hawkins, whose chronology is very much at fault, does not state the amount which Handel is supposed to have lost, neither does Burney in his *History of Music*, where, after dealing with the production of *Serse*, he states: "Handel had been so great a loser by striving against the stream of fashion and opposition the preceding season, that he was obliged to sell out of the funds the savings of many former years, to pay his performers, and was still in some danger of being arrested by the husband of Strada, for the arrears of her salary. It was at this time that his friends with great difficulty persuaded him to try public gratitude in a benefit, which was not disgraced by the event; for on Tuesday, in Passion-week, March 28th [1738], was advertised at the Opera-house in the Hay-market an Oratorio, with a Concert on the organ, for the benefit of Mr. Handel; pit and boxes put together at half a guinea each ticket, and 'for the better conveniency, there will be benches on the stage.' The theatre, for the honour of the nation, was so crouded on this occasion, that he is said to have cleared £800."

It is of interest to note that it was in April, 1738, that the Roubiliac statue of the composer was completed for Vauxhall Gardens, to the order and at the expense of Jonathan Tyers. The statue was reported to have cost not less than £300, and in a notice about it in *The Daily Post*, April 18, 1738, it is stated that Tyers very generously took fifty of the tickets for Handel's benefit on March 28. One would like to know the reasons for Tyers's admiration of Handel and his generosity to him.

In Coxe's *Anecdotes of Handel* we are told that at this time (c. 1737) "he had lost ten thousand pounds, the produce of his youthful exertions, and was besides so greatly in debt, that he was in daily fear of being arrested for the salaries of his performers; with whom, however, he contrived to settle by bonds, which were afterwards duly discharged."

Schœlcher and later writers have described Handel as bankrupt, but there is not the slightest evidence that he was a bankrupt at this period or in 1745, however difficult it may have been for him to meet all of his debts with immediate cash payments. Mainwaring says he received £1,500 from the benefit, and other writers £1,000.

A very interesting piece of evidence of Handel's financial position soon after his benefit is given in a letter of Jennens to the Earl of Guernsey, dated 19th September, 1738, and published for the first time by Flower: "Mr. Handel's head is more full of maggots than ever. . . . His second maggot is an organ of £500 price which (because he is overstocked with money) he has bespoke of one Moss of Barnet." Was Jennens describing Handel's financial position accurately or only making fun of him? Perhaps the composer was able to indulge in the purchase of a new organ as a direct result of the benefit.

Abdy Williams says (on what authority is not stated): "The King, annoyed at the favour suddenly shown to Handel by the Prince of Wales after the wedding anthem and *Atalanta* [1736], ceased his annual subscription of £1,000. Handel had spent the whole of the £10,000, the savings of many years, with which he began his management."

Against all these various opinions we have definite evidence in the Treasury Papers that the royal subscription of £1,000 to the Royal Academy of Music (the Undertakers of the Opera) was paid in each of the years 1736, 1737 and 1738, covering the period of Handel's supposed financial collapse and bankruptcy; although there is no evidence that these payments supported Handel's company when he was not producing Italian opera at the King's Theatre.

Mainwaring tells us that Lord Middlesex undertook the direction of the Opera, and that Handel produced for his Lordship "*Faramondo* and *Alessandro Severo* . . . in the year 1737. For these he received 1,000l." Mainwaring's details are wrong. The date should be 1738, and there is no evidence in the Treasury Papers of payment of £1,000 to Handel, but only of the royal subscription of £1,000 to the Royal Academy for the Undertakers of the Opera (July 5, 1738); and the Earl of Middlesex apparently did not take over until 1741. (Burney.) Mainwaring does not mention *Serse*, which was produced on April 15, 1738, and only played five times.

There are no references in the Treasury Papers to opera payments during the years 1739–41, but the annual subscription was paid again in 1742 (June), 1744 (February and August) to The Royal Academy of Music (Undertakers of the Opera); but Handel at this time was not interested in Italian Opera. It is worth noting, that from 1722 until 1744 the royal subscription to the Opera was almost invariably made to The Royal Academy of Music, thus indicating that in spite of changes in direction, management, and personnel, some definite company or organized body was in control of Italian opera at the King's Theatre during the whole period, in spite of the reported collapse of the first Academy in 1728.

So much for Handel's operatic career. The last twenty years of his life were mostly concerned with oratorios, and in spite of the difficulties in the initial stages of popularizing this form of work against considerable prejudice, some determined opposition, and the vicissitudes of certain seasons, the composer must have found, on the whole, sound financial advantage in his performances, of which he gave something like 200 from 1743–59. He must have financed these himself, and was not bothered with the excessively high fees that were customary to the leading singers in Italian opera. As we know, he found it difficult at times to complete the number of subscription performances, but there is no reason to think that as a rule the oratorios, especially in his later years, did not pay. It is clear from certain reports that the receipts from single performances were from £300–£400. Most of the works were published soon after production, and there must have been a return from this source both to composer and publisher, although, as with the operas, the average edition could only have been a hundred or two.

Handel's successful visit to Ireland, 1741–42, when the first performance of *Messiah* produced upwards of £400 for charity, must have been financially advantageous to the composer. From the most reliable sources, it is known that all of his concerts before and after the production of *Messiah* were most enthusiastically supported; and it must have been a surprise for the composer to find that on his return to London he had difficulty in making a similar impression on his English public. The story has been told elsewhere of his series of subscription performances of oratorios that culminated, according to some writers, in a second bankruptcy in 1745, a statement for which there is no real evidence. (See Chapter V.) Although the next year was not too successful for the composer, from this time onwards he must have become increasingly free from financial anxiety, able to devote himself to his friends and his charities, performing and composing as he felt inclined, and with the sure knowledge that his reputation was secure.

Hawkins tells us, that in his later years "the produce of his oratorios amounted to more than two thousand pounds a season", and that he invested his money in the city "at the end of the Lent season, under the direction of Mr. Gael Morris, a broker of the first eminence, whom he used to meet and confer with at Garraway's or Batson's coffee-house". Burney (*Sketch*, etc.), referring to the season of oratorios before Handel's death, says: "One of my friends, who was generally at the performance of each Oratorio that year, and who used to visit him after it was over, in the treasurer of the theatre's office, says, that the money he used to take to his carriage of a night, though in gold and silver, was as likely to weigh him down and throw him into a fever, as the copper-money of the painter Coreggio, if he had had as far to carry it."

Whatever the facts are about Handel's personal gains and losses, it cannot be denied, that he was instrumental in raising considerable sums for charitable purposes. It is not necessary to tabulate here details of his personal gifts and generous actions to relatives and friends, but two of his major interests

The Foundling Hospital and The Fund for the Support of Decay'd Musicians, afterwards The Royal Society of Musicians, must be mentioned. Burney says that the Hospital benefited to the extent of £6,935 from the eleven performances of *Messiah* which were given by the composer from 1749 to 1759, and the round sum of £7,000 is given in the *History of the Foundling Hospital* (Nichols and Wray) as the proceeds to the charity resulting from Handel's performances on its behalf.

From the interesting details of the expenses of the performance of *Messiah*, May 3, 1759, it is possible to get an accurate account of the orchestra, singers, and the fees they obtained. The average of the instrumentalists was about 10s. 6d.; the singers, principals £1 1s., to £6 6s. the others 10s. 6d., and J. C. Smith, junr., who directed the performance in place of Handel, £5 5s.

It is probable that Handel received, as a rule, an "honorarium" for his performances, as recorded in the Foundling Hospital minutes on May 31, 1749 (*Musical Times*, May, 1902). On that occasion it is stated "That Mr. Handel be desired to return thanks of this Committee to the performers who voluntarily assisted him upon that occasion . . . That the treasurer do pay the secretary £50 for Mr. Handel to dispose of in such manner as he shall think fit." Probably Handel distributed part, at any rate, of this sum among the voluntary performers.

Handel was a subscriber to the Musicians Fund from its inception in 1738, and in addition, from 1739 onwards frequently gave performances of his works for the benefit of the institution, even at times when his own affairs were not too prosperous. It seems reasonable to suppose, however, that he was never quixotic enough to be raising large sums for charities when he was on the brink of financial ruin himself; and as recorded in the details of the Foundling Hospital performances, he did receive payment on some occasions—no reflection on his generosity—probably in recognition of the expense he was put to.

In his will and codicils, which included many personal legacies, Handel did not forget his favourite charities. To the Foundling Hospital he left a fair copy of the Score, and all the Parts of *Messiah*, probably to ensure that the annual benefit performances of the work should go on. "To the Governours or Trustees of the Society for the support of decayed Musicians and their Families" he left £1,000.

Handel is reported to have died worth £20,000 (Hawkins, Burney, Coxe). On this point we have definite contemporary evidence in the letter of James Smyth to Bernard Granville dated April 17, 1759 (Mrs. Delany, *Autobiography*, etc.), from which source we also learn that Handel made £1,952 12s. 8d. from his oratorios that year.[1]

The London Evening Post (April 14–17, 1759) stated: "By the death of the celebrated Mr. Handel a considerable Pension reverts to the Crown." While thus endorsing the evidence that the composer did receive a pension, this brief reference annoyingly omits the amount, and it is still therefore a matter for speculation as to whether it was only the £200 paid as music-master to the Princesses, or the grand total of £600 as frequently stated—£200 granted by Queen Anne, £200 granted by George I, and £200 as music-master. The details of the composer's will are too well known to be repeated here.

This survey leaves out of account the large circle of professional and private friends, influential and otherwise, who came into the composer's life, but about whom there is no definite evidence that they assisted him financially or otherwise. From what has been said, it seems perfectly clear, that in a purely material sense, Handel was a most fortunate musician. He was always in touch with people able to help him with their patronage or financial support. He must have made friends easily, and retained them. In spite of temporary setbacks, he was generally above want with its attendant fears, and was therefore able to express in his music the outstanding qualities of his personality—large heartedness—dignity—good nature—a cheery, healthy, human outlook without jealousy, bitterness, or pessimism.

---

[1]Fuller details of Handel's estate are given in Percy M. Young's biography of Handel.

III
THE EARLIEST EDITIONS
OF *MESSIAH*

THE
EARLIEST
EDITIONS
OF
MESSIAH

So much has been written about Handel, Walsh and *Messiah*, that it may seem futile to attempt to add anything of importance to what has already been published. In addition, however, to the fact that many of the popular statements on the matter are conflicting and inaccurate, there is a further reason for continuing the inquiry. Behind the few certainties and many speculations about the earliest appearances in print of *Messiah* there is a mystery still awaiting solution.

The purpose of the present article is to reopen the question in the light of some recent investigations that may help towards an ultimate settlement, and at any rate, a summary of the existing evidence for this or that theory should be useful.

Readers of Handel literature will be familiar with the statements that *Messiah*, in its complete form with the choruses, was first published by Randall & Abell, in 1767, and that a rare version of *Songs in the Messiah*, was published in 1760 or 1763, these editions being the first of the numerous issues of the immortal masterpiece.

The authority for the information with regard to the 1767 edition appears to be unquestionable. The work was advertised in *The Public Advertiser* for July 23, 1767, as being ready to be delivered to the subscribers, an earlier announcement on July 4, stating that it would be ready for July 7. For a fuller account of this part of the story the reader is referred to the excellent article by the late F. G. Edwards, in *The Musical Times*, November, 1902, although further reference will be made to the subject later on.

As to the actual date of the first edition of the *Songs in Messiah*, said to have been published in 1760 or 1763, there is unfortunately a good deal of repetition and contradiction in the statements of the authorities, but very little evidence. The matter is not referred to by Mainwaring, and apparently it did not attract attention until well on in the nineteenth century.

Sir George Macfarren, in a series of articles in *The Musical World*, 1849, refers to "the edition of Walsh, published in the life-time of the composer, in which the oratorio is printed 'as it was originally composed', namely according to Handel's MS., and the 'various alterations', namely the resettings of several pieces . . . form an appendix". "As it was originally composed" seems to be a corruption of "As it was Originally Perform'd" which appears on the Randall and Abell Score, the first edition to contain an appendix. The statement of Macfarren is qualified in his introduction to the libretto of the work, published by the Sacred Harmonic Society in 1853, and which reads as follows: "It is remarkable that the *Messiah* was not printed in the life-time of the author. This may be inferred from his legacy of the manuscript copy to the Foundling Hospital, and it is more directly proved by the catalogue of Walsh, his publisher, dated 1760, in which it is not included. A very scarce edition of the songs only, which has none but the first settings of the pieces that were recomposed, bears Walsh's imprint; this, however, is never advertised during Handel's life, neither does it appear in Walsh's catalogue to which reference has been made, whereas, of all the other Oratorios, the publication of the songs is announced in the journals immediately after the production of the works. The earliest printed copies of the entire work bear the imprint of Randall, Walsh's successor, and they are chiefly printed from the same plates as this edition of the songs, but the choruses are as obviously printed from plates engraved at a later time."

FRANCESCA CUZZONI

CHALK DRAWING BY PHILIPPE MERCIER

From the original in the British Museum

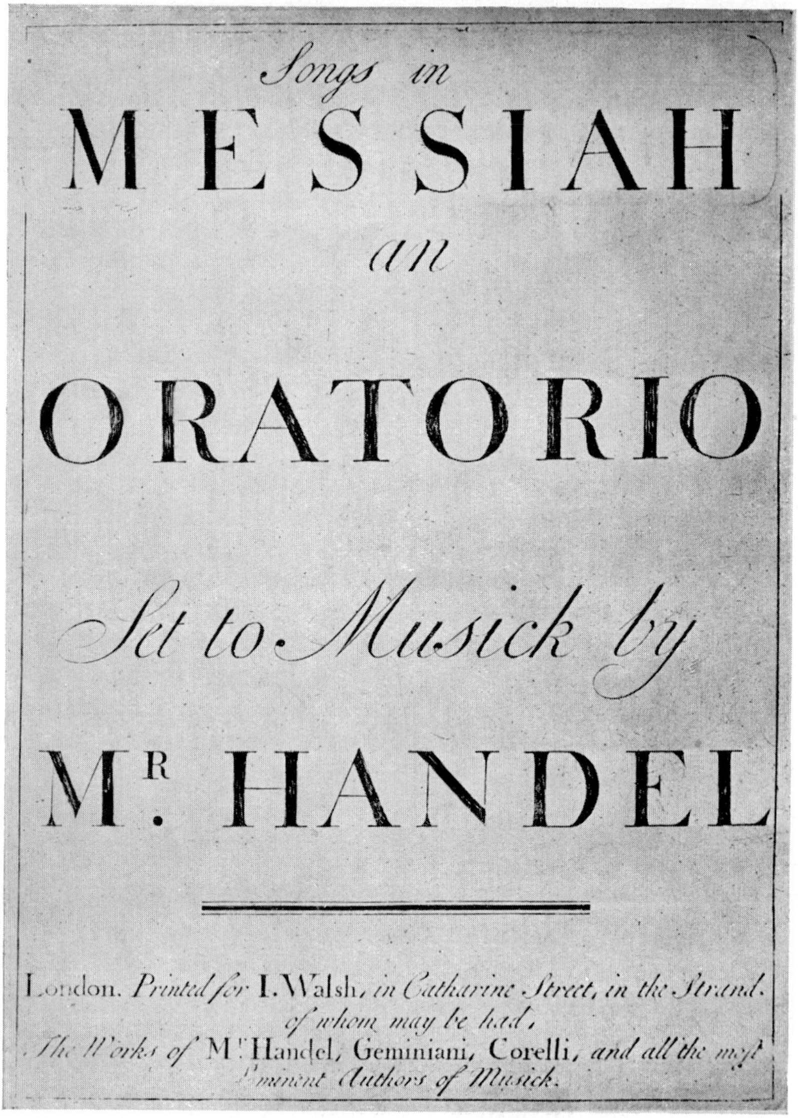

TITLE-PAGE OF THE FIRST EDITION
OF "SONGS IN MESSIAH" *c.* 1749

From an extremely rare copy in the possession of Wm. C. Smith

PLATE NO. 4

Still another modification was made by Macfarren in the preface to the vocal score of *Messiah*, published by R. Cocks & Co., London, in 1884. In this case it is stated that "The first publication of the songs in *Messiah* was advertised by Walsh, the music-seller, in 1760, the year after the composer's death." Schœlcher, in his well-known biography, says: "The first collected edition, entitled *Songs in the Messiah*, does not date further back than 1763, four years after the author's death. Even in this, there were wanting five recitatives and all the choruses, and still we find all the airs as they had been composed originally, and without any of the changes which Handel had made. The first edition which is really complete is that of Randall, Walsh's successor, and it belongs to the year 1768."

Some of the statements in these quotations need qualification.

Macfarren contradicts himself, and as no copy of the Walsh catalogue dated 1760 appears to be known, the statements must be taken for what they are worth. Walsh did advertise in November and December, 1760, *A Compleat Catalogue of Vocal and Instrumental Music. Price 6d.* Similar notices appeared in 1761, and subsequently, of what were probably other editions of the catalogue advertised as early as 1743; and from time to time Walsh issued catalogues of his publications at the end or beginning of some of his works.

The newspapers up to the end of 1760 did not advertise the publication of *Messiah* except in the 1743 references to the Overture, where the work is entitled: *The Sacred Oratorio* and also *Messia*.

Both Macfarren and Schœlcher are wrong in giving Randall as the publisher of the first printed Score. This was issued in 1767 and bears the imprint of Randall and Abell. Although this partnership ceased in 1768 owing to the death of Abell, Randall continued for a number of years to issue editions of the work with the two names still in the imprint.

Continuing his story of the publication of *Messiah*, Schœlcher mentions how he met John Caulfield, the son of Walsh's apprentice, and that Caulfield, in recalling the conversation of his father on the question of the publication of the work, said that "Walsh demanded the MS., sending, at the same time the usual *honorarium* of twenty guineas, which was the stipulated price of every oratorio which he printed. But the composer would not accept them, saying that rather than receive such a sum he would not publish the oratorio."

In considering the motives which may have prevented the early publication of *Messiah*, Schœlcher suggests "that Handel valued this work from the beginning, much beyond any other, in spite of the indifference of the public," and later on says, "It must even be supposed that Walsh was in some manner religiously bound, since, in spite of the certainty of profit, he only engraved his book of *Songs in The Messiah* four years after the death of the composer."

With reference to Schœlcher's remarks about Walsh, Frank Kidson, in his very interesting article, "Handel's Publisher, John Walsh, his Successors and Contemporaries" (*Musical Quarterly*, July, 1920), says: "It is obvious that Walsh junior is here meant for the elder Walsh died in 1736 when but few of the oratorios were issued. *The Messiah* in its entirety was not published until after the death of the younger Walsh, though one curious folio edition, *Songs in Messiah an oratorio, set to musick by Mr. Handel*, bears a Walsh imprint. There is reason to believe that this was published by William Randall, who has used an old title-page, the first three words being inserted from a different plate in one which seems to have been used for all the oratorios as they came out."

Mr. Kidson's reputation as an authority on music publishers is well known, but it is difficult to understand why he suggested Randall as the publisher of the *Songs*. The evidence appears to be in favour of a much earlier date than has been usually accepted, and there seems to be no apparent reason for ascribing the first edition to Randall, although he did publish some later issues of the work.

It may be as well to point out also, that Walsh used more than one kind of plate for the title-pages of Handel's oratorios, although the one referred to by Mr. Kidson is very common and was first used in 1747 for *Judas Maccabæus*. Another plate was used for *Joseph* (1744), and another for *Belshazzar* (1745), *Theodora* (1751), and *Jephtha* (1752), the imprint in each of these two plates reading the same except for punctuation: "Printed for I. Walsh . . . of whom may be had, all Mr. Handel's works." While admitting that it is unsafe to interpret Walsh's statements too literally, it is nevertheless interesting to find that subsequent to the production of *Messiah*, the publisher was advertising "all Mr. Handel's works".

F. G. Edwards, in the article already referred to, says:

"The Messiah" was not published in its complete form during Handel's life-time. The Overture is said to have appeared in 1743, as one of a set of overtures published by Walsh, who between the years 1749 and 1759, also issued eighteen of the vocal solos in a collection of 'Handel's songs (400) from the oratorios.' It is significant that while these 400 songs bear the titles of the oratorios from which they are taken, those from 'The Messiah' are printed without such headings."

The Overture to *Messiah* did appear (in eight instrumental parts, and also for the harpsichord) for the first time in 1743, in Walsh's Eighth Collection of Handel's Overtures.

The four hundred songs (first issued 1748-59) went through several editions, and instrumental parts were issued with them by Walsh. In the index to the volumes of these parts, the name of the oratorio is given to *Messiah* items, and in one or two of the parts the word *Messiah* also appears in connection with the aria, "But who may abide". Evidently there was some definite objection to publishing *Messiah*, or even items from it, with the same freedom as other works by Handel.

Romain Rolland, in *A Musical Tour Through the Land of the Past* (1922), says that "Handel had forbidden his publisher Walsh, to publish any part of this work [*Messiah*], the first edition of which did not appear until 1763, and he bequeathed to the [Foundling] Hospital a copy of the full score. He had given another copy to the Dublin Society for the Relief of Debtor Prisoners, with permission to make use of it as often as the Society pleased in the interest of their beneficiaries."

Other quotations could be furnished showing how contradictory the statements are as to the date of publication of *Messiah*, and the equally conflicting opinions as to why publication was delayed.

J. Allanson Benson, in his most interesting booklet, *Handel's Messiah: the Oratorio and its History*, offered, with much that concerns the practical interpretation of the work, a new suggestion that the *Songs* were first published as early as 1743–44, but were not advertised at the time owing to the objections which existed against the use of such a sacred subject as an entertainment. The question of date is important, and it is necessary to quote Allanson Benson on this point:

"It has been stated that the 'songs' in 'Messiah' were not printed till 1760 at the earliest. This seems to me to be very unlikely. The appearance of 'O thou that tellest' and 'He was despised', an octave higher in the G clef (the usual way of printing 'counter' parts for the use of the general public) long after they had ceased to be sung by that voice, cannot be accounted for. Then why should the original version of 'But who may abide', which Handel had certainly discarded after the first London performances (we gather from a pencilled note in the autograph that he had tried a transposition in E minor for Lowe) be inserted, when the version with the *prestissimo* movements had been in use both as contralto (artificial) and soprano for years? The air, 'But lo!' which he wrote for Mrs. Clive, must have been written for the early performances in 1743, or possibly 1745, as she did not sing for Handel after 1746; and this was printed instead of the original recitative (14a) which had been reverted to long before 1760. Again, the version of 'Thou art gone up' (the mezzo-soprano version—not the original bass) seems to have been written for early performances, for it must have come before the 'Guadagni' version, as it is in this collection; the 'Guadagni' not having been printed till Randall's score of 1767."

Although the evidence offered by Allanson Benson is extremely valuable in support of the theory that the *Songs* were published earlier than 1760, it will be shown later that his date of 1743-44 cannot be accepted.

The present writer in his original article on the subject, which appeared in *The Musical Times*, November, 1925, listed six early editions of the *Songs*, owned as follows:

No. 1.   Newman Flower. (First edition.)
No. 2.   Allanson Benson.
No. 3.   Newman Flower. (Another edition.)
No. 4.   Harold Reeves.
No. 5.   British Museum. (G. 160. p.)
No. 6.   British Museum. (G. 160. l.)

The conclusions arrived at in 1925 as to the number of known editions and the chronological order of them were based on the then available information. It is now necessary to reconsider the whole question in the light of later discoveries by the present writer.

The number of editions is now known to be at least nine, and the copies of them, listed here in chronological order, are owned as follows:

No. 1. William C. Smith.
      Newman Flower.   (No. 1. *Musical Times*, November, 1925.)

No. 2. William C. Smith.

No. 3. Mrs. Allanson Benson. (No. 2. *Musical Times*, November, 1925.)

No. 4. Newman Flower.   (No. 3. *Musical Times*, November, 1925.)

      Harold Reeves.   (No. 4. *Musical Times*, November, 1925.)

No. 5. British Museum. (G. 160. p. No. 5. *Musical Times*, November, 1925.)
      William C. Smith.

No. 6. The King's Music Library. (British Museum, R.M. 6. h. 15.)

No. 7. British Museum.   (G. 160. l. No. 6. *Musical Times*, November, 1925.)

No. 8. British Museum.   (G. 160. w.)

No. 9. An issue published with Pergolesi's *Stabat Mater*, with Walsh title-page, which cannot be placed exactly. No copy available. Walsh advertised the *Stabat Mater* in May, 1749.

In support of this chronological arrangement, the following evidence is offered.

The title-pages of Nos. 1-3 are similar and read as follows:

Songs in Messiah an Oratorio Set to Musick by M^r. Handel London. Printed for I. Walsh, in Catharine Street, in the Strand. of whom may be had, The Works of M^r. Handel, Geminiani, Corelli, and all the most Eminent Authors of Musick.

The title "Songs in Messiah" in the first three editions is from a supplementary plate; the title-page having been adapted from that used for *Judas Maccabæus*.

All the other editions have *The Songs in Messiah*, this title being from a different supplementary plate from that used for Nos. 1–3. Otherwise the title-pages of the first seven agree, all having the same Walsh imprint. No. 8 has simply the title, *The Songs in Messiah* in the middle of an otherwise blank page, without description or imprint. Other differences besides those on the title-pages distinguish the three earlier issues from the others. The earlier ones are paginated 1–70 at the bottom of the pages, in the centre, and have no additional paginations, such as occur in the later issues. Moreover, Nos. 1–3 are the only ones with the aria, "He was despised" printed in the G clef with the direction "To be Sung an Octave lower". The recitative "Then shall the Eyes of the blind" (p. 31), the heading "Part the Third" (p. 57), the separating stave marks (//) which occur in the other editions are all omitted from Nos. 1-3, and although these all differ from one another in details noted later on, they can be roughly grouped together as having been engraved and issued probably a good deal earlier than Nos. 4-8, with No. 1 unquestionably first.

Any student of the bibliographical and historical problems connected with Handel research must be prepared for surprises. When the original article on the subject of *Messiah* appeared in *The Musical Times*, November, 1925, the writer dealt with all the available editions and gave, quite rightly in the light of the then-existing evidence, priority of date to the issue represented by an extremely rare copy in Newman Flower's collection, one other copy of which has been discovered since and subsequently acquired by the present writer, who contributed a supplementary article on the subject to *The Musical Times*, December, 1941. At that time it was impossible to collate the two copies, and it was assumed that they were of different editions. Subsequent examination has now shown that they are alike, and are therefore the only two copies of the first edition of Handel's universally accepted masterpiece that have been identified up to date.

Bearing in mind what has already been said about editions Nos. 1–3, the earliest of these is easily distinguished from the other two by having less or different figurings in the Bass throughout. Some two hundred bars are different in this respect, of which the following examples taken at random will be sufficient for purposes of identification.

In this last example it will be noticed that the third note B was altered to A in the second edition.

The question of the changes in figuring in various editions of Handel's works is one on which there is little reliable information, and it is a subject for fruitful speculation and worthy of expert and detailed consideration. After the issue of Walsh's first edition of *Songs in Messiah* the figurings were drastically revised for the later editions, presumably by Handel himself, or under his direction by J. C. Smith, Walsh or one of his assistants.

Similarly the various editions of the Randall Scores of *Messiah*

75

show considerable differences in the figurings, as recorded later on.

The autograph (King's Music Library, R.M. 20. f. 2.) contains many figurings less than the editions of the *Songs* and the Randall Scores, but in the manuscript copy of the Full Score (R.M. 18. b. 10.) more figurings are given than in the autograph.

Songs in Messiah (Edition No. 1) consists of title-page, verso blank + pp. 1–70, without index. Page 1 is headed "Overture".

At the bottom of p. 35: "End of Act first"

At the bottom of p. 56: "End of Act 2d."

At the bottom of p. 70: "End of Act 3d."

These details are the same in the first three issues.

Contrary to the general practice observed in Walsh's other publications of Handel's vocal works, the singers' names are not given. In view of the uncertainty as to some of those who took part in the earliest performances, it is a pity that the singers' names are not mentioned. As pointed out later on, the first edition of the *Songs* was issued some years after the first performance of the work, which may explain the omission of the names.

Unquestionable proof that the issue described here as the first edition is really the earliest, is provided by the fact that the plates as altered with the new figurings in the Bass for the issue described as the second edition, were used in all of the subsequent editions of the *Songs*, and in the various editions of the Full Score from 1767 onwards, although in many cases further modifications were made to the plates.

As already pointed out, the first three editions have similar title-pages. (See Plate No. 4.)

The second edition, a copy of which is in the collection of the present writer, can be easily distinguished from the first by variations in the figuring referred to above. There are records of some half-a-dozen or so copies of this second edition elsewhere, that have hitherto been accepted as first editions. Until these have all been carefully examined in the light of the present study of the subject, it is impossible to identify them accurately.

The third edition, of which the only copy available for examination was formerly in the possession of Allanson Benson, is to be distinguished from the second by the re-engraving of p. 66 necessitated by the inclusion of the recitative, "Then shall be brought about the saying".

The plates of pp. 66–67 of this edition were not used in the main body of Randall and Abell's Score (1767) and subsequent editions of it. Page 165 of that work contained the recitative, "Then shall be brought to pass" and the shortened version of "O Death, where is thy Sting," while the versions of these numbers as they appeared on pp. 66–67 in the third edition of the *Songs* (Benson) were reproduced as pp. 34–35 of the Appendix to Randall and Abell's Score.

Editions Nos. 2 and 3 of the *Songs* have, in places, different figurings in the Bass from those of No. 4 and later editions, as the plates of No. 4, and after were as revised for use in the Randall and Abell and Randall editions of the Score.

Two copies of No. 4 have been examined, and were formerly listed as No. 3 (Newman Flower) and No. 4 (Harold Reeves), but the only difference between them is in the direction of the wire-lines in the paper, suggesting issues from the same plates at different times. For bibliographical purposes they can be considered together as one work, certainly later than Nos. 1–3. Besides the variations in figuring as compared with Nos. 2 and 3, No. 4 can be identified and definitely placed by having in addition to the original pagination (1–70) at the bottom of the pages, a second pagination at the top inner or outer corners, or top centre, running consecutively through the volume as follows: 1–10; 18–23; 37–41; 53–55; 60–67; 78–81; 106–109; 121–122; 126–134; 142–143; 153–155; 159–164; 34–35; 172–174. Pp. 17–19 (bottom pagination) have, however, no top pagination. The second (or top) pagination was added to the plates when they were prepared for Randall and Abell's complete edition with the choruses, published in 1767. The Appendix, issued as part of that work, and containing alternative settings of certain items, was paginated 1–35, and the pages 66 and 67 of the *Songs* (No. 4) with the top centre pagination 34, 35 contain the lengthened form of "O Death, where is thy Sting" which was printed as pp. 34–35 of the Appendix to the 1767 edition, the shortened version being inserted in its place in the body of that work. All the editions of the *Songs* (No. 1–3) have the longer version, but in the issues (No. 4 etc.)

subsequent to the preparation of the plates for the 1767 edition the pages have the second pagination (34, 35) of the Appendix of 1767 and later. Except for the removal of this number to the Appendix, and the following variations, the plates of the *Songs* with pagination at the bottom were used throughout for the 1767 edition:—Pp. 17–19 (O! thou that tellest) were from new plates, the aria for contra-tenor being lowered an octave for contralto voice, and the recitative, "Behold a Virgin", being included. This re-engraved version appears as pp. 30–32 of the 1767 edition, without any pagination at the bottom of the pages, although later issues of the *Songs* still retained the contra-tenor setting from the original plates. Pp. 36–39 ('He was despised") of editions Nos. 1–3 of the *Songs* were not used in the 1767 edition of the Score, because the number was re-engraved for the Score, and pp. 78–81 of that work (First and Second editions) have therefore no pagination (36–39) at the foot of the pages. As explained above, the first three editions of the *Songs* contain this aria printed an octave higher than it was to be sung, but in the full edition of 1767 it was given the lower setting, and this version with extra figurings was included in issues Nos. 4–8 of the *Songs*, with top pagination 78–81 and bottom pagination 36–39.

When the plates of the *Songs* were used for the Randall and Abell Score, the words, "End of Act first", "End of Act 2^{d}." and "End of Act 3^{d}." were erased from the plates as they did not apply to the Score, but as they were not completely obliterated some of the words still remain faintly legible in copies of the Score.

The next edition to be considered (No. 5, British Museum, G.160.p. and the author) has the same double paginations as No. 4, and in places a third pagination. This third pagination, added to the top centre of pages 14–16; 20–24; 48–54; 60–65, of the original edition is correspondingly as follows: 19–21; 22–26; 27–33; 34–39. This requires further explanation. In 1743, Walsh published a volume, entitled:

Handel's Bass Songs from all the Operas Price 5^{s}. London Printed for & Sould by I: Walsh Musicall Instrument maker in Ordinary to His Majesty at the Golden Harp & Ho=boy in Catherine=street near Summerset=house in y^{e} strand

This was followed in 1747 by:

> A Second Set of Favourite Bass Songs Collected from the Late Oratorios Compos'd by M^r. Handel. These Songs are proper for two Violoncellos. N.B. The First Set of Bass Songs are Collected from the Operas. London. Printed for I. Walsh, in Catharine Street in ye Strand.

This volume also bears another imprint in the form which appeared on the First Set as above.

In 1754 another volume appeared with a title-page like the First Set, but preceded by the words "A 3^d Set of", written in manuscript.

These three sets of Bass Songs were well advertised on various Walsh publications. They contain no items from *Messiah*.

Then in August, 1769, there appeared another volume entitled *A Fourth Set of Favourite Bass Songs*, with a similar title-page to that of the Second Set published in 1747 and with the two Walsh imprints, although the work must have been issued by Randall and not by Walsh.

The distinguishing feature of this Fourth Set is that it contains numbers from *Messiah*. It is paginated 2–51 consecutively, and the pagination of the *Messiah* items in this work is that which reappears as the third pagination on the later editions of the *Songs* (No. 5 and after) referred to above.

In addition to the consecutive and complete pagination, 2–51, every page of *A Fourth Set of Favourite Bass Songs* also bears at the top the pagination of the particular song as it appeared in, presumably, an earlier edition of the complete oratorio, or in an edition of the songs from the particular oratorio in question. In the case of the *Messiah* items, there are the three paginations, i.e., those of the *Songs*, of the 1767 edition of the Score, and of *A Fourth Set of Favourite Bass Songs*.

Although Randall's imprint appears on a number of his publications, he re-issued some of Walsh's works with the Walsh imprint, and as in the case of *A Fourth Set of Favourite Bass Songs*, Randall did not hesitate to adapt a Walsh title-page for use in an original publication of his own.

It is significant in this connection to note, for later consideration, that *A Fourth Set of Favourite Bass Songs* does not bear on the music pages of the *Messiah* items the word "Messiah", and neither the initials "W.R." nor the name "Randall", such as the same pages have in the later editions of *The Songs in Messiah*.

The items in *A Fourth Set of Favourite Bass Songs* include, in addition to those from *Messiah*, numbers from *Judas Maccabæus*, *Samson*, *Susanna*, and *Theodora*.

When the original article of this present study of *Messiah* was written, it was suggested that Randall's Score of *Samson* was contemporary with *A Fourth Set of Favourite Bass Songs*, because the double paginations were the same on the numbers that occur in both works. It is now clear, that there were two issues of the Randall *Samson*—one in 1769 before the *Bass Songs* and without the double paginations, and one in 1769–70 or later after the *Bass Songs*, and with the double paginations.

Returning to the question of editions of the *Songs*—No. 6 (King's Music Library, R.M. 6. h. 15.), not previously described in *The Musical Times*, November, 1925, differs from all previous issues in two respects. The first is the frequent use at the top of the pages of the word "Messiah". Whether there was formerly any reason for suppressing the advertisements of the oratorio under its correct name or not, they had evidently disappeared by the time this volume was issued. The second point is the addition at the bottom of some of the pages of the initials "W.R.". These initials stand for William Randall and might be considered conclusive evidence that the issue was by him. But from other evidence (water-marks, etc.) it is possible that the work was put out by Elizabeth Randall, his widow, in business (1776–1783?), the numbers of the work bearing the initials W.R. having been previously sold separately by William Randall.

The seventh edition of the *Songs* (British Museum, G.160.l.) is similar to No. 6, but with the addition of "Messiah Pr. 9^d" added to page 6, and "Randall" at the end of page 10; clearly supporting the theory already expressed about the sale of single numbers from the oratorio. This issue may also have been by Elizabeth Randall or even by her successors, Wright or Preston.

The eighth edition (British Museum, G.160.w.) is different from all the previous issues. The title-page, without imprint, simply contains *The Songs in Messiah*, impressed in the middle of the page, from the supplementary plate of the previous issues. The volume is a made-up copy from impressions of earlier plates, with some newly engraved, and with a number of blanks and other differences. Comparing the work with the previous issue some variations which will aid identification are:

Page 8 is from the plate newly engraved as page 8 of Wright's second issue of the Score (c. 1800) with Wright's pagination at the top.

Pp. 11–13 are omitted.

Pp. 27–28 are from the plates of the Second edition of the *Songs*.

There is a second page 28, with slight modifications in the figurings, from the plate as used in the Fifth edition of the *Songs* and with the pagination 60 at the top, from the Randall and Abell and Randall Scores.

Page 29 (the second page of "Rejoice greatly") is from the plate newly engraved as page 61 of Wright's first issue of the Score (c. 1785) with Wright's pagination at the top.

Pp. 16, 19, 21, 24 and 25 are followed by blank pages, and there are other blanks and details, distinguishing the work from other editions.

The copy must have been made up from whatever stock sheets and plates were available at the time, and was contemporary with or a little after the second Wright Score (c. 1800).

The edition listed here as No. 9, is only known to the present writer as an item in the sale catalogues of W. Reeves, London (Part 29, 1910; Part 30, 1911) where it is given as:

> Handel (Mr.), The Songs and Overture in the Messiah, an Oratorio, set to Musick, with the Stabat Mater of Pergolesi, Full Score, with Fig. Bass, folio, old calf, 10s. *Lon., I. Walsh.*
>
> The Stabat Mater referred to has its own separate title as well as being noted on the Messiah title.

Until a copy of this work is available for examination, little can be added to the information given in the Reeves catalogues. Walsh advertised a score of the *Stabat Mater* in 1749, which had already appeared in 1748 as part of "Le Delizie dell' Opere" (Vol. V), but no advertisement has been traced of *Messiah* and the *Stabat Mater* as being published together.

It is, moreover, quite impossible to suggest a date for the dual Walsh item. It may have been issued by Randall or his successors, in spite of the Walsh title-page. For the present, therefore, it cannot be considered as being placed in its proper chronological order.

In addition to the editions already mentioned, the following particulars of unidentified, or inaccurately catalogued copies, have been taken from various catalogues:

1. A copy, with title-page in manuscript *Songs in Messiah*. Walsh. (A ylesford Collection.)

2. A copy, unpaginated. Walsh. (Joachimsthal Gymnasium.)

3. A copy with the title *Messiah, an oratorio, set to musick*. Walsh. (Cummings, Sale catalogue.)

Of these No. 1 probably refers to an imperfect copy wanting the ordinary engraved title-page, or to an issue from Walsh's shop with an original manuscript title-page by the publisher, in keeping with a practice that he adopted sometimes with regard to other works; and Nos. 2 and 3 may be examples of inaccurate cataloguing, No. 3 being presumably the *Songs in Messiah* acquired by Ellis at the Cummings sale. (Ellis XXI, 1918.)

As a rule the publication of Handel's works was very well advertised, as even a cursory glance at the newspapers of the time will show. With few exceptions, soon after an opera or oratorio was produced, Walsh announced an edition of the work, or the songs from it, and on many of these publications there is a catalogue of earlier works also to be had of the publisher. As the oratorios continued to be produced, so the advertised list of them was extended, but up to the present the most diligent search has failed to find any mention of the *Songs in Messiah* or of the complete work in the advertisements before 1763.

If, as there is reason for thinking, the *Songs* were issued some years before the Score of 1767, why was the work not advertised in the usual way?

It is well known that the oratorio was produced in Dublin in April, 1742, when it was announced as "Mr. Handel's new Grand Oratorio, called the Messiah" (Faulkner's Journal, March 23–27—H. Townsend), but described on the word-book as "Messiah. An Oratorio". Performed in London three times in 1743, and twice in 1745, it was billed on these occasions as "A New Sacred Oratorio" or "The Sacred Oratorio". It was not performed again, apparently, until 1749, when it was advertised as "An Oratorio, call'd Messiah".

On July 19, 1743, *The Daily Advertiser* announced:

> New Musick. This Day are publish'd, Handel's Six Overtures for Violins, &c. in eight Parts, from the Operas and Oratorios of Samson, the Sacred Oratorio, Saul, Deidamia, Hymen and Parnasso in Festa. The eighth Collection . . . Printed for J. Walsh, &c.

This notice appears to be the earliest advertisement of the Overture to *Messiah*, although described as "The Sacred Oratorio". Other advertisements of a similar nature appeared in the newspapers on July 20 (*The Daily Advertiser*), July 21–23; July 26–28 (*The London Evening Post*) and an abbreviated notice December 14 (*The Daily Advertiser*), 1743. The same six Overtures for the Harpsichord were advertised for the first time apparently on December 2, 1743, when *The Daily Advertiser* announced:

> Musick. This Day are publish'd, Handel's Six Overtures from the Operas and Oratorios of Samson, the Sacred Oratorio, Saul, Deidamia, Hymen, and Parnasso in Festa, set for the Harpsichord. The eighth Book. The same Overtures may be had for Violins, in eight Parts. Printed for J. Walsh, &c.

On December 12, 1743, *The London Daily Post and General Advertiser* announced the work as:

> This Day is published, Price 3s. Six Overtures from the Opera and Oratorio's of Sampson, Messia, Saul, Deidamia, Hymen, Parnaso; set for the Harpsicord. Compos'd by Mr. Handel. The 8th Book . . . Printed for J. Walsh, &c.

This notice is of particular interest as it appears to be the only one of the period using *Messia* [i.e. Messiah] instead of "The Sacred Oratorio". On the title-page of the *Six Overtures*,

Messiah is given as "*The Sacred Oratorio*", but in the body of the work it appears as *Overture in Messiah*. A few years later, when Walsh issued new editions of the sets of Overtures, he invariably used the title *Messiah*.

During the period 1726–60? Walsh published (in separate parts with various title-pages) a work which in its completed form of seven volumes had the following title to the later issues:

> Sonatas, or Chamber Aires, for a German Flute, Violin, or Harpsicord. Being the most Celebrated Songs, and Ariets, Collected out of all the Late Oratorios and Operas. Compos'd by Mr. Handel.

Vol. 5 of this set, first published in parts 1743–44, contains one item from *Messiah*, namely, "He was despised". In the index to Vol. 5 of an early issue of the complete edition of the seven volumes of the "Sonatas or Chamber Aires" etc., this aria is given as "He was rejected" from *Messiah*, but on the page of the work it is described as "Air by Mr. Handel in the Sacred Oratorio". In a later issue of Vol. 5 the item is given in the index as "He was despis'd" from *Messiah* and in the body of the work as "Nº. 398. Air by Mr. Handel in the Sacred Oratorio. He was despised." No *Messiah* numbers occur in the sixth volume of the series, but there are nine in the seventh volume, published about 1760. In this latter volume the items are described in the index as being from *Messiah*, but in the body of the work there is no indication to that effect.

The omission of the source of the *Messiah* excerpts included in the collection *Handel's Songs Selected from his Latest Oratorios*, published from 1748–59, has already been referred to. It is only mentioned again here, as part of the evidence that exists to show that there must have been some significant fact behind the very occasional use of the word *Messiah* as the title of the oratorio.

The first definite advertisement of the publication of *Messiah* appears to be that in *The Public Advertiser* of March 29, 1763, which runs as follows:

> This Day is published, A second Set of Handel's Grand Songs in Score, introduced in his Oratorios, not printed before.

> 2. Handel's Oratorios in Score of Judas Maccabæus, Samson, Occasional Oratorio, Messiah, Alexander's Feast, Acis and Galatea. Also a complete Set bound, 14 Vols.
> . . . Printed for J. Walsh, &c.

Messiah was also advertised on this *Second Set of Handel's Grand Songs in Score*, the title-page of which reads *A 2ᵈ [ms] Grand Collection of Celebrated English Songs*, etc.; this being apparently the earliest advertisement of the oratorio on another Walsh publication.

The Walsh advertisement of March 25 (*Public Advertiser*), preceding the significant one of March 29, 1763, mentions *Handel's Oratorios in Score of Judas Maccabæus, Occasional Oratorio, Samson, Alexander's Feast, and Acis and Galatea, Also a complete Set bound, 14 vols. Messiah* is not specially mentioned, but it may easily have been included in the fourteen volumes advertised on March 25, and in the similar advertisements with slight differences that appeared for the first time on March 10, then on March 11, 12, 15, 17 and 18. As the advertisement of February 17, 1763 (*Public Advertiser*), announced the *Oratorios in Score, in 13 vols.*, it may be considered reasonable to assume that *Messiah* was first included in the fourteen volumes from March 10, 1763, onwards, but the Walsh advertisements are contradictory at times and are not accurate guides. For instance, as early as June 27, 28, 29, 1751, it was announced (*General Advertiser*) that *A Complete Set of all Mr. Handel's Oratorios may be had neatly bound in eleven volumes*, and on February 8, 1753 (*Public Advertiser*), *Handel's Oratorios in Score, in all 22, bound in 12 volumes*. Similar advertisements at other times, suggesting that Walsh was offering all the oratorios to date, could be quoted, but none of these would throw any further light on the query as to whether the advertisement of March 29, 1763, was coincidental with the publication of *Messiah* (songs or complete work), or whether the oratorio was published earlier and not advertised by name.

There was an advertisement in *The Public Advertiser* of September 16, 1763, which seems to sum up the position with regard to the oratorios. It mentions *24 Oratorio in Score, five of which are compleat with Recitatives and Chorusses*. Similar notices appeared on October 1 and 15, 1763. The reference to five of the Oratorios being complete might be considered to provide a clue, but when it is remembered that on the Randall and Abell Score of *Messiah* the only other complete scores mentioned as being available are *Samson*, *Alexander's Feast*, and *Acis and Galatea*, the uncertainty about *Messiah* still remains.

An attempt can now be made to approximate the dates of the various known issues of the *Songs in Messiah* reviewed above:

No. 1: Most probably first issued c. 1749, not c. 1733-4 as previously suggested in the *Musical Times*, November, 1925. The reason for this assumption is that the title-page is from an adaptation of the plate used by Walsh first of all for *Judas Maccabæus* in 1747. From a critical examination of the title pages of all the available copies of *Joshua* (1748), *Alexander Balus* (1748), *Susanna* (1749) and *Solomon* (April, 1749), all of which were from the same original *Judas Maccabæus* plate as *Messiah*, it seems clear that *Messiah* was issued soon after *Solomon*, and can therefore be reasonably dated 1749 or 1750. Unless a definite contemporary advertisement comes to light, this is as near to the actual date as one can get at present, and it is particularly interesting to note that 1749 was the year when the work was performed and announced in London for the first time under the title "An Oratorio, call'd Messiah", (*General Advertiser*, March 23) and the London libretto was issued at the same time with the title "Messiah: An Oratorio," &c.

No. 2: A little later, perhaps a year or two after No. 1.

No. 3: A few years later than No. 2. Perhaps it is the issue referred to in the advertisement of March 29, 1763, but there is no definite evidence on this point.

No. 4: Formerly listed as Nos. 3 and 4 and dated about 1763, in spite of earlier conclusions must now be considered as a Randall and Abell, or Randall issue, contemporary with the third edition of the Full Score, i.e. about 1768.

No. 5: 1769–70, a Randall issue contemporary with *A Fourth Set of Favourite Bass Songs*, but not bearing Randall's initials or name.

No. 6: c. 1775–80, a later Randall issue, or even put out by Elizabeth Randall, who succeeded her husband in 1776.

No. 7: Listed as No. 6, (1770 or later) in the *Musical Times*, November, 1925, but now considered to be by Elizabeth Randall or her successors, 1780?—1800?

No. 8: Publisher uncertain, c. 1800 or later.

No. 9: Cannot be dated.

These suggestions are put forward tentatively, but at least there is some bibliographical evidence for them.

Before leaving the question of *Songs in Messiah*, perhaps it may be of interest to record that in a letter of Mrs. Dewes to Bernard Granville, December 3, 1750 (Mrs. Delany, *Autobiography and Correspondence*) she says, "When I wish to raise my thoughts above this world and all its trifling concerns, I look over what oratorios I have, and even my poor way of fumbling gives me pleasing recollections, but I have nothing of the *Messiah*, but "He was despised." This extract suggests that the aria, unless the reference is to a manuscript, or to the arrangement in 'Sonatas or Chamber Aires' referred to above, had been published separately, but there is no evidence elsewhere that this was the case, although Walsh did sell single numbers of earlier works, and Randall continued the practice, including items from *Messiah*.

The 1767 edition of the Score of *Messiah*, published by Randall and Abell, is so well known to collectors that it might seem to be unnecessary to do more than merely mention it here. Hitherto it has been generally accepted as the only issue of the Full Score put out by Walsh's immediate successors and having the imprint of Randall and Abell. It can now be shown that there were at least five or six editions of this famous work; the later issues having been generally wrongly described as first editions. Details of the editions are given below, and from an examination of available copies it is apparent that genuine examples of the first edition are almost as rare as copies of the first edition of the *Songs*. The present writer is fortunate in possessing a fine specimen of the first edition of the Score with a fairly early, if not contemporary, finely decorated binding.

It is not intended to give here all the distinguishing features of the various editions that have been traced, but only enough information to enable copies to be accurately identified.

The title-page of the first, which, with engraving slightly

modified, was also used in the next four or five editions, reads as follows:

> Messiah An Oratorio in Score As it was Originally Perform'd. Composed by M^r. Handel To which are added His additional Alterations. London. Printed by Messrs. Randall & Abell Successors to the late M^r. J. Walsh in Catharine Street in the Strand—of whom may be had the compleat Scores of Samson, Alexander's Feast, and Acis & Galatea.

The first state of the title-page is as that of the present writer's copy, the only one identified up to the present. In it the "add" of "additional" is rather thickly and roughly engraved, and the two "t's" of "Alterations" are crossed differently from these letters in later issues. (See Plate No. 5.)

The work is paginated at the top outer corners 1–188, followed by Appendix with top centre pagination 1–35. "End of the First Part." occurs at the bottom of p. 73; "Part the Second." at the top of p. 74; "End of the Second Part."at the bottom of p. 152; "Part the Third" at the top of p. 153; "Finis" at the bottom of p. 188. Throughout the volume, with some exceptions, the separating stave marks (//) are given, which do not occur in the preceding editions of the *Songs*. As already pointed out the plates of the *Songs* were used where possible in the preparation of the Score, and the pagination of the *Songs* therefore appears at the bottom of the pages in the Score that were printed from these plates. The pages used from the *Songs* are 1–16, 20–35, 40–65, 68–70 in the body of the work, and 66–67 in the Appendix. The pages 17–19 of the *Songs* were not used in the Score as new plates were engraved for this number ("O! thou that tellest") which was lowered for a contralto voice, and the recitative "Behold a Virgin", added. Similarly the original plates of pages 36–39 of the *Songs* were not used in the Score, the number ("He was despised") being reset an octave lower in the Score than in the *Songs*. The pages 66–67 as revised for No. 3 etc. of the *Songs* appear in the Appendix to the Score, a shortened version of the number ("O Death, where is thy Sting") being used at page 165 in the body of the work, with the recitative "Then shall be brought to pass" instead of "Then shall be brought about".

The work contains "A List of the Subscribers" (92 for 129 copies, on 2 pages) and "Index" leaf; and although these features appear in the later editions also, there are variations to be noted which will aid identification:

> Mr. Samuel Arnold
> Mr. Samuel Dyer
> Mr. Morrice Dreyer
> Mr. Samuel Howard
> The Singers at Ossett

are names of the subscribers amongst others, the form of which varies in some of the later editions. The printer's ornaments of the "List of the Subscribers" and of the "Index" in the first edition differ from those in some of the later editions. In the first and second editions rests are omitted from the second and third bars of the Bass vocal part of the bottom stave of p. 180. These have been supplied in manuscript to the author's copy of the first edition. It is not known whether the rests were added to the plate for the third and fourth editions, but they are in the fifth and subsequent editions. The differences in figuring of the first and second editions are indicated under the latter.

Of the pages in the Score printed off from the plates as used in the second and third editions of the *Songs* some hundred and twenty bars have different figurings in the Bass from those in the second edition of the *Songs*. These further modifications could not have been made by Handel as the Score appeared eight years after his death.

Three copies at least of the first edition of the Score were specially issued in three volumes or parts. A complete copy in this form is in the King's Music Library (R.M.7.g.6.), and may have been prepared as the subscription copy for George III. The first volume ends at page 73, the verso of which is blank. The second volume commences with a blank page, the verso of which is page 74, and the part ends at page 152. The third volume has no title-page, but commences at page 153 and concludes with page 35 of the Appendix, the verso of which is blank. This copy has the slight modifications in the engraving of the title-page as referred to below, and which exist in all of the subsequent impressions from the same plate.

A copy of the second volume of the three volume issue is in the possession of Gerald Coke. On the blank page at the beginning of the work is the description "2d Act" in manuscript.

It seems fairly safe to assume that the well-known Houbraken portrait of Handel was not issued with the first edition of the Score and probably not with the second or third editions, or at any rate not with all copies.

The second edition of the Score, a copy of which is in the British Museum (I.112.), has two or three variations, not very important, but which distinguish it from the first edition. The letters "add" of "additional" on the title-page have been thinned, and the crossing of the "t's" in "Alterations" has been modified as in the three volume issue of the first edition in the King's Music Library. This later revised title-page was used for all of the subsequent Randall editions. On page 19 of the Appendix of the second edition, bars 6, 7, 8 and 10 have additional figurings in the Organs from those given in the first edition.

Appendix p. 19. Bars 6–10.

First edition.

Second edition.

These slight, but significant differences, place the work a little later than the first edition, probably in 1767 or 1768.

The third edition (a copy of which was formerly in the possession of Harry Wall, Sittingbourne), has title-page, contents and pagination as in the second edition, except that pages 78–81 are from modified plates and have an additional bottom centre pagination 36–39. This is explained by the fact that this number ("He was despised") in the newly engraved form with additional figurings was used for the fourth and subsequent issues of the *Songs*.

The "List of the Subscribers" gives "Samuel Dyer, Esq." instead of "Mr. Samuel Dyer"; "Mr. Maurice Dreyer" instead of "Mr. Morrice Dreyer"; the ornaments of the "List" are different from those used in the earlier editions, and there may be further modifications in the figurings. The details given here are sufficient, however, to identify copies. These may or may not have had the Houbraken portrait. This third edition of the Score may be assumed to be about 1768.

A fourth edition of the Score can be distinguished from the previous issues by the extra top centre paginations:

$$
\begin{array}{lll}
19\text{–}21 & \text{on pp.} & 21\text{–}23 \\
22\text{–}26 & ,, & 37\text{–}41 \\
27\text{–}33 & ,, & 128\text{–}134 \\
34\text{–}39 & ,, & 159\text{–}164
\end{array}
$$

These extra paginations are from *A Fourth Set of Favourite Bass Songs* issued in 1769, and are referred to under the *Songs in Messiah*.

The ornaments on the "List of the Subscribers" and "Index" page are different from those in previous editions, and amongst the subscribers appear "The Singers at Osset" instead of "Ossett".

Samuel Howard appears as "Mr." He became "Dr." Samuel Howard in 1769. It is reasonable therefore to place this edition at about 1769, and it may be identified with that advertised in May, 1770, as being on "Imperial Paper". The copy examined contains the Houbraken portrait, which does not appear to have been included in the earlier editions.

What can be considered as another issue of the fourth edition is recorded, the only variations being different ornaments in the "Index" and "List" from those in the preceding issue, and one minor change at least in the subscriber's names: "Perkins, Organist of Finedon" instead of "Findon". As this reported copy is not available for examination, the detail given here must be taken with reserve, and further information may entail reconsideration as to approximate date and description.

A fifth edition was issued with further alterations in the "List of the Subscribers": "Dr. Samuel Arnold" instead of "Mr.", "Dr. Samuel Howard" instead of "Mr.", "Mess. Thompson" instead of "Thompsons", "Rev. Mr. Pinder" instead of "Pindar", and the names under "H" are in the order, "Heaton, Hurdis, Howkins", etc. The "Index" is differently set up, and the ornaments on "List" and "Index" pages are again different from those used in earlier editions, and there are other minor variations in spelling, type, etc. Over fifty bars show different figurings compared with those of the second edition, although some of these variations may occur in the third and fourth editions, which have not been compared in this respect. Two or three examples which may help identification of copies are as follows:—

	Second edition.	Fifth edition.

Page 7. Stave 1. Bar 1.

Page 8. Stave 1. Bar 2.

Page 14. Stave 2. Bar 7.

Page 180 has the rests supplied to two bars of the Bass vocal part, bottom stave, omitted from the first and second editions, but which may be in the third and fourth.

As Arnold became "Dr." in 1773, this edition must be of that date or later. Copies of this edition presumably had the Houbraken frontispiece although missing from the present writer's copy.

Elizabeth Randall, the widow of William Randall, continued the business after the death of her husband probably early in 1776, until May, 1781, at anyrate, and perhaps until early in 1783, when Wright & Wilkinson (Wright & Co.) advertised as the "Successors to Mr. Walsh" at the Catharine Street address, and as the "Proprietors of all Handel's Works and Manuscripts". They issued a number of Scores of Handel works in a form similar to those of Randall's. H. Wright, after Wilkinson died or left the firm, put out three issues of *Messiah* from Randall's plates with modifications, two with the address "Catharine Street", the first c. 1785, the second c. 1800, not later than the end of 1801, and the third, with the address "386, Strand", about 1802. These issues had bad impressions of the Houbraken frontispiece, and the title-pages were adapted from Randall's, with the addition of the price £1 11s. 6d. on copies of the first £1 1s. on copies of the second and third, but probably with the price erased entirely or amended in some cases. Randall sold the work at £2 2s. Wright issued some Handel oratorios at £2 2s. but at £1 11s. 6d. to subscribers, and in 1786 he reduced the price of oratorios generally to £1 1s.

The first Wright edition (c. 1785) has the same title-page, except for imprint and price, as the last Randall, and includes the Houbraken portrait, "List of Subscribers" and "Index" as in that edition, which it follows generally, except that page 61 is from an entirely new plate afterwards used for page 29 of the *Songs*. (No. 8.) A number of the pages have the addition of "Messiah" at the top, and some "W.R." and in one case (page 10) "Randall" at the bottom, as in editions of the *Songs* (Nos. 6 and 7), these items having been issued previously and sold separately.

The second Wright edition (c. 1800) is similar to the first, except that the price is different, the "List of Subscribers" is omitted, the "Index" differently set up is on the verso of the title-page, and page 8 is from an entirely new plate, afterwards used for page 8 of the *Songs*. (No. 8.)

The third Wright edition (c. 1802) is generally the same as the second, except that the imprint has the address changed to "No. 386, Strand".

When Wright ceased publishing about 1803 or later, Thomas Preston, who succeeded his father John Preston at 97, Strand, c. 1798, acquired Wright's stock of plates. Somewhere about 1805–10 he issued the Score of *Messiah* from the Randall and Wright plates, with his own imprint on a newly engraved title-page carefully copied from Wright, and with the Houbraken portrait as frontispiece.

This was the last of the early editions that had a direct connection with Walsh's publications and in which impressions from his original plates appeared, but some use of these plates was made by J. Alfred Novello as late as 1850, after he had acquired them at the sale of Coventry and Hollier's stock in December, 1849. This issue is referred to again later on.

Although not of particular importance for the purposes of this study, an edition of the Score of *Messiah*, issued by Bland and Weller about 1813–15 may be briefly noted. It is a folio volume with the following title-page:

> New Edition Messiah An Oratorio. (In Score) As it was Originally Performed Composed by M^r. Handel, To which are added His Additional Alterations. Pr. 1^L. 1^s. 0. London. Printed & Sold at Bland & Wellers, Music Warehouse, 23 Oxford Street.

The whole work (including title-page) although set up from entirely different plates, was made to look as much like the Randall, Wright, Preston issues as possible, having the same top page pagination as its predecessors: (1–188 + Appendix 1–35) and following them generally in layout, figurings, etc.

Details of other early nineteenth century editions of *Messiah* or parts of it by various English publishers (G. Walker, Lavenu & Mitchell, Goulding & D'Almaine, Button & Whittaker, R. Birchall, etc.,) are omitted from this examination of the subject, which is primarily concerned with editions by Walsh and his successors and competitors up to the end of the eighteenth century. It may be pointed out, however, that Robert Birchall issued c. 1800–01, *Handel's Oratorios in Parts for a Full Band*, including *Messiah*, of which he also published the Score.

Before dealing with the more important editions of Harrison, and Arnold, it is necessary to make brief reference to the publications of John Bland (114 Long Acre, c. 1776–78; 45 Holborn c. 1779–95), a different firm from that of A. Bland (23 Oxford Street, 1784–92), afterwards Bland and Weller (1792–c. 1818). Each of these firms published Handel's Songs, Overtures, etc., in sheet form and John Bland advertised, c. 1782, an edition of the "Overture and Airs in the Messiah for the Hp^d. [Harpsichord] 3s. 6d.", also "Songs in Messiah, 3s. 6d.". These editions were simply previously published numbers brought together in one volume, each number headed with its own title and imprint, "London. Printed for J. Bland," etc. The edition of "The Overture and Songs . . . for the Harpsichord" was re-issued, c. 1797, by Francis Linley, from Bland's plates, and subsequently by Preston & Son, with the imprints changed accordingly. The separate items, of which these editions were made up, were rather roughly engraved, and were sold separately at a penny a page; and form an interesting link between the expensive Randall, and Wright editions, and the highly successful and popular vocal scores of Harrison.

The first serious attempt to issue an edition of *Messiah* in competition with the Walsh and Randall issues was made by Harrison & Co. (James Harrison) of 18 Paternoster Row in 1783–84. This energetic firm, whose activities have been generally overlooked, published most of Handel's Oratorios besides works by other composers. From 1783 to 1792, if not later, frequent advertisements of *The New Musical Magazine* appeared in the press. The announcements are confusing, and in the absence of a complete file of the work it is difficult to say whether there were any differences in the various issues. In November, 1783, the publisher announced *The New Musical Magazine*, as a proposed monthly series of well-known musical works to be issued in parts, each part with a sheet of letterpress. The scheme was modified and a new edition, to be continued weekly, was announced March 15, 1784, after sixteen numbers had appeared. Of these, numbers 2–6 contained *The Messiah . . . with the Chorusses in Score*. The five parts were issued separately at 1s. 6d. each, the whole work for 7s. 6d. Harrison's plan was definitely competitive, as he published lists of his prices for various works in contrast with the prices of other publishers. In the list of March 15, 1784, he compared his *Messiah* at 7s. 6d. with other editions at £2 2s., thus clearly referring to those of Randall and Wright, without mentioning their names, and in a "Contents" sheet of the first sixteen numbers of *The New Musical Magazine* he compared his price of £1 4s. with other music-sellers' prices of £5 12s. 6d. Harrison's cut prices seem to have had some effect, for on June 9, 1786, H. Wright advertised himself in *The Morning Herald* as the real proprietor of all Handel's works and manuscripts, and added that "his complete Oratorios in score, for the easier accommodation of the public are this day reduced to £1 1s. each."

The title-page of Harrison's *Messiah* reads as follows:

> The Messiah; An Oratorio. Composed by Mr: Handel, For the Voice, Harpsichord, and Violin; with the Chorusses in Score. London: Printed for Harrison & Co. No. 18, Paternoster Row.

The volume is an oblong folio, in style and size similar to Harrison's issue of *Acis and Galatea* and other works in the series. It consists of title-page, verso blank + blank, verso pp. 4–88 of music, + p. 89 "Contents" page, verso blank, paginated at the top outer corners. It is divided into three parts, with an "Appendix" commencing at page 84, which consists of the Chorus, "Their sound is gone out" and the Duet and Chorus, "How beautiful". The body of the work includes the continuous solo setting of "How beautiful . . . Their sound is gone out" as in the body of Randall's edition pp. 126–127. The serial numbers of *The New Musical Magazine* appear at the bottom of the pages, 2 on pp. 4–18, 3 on pp. 19–34, 4 on pp. 35–50, 5 on pp. 51–66, 6 on pp. 67–89. The figuring to the Bass does not agree as a rule with that of the later Randall issues.

In February and March, 1785, there were announcements in *The Morning Post and Daily Advertiser* of a "New Edition of the New Musical Magazine . . . comprehending the Entire Works of Handel, Arne and other celebrated Composers. . . . Carefully revised by and published under the immediate inspection of Dr. Arnold".

On June 1, 2, 1785, Harrison & Co. advertised (*Morning Post and Daily Advertiser*) in connection with the Musical Festival, Westminster Abbey, "The Messiah, for the Voice, Harpsichord & Violin, with the Choruses in Score. . . . Elegantly and correctly engraved. Under the inspection of Dr. Arnold." There are further general advertisements of *The New Musical Magazine* in 1785. In February, 1786 (*Morning Chronicle and London Advertiser*; *Morning Herald*) there are notices of "The six select Oratorios of Handel, as they are to be performed during the Lent Season. . . . Messiah, 7s. 6d., Israel in Egypt, 15s. . . . The whole elegantly and correctly engraved with the

Chorusses in Full Score, under the Direction of Dr. Arnold. . . . Printed for Harrison and Co. . . . of whom may be had other compleat Works of the Immortal Handel, at considerably less than half the usual Prices, all carefully corrected by Dr. Arnold."

Contemporary with one or another of these notices of 1785–86, Harrison put out another edition of *Messiah*, although there is no indication on the work itself that it was published "under the Direction of Dr. Arnold." The title-page is the same as in the first Harrison edition, but the work, although generally similar in style, is an entirely new edition from new plates not bearing the part numbers of *The New Musical Magazine*. It consists of title-page, verso blank + blank, verso pp. 4–87, verso "Contents" page. It is in three parts. Besides variations in figurings, symphonies, etc., the chief difference between this and the earlier edition is the inclusion in the main body of the work, of the two numbers in the "Appendix" of the earlier edition, followed by the additional air "Their sound is gone out", which is in the Appendix to Randall's edition (p. 33), and in Arnold's later edition of the score (p. 151). Harrison's cheap and handy editions of *Messiah* and other Handel works must have sold very well, being the only cheap editions available at the time of the Handel Festivals, 1784, 1785 and onwards.

Harrison was still advertising *The New Musical Magazine* . . . *The whole Corrected by D*ʳ. *Arnold* as late as 1792, although by that time Arnold had probably given up his active connection with the work, as he was then busy on his monumental and well-known edition of Handel. In fact, it is possible that his association with Harrison gave Arnold the idea of the more ambitious project.

The independent sheet of letterpress which Harrison advertised as issued with each work of *The New Musical Magazine*, is assumed, not without reason, to have been the libretto of the particular work, as a number of such libretti without title-pages exist in the British Museum (11770.g.1.–5.) catalogued separately from the music.

On May 22, 1786, *The Morning Post and Daily Advertiser* and other papers announced:

> Handel's Songs Complete. (Harrison's Edition) Corrected by Dr. Arnold. Dedicated to their Majesties. On Saturday next, May 27th, will be published, embellished with a most splendid Vignette Title-page, designed by Mr. Burney, and engraved by Heath. Number I. To be continued Weekly, Price only 1s. 6d. of The Songs of Handel Complete; for the Voice, Harpsichord, and Violin. Beautifully and uniformly engraved on large Folio Plates, under the direction of Dr. Arnold, Organist and Composer to his Majesty. ·.· The two first Numbers of this valuable Work will contain the Overture and all the Songs in the Messiah complete, though inferior Editions are sold at the Music-shops for Half-a-Guinea. Printed for Harrison and Co., No. 18, Paternoster-row.

The title-page of this Harrison edition of *Messiah* reads as follows:

> Harrison's Edition, Corrected by D^r: Arnold. The Overture and Songs in the Messiah, An Oratorio; for the Voice, Harpsichord, and Violin. Composed by M^r. Handel. London: Printed for Harrison and C^o. N°. 18, Paternoster Row.

The volume is an oblong folio, in style and size similar to the vocal scores of Harrison's *New Musical Magazine*, but it contains only the Overture, Recitatives and Songs, with figured Bass. It consists of title-page, verso blank + blank, verso 4–32 of music + "Contents" page, verso blank, and was issued as parts 1 and 2 of the series of Handel's Songs, the serial part numbers 1* and 2* appearing at the bottom of the pages.

With the first part of this *Messiah* Harrison issued a finely designed title-page of the series by Burney, engraved by Shepherd and Heath, followed by a dedication to the King and Queen, by James Harrison, dated May 27, 1786, bearing the Royal Arms, designed by Sharp and engraved by Walker. This title-page reads:

> Harrison's Edition, Corrected by D^r. Arnold. The Songs of Handel. Volume the First. Containing all the Overtures, Airs, Duetts, &c. in The Messiah, Judas Maccabæus, Acis and Galatea, Samson, Alexander's Feast, and

98

Dryden's Ode on S^t. Cecilia's Day. For the Voice, Harpsichord, and Violin. London: Printed for Harrison and C^o. N°. 18, Paternoster Row. Published as the Act directs, May 27, 1786.

One copy of *Messiah* is listed as containing a four page catalogue of music published by Harrison, this also bearing the Royal Arms, which also appear again on a front wrapper of this particular volume. The British Museum copy is without the wrapper or catalogue.

On May 29, 1786, the Harrison advertisement of *Handel's Songs Compleat . . . corrected by Dr. Arnold*, as given on May 22, appeared in *The Morning Herald*, immediately above the notice of Arnold's proposals for his subscription edition of Handel's works, the project which may have caused Arnold to sever his connection with Harrison about this time; the first notice of Arnold's edition having appeared in *The Public Advertiser*, May 25, 1786.

Kidson says that "it was James Harrison who was thoughtful enough to provide for the gentleman amateur a full copy of the *Messiah* for a single German Flute". No copy of this work has been traced.

Arnold's well-known collected edition of Handel's works was issued in parts commencing May, 1787. The title-page of *Messiah* reads as follows:

> Messiah A Sacred Oratorio In Score With all the Additional Alterations Composed in the Year 1741. By G. F. Handel.

The work consists of title-page, verso blank + pp. 3–218 of music, followed by page 219 containing "But who may abide", with the note "N.B. This Recit was originally Performed in Ireland", and "Contents" in two columns on the same page, verso blank. The Arnold serial numbers 9-13 occur throughout the volume at the bottom of the pages. There is no appendix of alternative versions, but the different versions of some numbers occur following each other in the body of the work. The figuring of the Bass differs in places from that in the Walsh and Randall issues. The five parts (Nos. 9–13) were issued during the months November, 1787– February, 1788, and with number 12 the well known engraving entitled: "Apotheosis of Handel", designed by Rebecca from a painting by Hudson and engraved by Heath, was presented to the subscribers. Arnold originally intended to give a copy of this with each class of Handel's works issued, in order for it to form a frontispiece, but he afterwards issued other engravings with the series which, from an examination of several sets of the edition, appear to have been inserted in various volumes according to the whim of the subscriber or owner.

It is not generally known that Arnold announced in August, 1788 "A New Edition" of Handel's works at 4s. a part "on Imperial paper" and 3s. "on inferior paper". On May 25, 1790, No. 1 of "A new Edition . . . Revised and corrected" was announced.

Another issue is supposed to have been made in 1797, and in 1802 Arnold advertised "A New, Revised and Corrected Edition of the Works of G. F. Handel . . . Each Volume, on Demy paper, Seventeen Shillings only;—on Imperial paper, One Guinea", etc. It is impossible to say with certainty to which issue a particular volume of Arnold belongs. The set in the King's Music Library can be accepted as a standard first edition, but most other sets have variations that make them difficult to date. In the later issues it is clear that *Messiah* underwent some changes. The British Museum volume (I.50. c. 1795 or later) has the same material and layout of the title-page as that of the King's Music Library copy, but the engraving is different and the words "Dr. Arnold's Edition" are added at the end of the title. More significant is the figuring in the two volumes, some sixty bars being different. The frontispiece of the King's copy is the "Apotheosis of Handel" (Rebecca–Heath) dated 26 of May, 1787, while the British Museum copy has the Cipriani–Bartolozzi portrait of Handel in ornamental setting, with the inscription underneath, "George Frederic Handel", etc., as in *Joseph* (c. 1794–95, King's Music Library copy), although this difference is not of significance in placing the work.

One other edition of *Messiah*, published by Harrison, Cluse & Co. of 78, Fleet Street (the successors of Harrison & Co.) c. 1798–99 must be noted. It formed Number 2 of Volume 6 of a popular periodical entitled *The Pianoforte Magazine*. The title-page reads:

> The Overture, Songs, and Recitatives; in the Messiah: A Sacred Oratorio. Composed by, G. F. Handel London: Printed for Harrison, Cluse, & Co. No: 78, Fleet Street.

The work is octavo, consisting of title-page, verso blank + blank, verso 4–41, verso blank + "Contents" page, verso blank. The pagination 4–41 is at the top outer corners, with the serial numbers 84, 85 of the Magazine at the bottom of the pages. It contains the Overture, Songs and Recitatives in Piano Score, without figuring to the Bass.

Mention has already been made of J. A. Novello's use of Walsh's and Randall's plates. Further details are given here. Novello's intention to issue a number of facsimile volumes of Handel's works from the original Walsh plates was a worthy one, but the publisher can hardly be excused of either ignorance or deception in carrying out his project. An outer jacket described the series as:

> Full Scores of Handel's Works, printed from the Original Plates engraved by Mr. Walsh, and which were corrected by Mr. Handel himself, and published in his lifetime, being the only five works which have been preserved &c.

The Novello folio score of *Messiah* is paginated 1–188 + appendix 1–35 as in the original Randall and Abell edition. As already pointed out, Walsh never issued a Full Score of *Messiah*, although his plates of the editions of the *Songs* were used in Randall and Abell's and the subsequent Full Scores, but no Walsh issue appeared with a title-page like that given in the pretended Novello facsimile.

Novello used Preston's plates, some of which were originally Walsh's, Randall and Abell's, or Wright's, for most of *Messiah* including the title-page, which was given a faked Walsh imprint. Fourteen pages were from entirely new plates, and the items throughout the work were numbered consecutively. (No. 1 etc.) Copies of this issue without Novello's outer cover to the series, are often inaccurately listed as Walsh editions.

As the popularity of *Messiah* increased and performances became common, various publishers, London and provincial, issued separate vocal parts of the work. A rather early and interesting example has the following title:

> The Chorus's (with the proper cues to each) in the Oratorio of Messiah Birmingham Engraved and sold by James Kempson Great Charles Street. MDCCLXXX. Price Six Shillings the Set.

Only the tenor part of this work is available. Originally consisting of about ten pages, printed on one side only, with manuscript and other additions, it formerly belonged to Charles Incledon, Michael Kelly, the Hereford Choral Society and others, before being acquired by the present writer from Cecil Hopkinson.

Of the eighteenth century continental editions, one must make mention of an extract by J. A. Hiller, issued in 1789, with the following title:

> Auszug der vorzüglichsten Arien, Duette und Chöre aus Georg Friedrich Händels Messias und Judas Maccabäus, in Claviermässiger Form, von Johann Adam Hiller . . . Dresden und Leipzig, verlegt von Johann Gottlob Immanuel Breitkopf. 1789.

It is a large oblong folio with seventy pages of music, including besides the numbers from *Messiah* and *Judas Maccabæus*, a chorus out of *D. Münters Oratorio*.

Later continental issues, including the well-known Mozart editions are outside the scope of this study.

Having dealt at length with the dates and issues of *Messiah*, there now remains the problem as to why the Oratorio was not issued in Handel's lifetime, assuming such to be the case. Three or four theories have been advanced:

1. That Handel quarrelled with Walsh about the price.

2. That the composer wished to retain the copyright of his work.

3. That as a production it was so unpopular in its earlier years that publication was not worth while.

4. That the use for an "entertainment" of incidents in Christ's life and Passion was objected to on religious grounds.

5. Personal animosity against Handel.

These theories are found scattered about in the literature of the subject, without very much evidence to support them. It remains to examine them systematically.

The first theory, that Handel would not accept Walsh's price, is not very tenable. Why should Handel continue to give Walsh his other successful works to publish? Moreover, avaricious as Walsh is supposed to have been, would he have risked losing the position as Handel's publisher for a single work, and one not over popular at that? As has been pointed out, there is good reason for thinking that the *Songs* were engraved about 1749, and as they were not advertised, it may be contended that a few copies were issued and the rest suppressed.

The second theory is not convincing in view of the facts, (a) that several copies of the manuscript existed in various hands; (b) that the overture was published in 1743; and (c) that the songs were included in Walsh's collection of *Handel's Songs Selected from His latest Oratorios* (1748–59).

The third theory has some weight as an explanation up to 1749 or 1750 only, as after that the popularity of the work is unquestioned.

Although there is little definite evidence for the fourth and fifth theories, they appear jointly as the most reasonable. The use of the title "Sacred Oratorio" instead of "Messiah", and the omission of the name of the work even when excerpts were openly published, are significant points. That Handel's genius and personality *did* provoke opposition is hardly to be disputed.

Mainwaring, whose dates and remarks are so often open to question, lived as a young man through the period; and it is reasonable to suppose that his statements in the following quotation at any rate are substantially correct: "In times when narrow notions were more in vogue, and when even men of

sense were governed rather by appearances than by realities,
Oratorios would not have been tolerated. In these happier
days the influence of prejudice was not indeed quite strong
enough to exclude these noble performances, yet it is even still
strong enough to spoil them. For are not the very same argu-
ments which prevailed for admitting Oratorios sufficient to
justify the acting them?"

Again:

"Indeed, in the year 1743, he had some return of his paralytic
disorder; and the year after fell under the heavy displeasure of a
certain fashionable lady. She exerted all her influence to spirit
up a new opposition against him. But the world could not
long be made to believe that her card-assemblies were such
proper entertainments for Lent, as his Oratorios. It is needless
to enlarge upon particulars which are easily remembered, or to
give a minute account of things generally known. It is sufficient
just to touch on the most remarkable. What is very much so,
his *Messiah* which had before been received with so much indifference, became from this time the favourite Oratorio."
Burney mentions Lady Brown, (probably the person referred
to by Mainwaring) "as a persevering enemy to Handel."

Schœlcher, Chrysander and Streatfeild all quote letters of
the period which show that Handel and his oratorios had
provoked controversy and opposition, and the letter of Mrs.
Dewes to Bernard Granville, December 3, 1750, already mentioned, especially refers to opposition to *Messiah*, as follows:
"It is only those people who have not felt the pleasure of devotion that can make any objection to that performance," etc.

It is possible now to give some more important contemporary
evidence as to the religious aspect of the matter (omitted from
The Musical Times article November, 1925), which shows that
there was definite objection to the use of the title "Messias".

Following a number of subscription performances at Covent
Garden during February and March, 1743, a performance of
Messiah, March 23, was advertised in *The Daily Advertiser*, and
also in *The London Daily Post*, March 19, as "A New Sacred
Oratorio", the word "Messiah" not being used.

Samson, which was the principal work in the preceding performances, was announced as "A new Oratorio, call'd Samson",
and the subscription season of six performances must have been

so far successful, because Handel advertised "Six entertainments more". The first of these later six was *Samson*, the second *L'Allegro ed il Penseroso with Additions, and Dryden's Ode on St. Cæcilia's Day*, the third, fourth and fifth (March 23, 25 and 29) *A New Sacred Oratorio*, and the sixth and last performance (the twelfth of the season) was *Samson*.

The music and the libretto of *Samson* were freely advertised, but there is no mention in the papers of the music or libretto of *Messiah* under any title.

On March 19, 1743, *The Universal Spectator or Weekly Journal* contained a long letter signed "Philalethes". Introducing the letter, the Author of *The Universal Spectator* [Henry Stonecastle] said:

"The following Letter may to many of my Readers, especially those of a gay and polite Taste, seem too rigid a Censure on a Performance which is so universally approv'd: However, I could not suppress it, as there is so well-intended a Design and pious Zeal runs through the whole, and nothing derogatory said of Mr. *Handel's* Merit. Of what good consequences it will produce I can only say—Valeat quantum valere potest".

"Philalethes" in his letter, which is too long to quote in full, says, in discussing the "diversions" of the time:

"But my Design, at present, is to speak to *one particular Diversion*, appropriated to this *Season* or Time of *Lent*; a Season design'd for every one to *humble* their *Souls*: But if one was to judge by the *busy Crowd*, and many *Diversions*, one should rather imagine it was a *Carnival*.

"But to my present Purpose, which is to consider, and, if possible, induce others to consider, the Impropriety of *Oratorios*, as they are now perform'd.

"Before I speak against them (that I may not be thought to do it out of Prejudice or Party) it may not be improper to declare, that I am a profess'd Lover of *Musick*, and in particular all Mr. *Handel's Performances*, being *one* of the *few* who never *deserted* him. I am also a great Admirer of *Church* Musick, and think no other equal to it, nor any *Person* so capable to *compose* it, as Mr. *Handel*. To return: An *Oratorio* either is an *Act* of *Religion*, or it is not; if it is, I ask if the *Playhouse* is a fit *Temple* to perform it in, or a Company of *Players* fit *Ministers* of *God's Word*, for in that Case such they are made.

"Under the *Jewish Dispensation*, the *Levites* only might come near to do the Service of the *Tabernacle*, and no common Person might so much as touch the *Ark* of *God*: Is God's Service less holy now?

"In the other Case, if it is not perform'd as an *Act* of *Religion*, but for *Diversion* and *Amusement* only, (and indeed I believe few or none go to an *Oratorio* out of *Devotion*) what a *Prophanation* of *God's* Name and Word is this, to make so light Use of them? I wish every one would consider, whether, at the same Time they are *diverting* themselves, they are not accessary to the break-ing of the *Third Commandment*. I am sure it is not following the Advice of the *Psalmist*, *Serve the Lord with Fear and rejoice unto him with Reverence*: How must it offend a devout *Jew*, to hear the great *Jehovah*, the *proper* and most *sacred Name* of God (a Name a *Jew*, if not a *Priest*, hardly dare pronounce) sung, I won't say to a *light Air*, (for as Mr. *Handel* compos'd it, I dare say it is not) but by a Set of People very *unfit* to *perform* so *solemn* a *Service*. David said, *How can we sing the Lord's Song in a strange Land*; but *sure* he would have thought it much stranger to have heard it sung in a *Playhouse*."

"But it seems the *Old Testament* is not to be prophan'd alone, nor *God* by the *Name* of *Jehovah* only, but the *New* must be join'd with it, and *God* by the most *sacred* the most *merciful Name* of *Messias*; for I'm informed that an Oratorio call'd by that Name has already been perform'd in *Ireland*, and is soon to be perform'd *here*: What the Piece itself is, I know not, and there-fore shall say nothing about it; but I must again ask, If the *Place* and *Performers* are fit? As to the Pretence that there are many Persons who will say their *Prayers* there who will not go to *Church*, I believe I may venture to say, that the Assertion is *false*, without *Exception*; for I can never believe that Persons who have so little Regard for Religion, as to think it not worth their while to go to *Church* for it, will have any *Devotion* on hearing a *Religious* Performance in a *Playhouse*," etc.

This letter provoked one reply at least, probably put out by the Covent Garden Theatre authorities, as it appears at the end of *The Daily Advertiser* announcement of the last Oratorio performance of the Season, *Samson*, on March 31, 1743. It is in verse, and quoted by Schœlcher, who unfortunately was unable to consult *The Universal Spectator*. It is as follows:

"Wrote extempore by a Gentleman, on reading the *Universal Spectator*.

"On Mr. Handel's *new* Oratorio, *perform'd at the Theatre Royal in Covent-Garden*.

"Cease, Zealots, cease to blame these Heav'nly Lays,
For Seraphs fit to sing Messiah's Praise!
Nor, for your trivial Argument, assign,
"The Theatre not fit for Praise Divine."
These hallow'd Lays to Musick give new Grace,
To Virtue Awe, and sanctify the Place.
To Harmony, like his, Cœlestial Pow'r is giv'n,
T'exalt the Soul from Earth, and make, of Hell, a Heav'n."

To this, "Philalethes" replied in *The Universal Spectator* of April 16, 1743, in another letter to Stonecastle, and after quoting the verse given above continued:

"As I could not forbear endeavouring to answer this, I send what I wrote for that Purpose, desiring you to dispose of it as you think proper, either to the *Flames*, or *publick Censure*.

"Mistake me not, I blam'd no heav'nly Lays;
Nor *Handel's* Art which strives a Zeal to raise,
In every Soul to sing *Messiah's* Praise:
But if to *Seraphs* you the Task assign;
Are *Players* fit for *Ministry Divine*?
Or *Theatres* for *Seraphs* there to sing,
The holy Praises of their heav'nly King?
Ah! no! for *Theatres* let *Temples* rise,
Thence *sacred Harmony* ascend the Skies;
Let *hallow'd Lays* to *Musick* give *new* Grace;
But when those *Lays* have *sanctify'd* the Place,
To *Use Prophane*, oh! let it ne'er be given,
Nor make that Place a *Hell*, which Those had made a
                                              Heav'n."

The writer goes on to suggest that special buildings set apart for the performance of oratorios by fit persons as "Acts of Religion" should be erected, and in a footnote points out that "Not the Poetry or Musick, the Place and Performers only are found fault with". It is quite clear, from what has been quoted, that the title "Messias" was also objected to by "Philalethes".

The extent to which these views found support is not known, but they persisted for some time, as evidenced by a long letter dated March 13, 1761, in *The Gospel Magazine*, February, 1775, entitled "Letter to a Friend, on going to hear the *Messiah*, at the Play-house". The writer of this letter states his objection to public performances of *Messiah* "because these sacred truths are exhibited, in their "turn, with the other diversions of the town, performed by the same people, with the same intent, in the same place." Apart from the main argument of the writer, the letter contains very early and definite evidence of the practice of audiences standing "at some of the chorusses in the *Messiah*" and "at the chorus at the end of the second part" (Hallelujah).

It is of interest to remember that, in course of time, Handel's *Messiah* became so generally accepted as a "religious" work by the mass of the British people, that the frequent and popular performances of it, in buildings of every kind—theatres, cathedrals, churches and halls—did much to exclude the performance and knowledge of the composer's other great choral works.

Whatever conclusion is arrived at, it is quite obvious that there was some reason why *Messiah* was treated differently from Handel's other Oratorios, and although all the available evidence has been brought together here, the uncertainty still remains. Surely it is not unreasonable to expect that some eighteenth century musical publication, diary, or collection of family papers may presently be discovered that will settle the question for all time. It will then be known whether the answer is to be found in Walsh's greed, in Handel's special affection for this supreme work, or in the strange spirit of the time which could see incongruity in the blending of such a sacred subject with the music of a master.

The writer can only suggest, in conclusion, that there is offered here sufficient evidence to dispute many of the previously accepted statements about the publication of *Messiah*, together with a considerable amount of new material essential to any further study of the subject.

IV

SOME HANDEL PORTRAITS
RECONSIDERED

SOME
HANDEL
PORTRAITS
RECONSIDERED

In spite of the fact that some of the recorded portraits of Handel existing in reputed contemporary paintings may be open to question as to date and authenticity, there remain a number of authoritative works which enable us to make up a reasonably accurate picture of the composer's physical appearance.

No study of this subject can be complete without reference to the exhaustive *List of Portraits, Sculptures, etc. of Georg Friedrich Händel*, published by Dr. J. M. Coopersmith in *Music and Letters*, London, April, 1932. It is not the purpose of the present writer to traverse the ground so admirably covered by Dr. Coopersmith, but principally to re-examine some of the portraits, particularly one of the best-known contemporary pictures of the composer, namely, the portrait in oils, attributed to Francis Kyte, 1742, which is now in the National Portrait Gallery, London. This painting has been generally accepted as an original portrait and the source of many subsequent prints and engravings. As the result, however, of recent investigations, details of which are given later on, it seems probable that the painting may be a copy or adaptation of an earlier painting or engraving, even if the signature and date upon it are correct. At any rate, it is perfectly certain that some hitherto accepted statements about engravings based on the Kyte portrait are inaccurate. Even if the painting is considered genuine, but not as an original portrait from life, it probably portrays Handel about 1737–38, when he was fifty-two to fifty-three years of age and not when he was fifty-seven, as the accepted date (1742) of the painting suggests.

Before considering recent discoveries on the subject, it will be of interest to trace the history and criticism of the picture as recorded by various writers prior to the death of W. Barclay Squire in 1927, when it passed, together with the Handel portrait by Hermann Van der Myn, into the possession of the National Portrait Gallery.

Of the early biographers of Handel, Sir John Hawkins, who was born in 1719, and knew the composer well, is the only one who gives any definite information about pictures or engraved portraits of the composer. Writing in his *General History of the Science and Practice of Music*, published in 1776, he says: "He was in his person a large made and very portly man. His gait, which was ever sauntering, was rather ungraceful, as it had in it somewhat of that rocking motion, which distinguishes those whose legs are bowed. His features were finely marked, and the general cast of his countenance placid, bespeaking dignity attempered with benevolence and every quality of the heart that has a tendency to beget confidence and insure esteem. Few of the pictures extant of him are to any tolerable degree likenesses, except one painted abroad, from a print whereof the engraving given of him in this work is taken: in the print of him by Houbraken, the features are too prominent: and in the mezzotinto after Hudson there is a harshness of aspect to which his countenance was a stranger; the most perfect resemblance of him is the statue on his monument, and in that the true lineaments of his face are apparent."

This statement appears to be the authority for many references by subsequent writers on Handel, but as will be shown, it has been so misunderstood and misquoted as to create a generally wrong opinion as to what Hawkins said or meant. Some of the relevant passages from later writers are given below, but it should be recognized that the information contained in them is based not only on Hawkins's statement, but also on a later work, the *Memoir relating to the Portrait of Handel by Francis Kyte* etc. issued by Keith Milnes in 1829. This *Memoir*, which is treated in fuller detail in due course, appears to be the first work to identify and record a portrait of Handel by Kyte. This artist's name does not appear in the early Handel biographies by Mainwaring, Hawkins and Burney, or in the *Anecdotes of George Frederick Handel, and John Christopher Smith*, by W. Coxe, issued anonymously in 1799.

The informative and interesting extracts from Schœlcher, Rockstro and Cummings which follow, all need qualification or correction on one point or another.

Schœlcher says: "One of the best-known portraits is that which proceeded from the admirable graver of Houbraken, for Randall's edition. It is after a picture of the same size as the engraving, and signed 'F. Kyte, 1742'. Handel was then fifty-eight years old. Hawkins has pronounced it to be 'the only good one, but that the features are too prominent'.

"Hawkins was probably not acquainted with that at Gopsall [Hudson] nor with that which has come into Mr. Ward's possession [Grafoni according to Schœlcher]. Houbraken's plate resembles the two latter, with the exception of that heaviness with which it is justly reproached. Mr. Keith Milnes, in a memoir published in 1829, explains that he accidentally met with Kyte's little picture, and had it engraved again, for his own satisfaction, by F. C. Lewis, who had endeavoured to correct the faults, without succeeding, in my opinion. These pieces of manufacture are never very happy, for a portrait cannot be made by guesswork. It is even better to have an imperfect original. Mr. Milnes, who is now advanced in years, is an enthusiastic Handelian, and shares his engravings with whosoever loves and venerates 'the greatest of musicians'."

The "Grafoni" painting referred to by Schœlcher is apparently that listed by Coopersmith and others, as by Giuseppe Grisoni.

Rockstro states in his *Life of George Frederick Handel* that: "A very fine portrait, though of small size, was painted in 1742, by F. Kyte, and is now [1883] in the Collection of Mr. Julian Marshall. In some respects this is the most valuable portrait of all. Hawkins seems to have thought so; but says 'the features are too prominent'. It was finely engraved by Houbraken, for Wright and Randall's edition of Handel's works; and reproduced for Sir John Hawkins' History. It has also been lately engraved by F. C. Lewis."

In the special Handel number of *The Musical Times*, December 14, 1893, Dr. Cummings gave a reproduction of the Kyte portrait with the following information:

"The portrait by Francis Kyte was painted in 1742, when Handel was fifty-seven years of age, and is noteworthy as having been executed from the life, that it might be engraved by Houbraken, at Amsterdam, for publication in London. The engraving subsequently appeared in numerous works, operas, etc., the plate finally after many printings and touches of renewal, producing a poor representation of the original picture. Sir John Hawkins, who knew Handel well, said that of all the portraits which had been painted, this conveyed the best likeness. The original oil painting is small (about 8 in. by 7 in.) and is inscribed on the back, Mr. Handel. It has had a somewhat chequered career, having been lost sight of for many years; it was recovered in a London shop by Mr. Keith Milnes, in 1824, who published a considerable account of it, with eulogistic letters from Sir Thomas Lawrence and Sir H. Beechy. At the death of Mr. Milnes the picture again disappeared, and was re-discovered at Sandwich a few years since by Mr. Julian Marshall, from whom I purchased it."

Schœlcher, Rockstro, Cummings and Keith Milnes tell us nothing about the history of the Kyte picture between 1742 and the date when the engraving is stated to have been made from it by Houbraken.

It will be noticed that Schœlcher misquotes Hawkins, confusing his remarks about a picture "painted abroad" and his reference to the Houbraken print.

Rockstro is wrong in stating that the Kyte was "reproduced for Sir John Hawkins's *History*". As is pointed out later on, the Hawkins portrait, though similar in some respects to the Kyte painting, was most likely based on another work altogether.

Cummings, like Schœlcher, does not quote Hawkins correctly, and assumes that the latter was referring to the Kyte portrait as the one "painted abroad", and which was a tolerable

114

likeness. Other inaccuracies also occur in the passages quoted.

Schœlcher is wrong in stating that Handel was fifty-eight in 1742.

Rockstro leads one to suppose that Wright and Randall were in partnership. Wright succeeded Mrs. Randall. Cummings states with assurance that the Kyte portrait was executed from "the life" for Houbraken to engrave at Amsterdam. This statement cannot be accepted if the genuine Kyte is the one dated 1742, now in the National Portrait Gallery.

In view of the importance of the Keith Milnes *Memoir*, it is necessary to give considerable extracts from this work, which is now somewhat scarce.

After referring to the print by F. C. Lewis engraved from the Kyte portrait, which Keith Milnes had issued in 1828, he continues the story of the original painting as follows:

"At a very early period of youth, it was my fate to be introduced to an elderly Gentleman, who in his own younger days had been personally acquainted with Handel, a visitor at his house, and constant frequenter of his Concerts and Rehearsals; and had been present at that Oratorio in which Handel made his last public appearance: viz., on the 6th of April, 1759,— within one week of his death. This extraordinary person and true Musician of the Old School, of whom, although so many years have since elapsed, I always preserve a lively and interesting recollection, was brother to the late Sir Edward Littleton, many years Representative in Parliament for Staffordshire. . . . It was his delight to talk of Handel, which he constantly did with the utmost enthusiasm: and if I had then possessed the sense and experience of a few more years, to have duly appreciated their value, many a curious Anecdote might have been noted down and preserved. One, however, which is applicable to my present purpose, I fortunately do recollect.—With the curiosity natural to a boy of fourteen, I eagerly inquired of him respecting Handel's personal appearance. His reply I perfectly remember to have been, that, although not well executed, nor doing any justice to the Original when living,—the likeness which most resembled Handel was Houbraken's Print of him, used as a Frontispiece to his Works. The impression this circumstance made upon me was probably deeper from the disappointment occasioned at conceiving that Handel should have had so coarse and heavy an aspect: for, Houbraken's Print, although without doubt containing the general outlines of resemblance, is miserably engraved, and indeed little better than a Caricature imitation of the original Picture: as it has since been my lot to ascertain.

"In after time I frequently felt a desire to know, what could have become of the Picture from which Houbraken's Engraving had been taken. The undoubted testimony I had received of its superior resemblance,—the difference in character and expression from any other representation of Handel upon canvass or paper,—the remarkable peculiarity of dress,—and, above all, the strong circumstance of being singled out in his own lifetime from among so many other Portraits which had been painted of him, and preferred as the fittest of them all, to be engraved for a Frontispiece to his Works,—combined in existing a very powerful interest with respect to this Picture. Little did I imagine, it would ever be my good fortune to become the Possessor of it;—or that I should have any share in rescuing so precious a relic from oblivion."

The writer, continuing, records his discovery of the painting in a picture dealer's shop in Great Newport Street in July, 1824. He says that immediately he saw it:

"It produced a sensation like the sudden re-appearance of a long-lost Friend.—Houbraken's Print had been so deeply impressed in my mind, that I was familiar not only with the general effect, but with every individual feature and almost every minute part of the dress. I beheld, indeed, a more pleasing and dignified expression of countenance than the Print had ever conveyed; but the resemblance was too strong to permit any feeling of doubt as to the identity.—It did however seem scarcely within the bounds of probability, that so valuable a document should have fallen into obscurity and neglect. I had naturally too imagined the original Picture to have been a full-sized Portrait; but this was small,—of the same dimensions with the present Print. [By F. C. Lewis,]—Could what was now before me be a Copy reduced for the purpose of engraving?—Yet there appeared a spirit in the touch, and an air of originality, not usually seen in Copies. I resolved, at all events, to risk the purchase upon my own judgment;—and never lost sight of

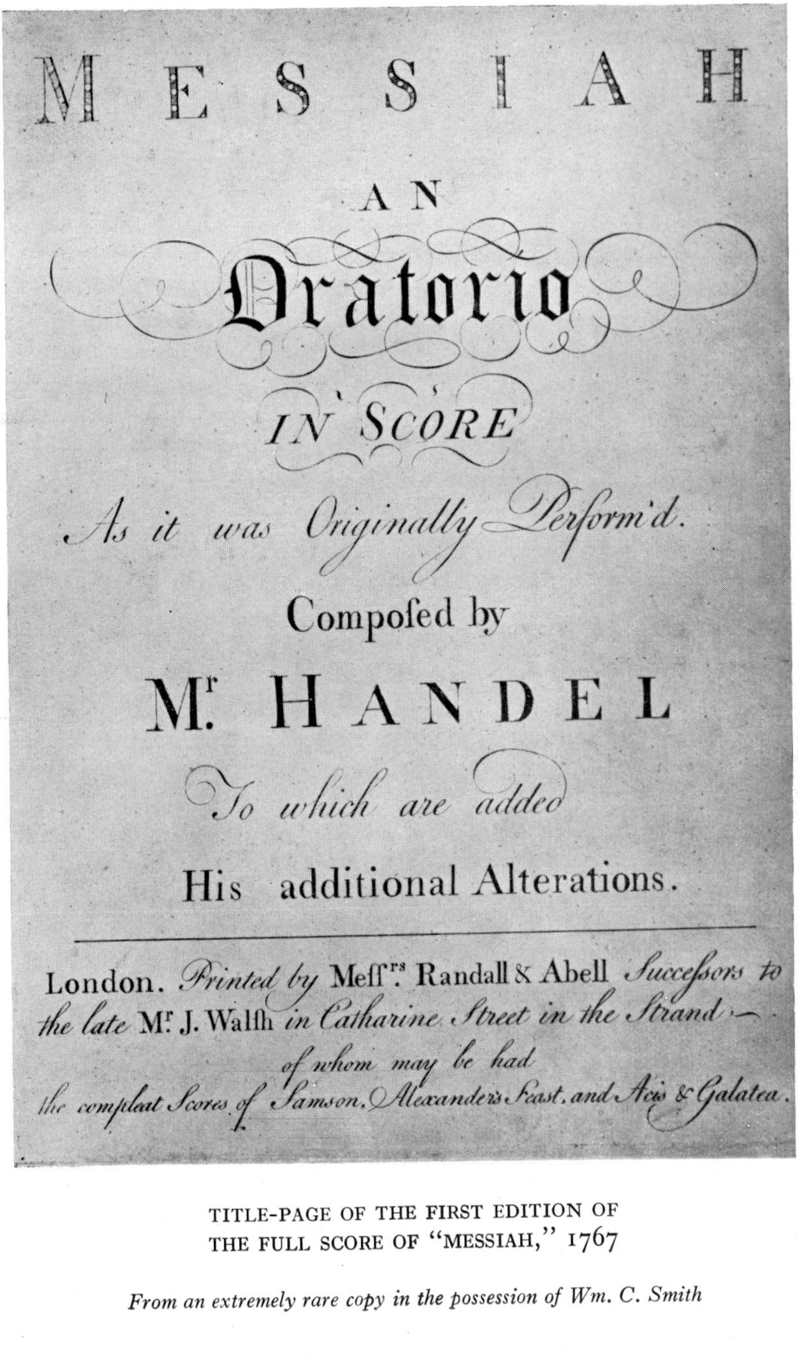

MESSIAH

AN

Oratorio

IN SCORE

As it was Originally Perform'd.

Composed by

Mr HANDEL

To which are added

His additional Alterations.

London. Printed by Mess.rs Randall & Abell Successors to
the late Mr J. Walsh in Catharine Street in the Strand.
of whom may be had
the compleat Scores of Samson, Alexander's Feast, and Acis & Galatea.

TITLE-PAGE OF THE FIRST EDITION OF
THE FULL SCORE OF "MESSIAH," 1767

From an extremely rare copy in the possession of Wm. C. Smith

PLATE NO. 5

HANDEL

ENGRAVING BY J. HOUBRAKEN, 1738

From a copy in the possession of Wm. C. Smith

PLATE NO. 6

the Picture till I had seen it deposited in my apartment. Indeed, during the examination an important discovery arose. Some dark characters were noticed on the back-ground, which upon closer inspection proved to be the Painter's name and the date, 'Fr. Kyte pinxt. 1742'.—This circumstance added a strong proof of originality : for, since the marking was so obscure as to be scarcely discoverable by a common observer, and the name, not of general celebrity as a Painter, there could be no grounds for supposing any deception.

"I took the earliest opportunity of showing my Prize to an accomplished and ingenious Friend, whose intimate acquaintance I am proud to trace as far back as the years of childhood ; and upon whose judgment I knew I could with certainty rely. It rejoiced me to find his opinion coincide with my own first impressions ;—and from him I received valuable assistance in the after investigation. We carefully examined some old Score Copies of Handel's Oratorios in Westminster Abbey, containing early Impressions of Houbraken's Plate. We also examined the worn-out mutilated Copper-plate itself still in existence at the warehouse of the Publishers, to whom it has been handed down from their predecessors who had the original Copy-right of Handel's Works.— All these researches still strengthened us in our opinion. But a farther convincing circumstance occurred, which seemed to remove every doubt. While putting on a little fresh varnish, of which the picture stood in need, Engravers' lines were discovered at equal distances round the margin of the Canvass. These lines had been carefully taken out where they interfered with the Portrait, but had been left upon parts of the back-ground.

"Another point may be glanced at here.—Were this only a Copy reduced from the Original for the purpose of engraving, it would naturally have been the exact size of the intended Print. We can scarcely imagine any Artist so inconsiderate as to hazard a double reduction, and thereby increase his risk of losing the likeness. But Houbraken's Engraving is smaller than this Picture in the proportion of about 16 to 19.

"In the Spring of 1826 I had an opportunity of submitting the Picture along with an early impression of Houbraken's Print to the inspection of Sir Thomas Lawrence, who, after attentively examining and comparing them together, without

I

the least hesitation pronounced it to be an original, and therefore interesting, Portrait;—and declared, there could be no doubt whatever that Handel had sat for it."

The writer of the *Memoir* then deals with the circumstances of the production of the print by F. C. Lewis, quotes the greater part of the passage from Sir John Hawkins's History, which has already been given above, and then continues: "It appears, that Sir John Hawkins had never seen the Portrait by Francis Kyte: because he refers only to '*the Print*' engraved from it '*by Houbraken*', and takes no notice of the Picture itself, which, had he been acquainted with it, he would surely have referred to rather than the Print. This Picture is much superior even to the *early* impressions of Houbraken's Plate: and it seems difficult to account for so great a failure as we find here in an Engraver whose works generally are held in high estimation . . . As no Painter's name is affixed as usual to the bottom of Houbraken's Print, Sir John might naturally enough have concluded, since the Engraving was executed abroad, and not taken from any Portrait known in this Country, that the Painting itself also was done abroad. There is another circumstance not a little remarkable. In the small Portrait engraved for Sir John's Work Handel appears dressed in the identical Coat (very distinguishable from being embroidered with lace of a peculiar pattern) in which he is painted by Kyte, although partly covered for the sake of picturesque effect with a loose mantle wanting in Kyte's Picture. The fashion of this Embroidery is quite singular, and has nothing like it among the numerous other Portraits of him. It does not appear, that Handel ever went abroad after the year 1736; and Sir John Hawkins states the Picture he alludes to in his History to have been painted abroad. But we can scarcely suppose, that Handel would be painted abroad in or prior to 1736 with the same Coat on him that he wore in England six years after when painted by Kyte in 1742.—Under all these circumstances, is it unfair to hazard the conjecture, that, from anxiety to produce a more favourable likeness of Handel than had been published, Sir John, assisted by his Engraver, Grignion, may have manufactured this Vignette, partly from Houbraken's Print and partly from his own recollection or the Statue, with the view of approaching to a more perfect resemblance of the Original? If so, they have failed in giving anything at all like the animated and dignified expression either of the Monument or the Picture. Sir John, it may be observed, only refers in very general terms to 'an Engraving from a Picture painted abroad'.—Now, if such Engraving ever existed (other than Houbraken's), there must be copies of it somewhere. But no such are known. Houbraken probably executed his at Amsterdam, and as the original Picture by Kyte, from remaining abroad, or some other cause, had certainly never been seen by Sir John, the latter might with some degree of plausibility imagine, and even state, that Houbraken's Print, which we are perhaps warranted in concluding was the only one really in his view, had been engraved from a Picture '*painted* abroad'."

In considering these extracts from the Keith Milnes *Memoir* the following points are worth noting. The reference to Sir Edward Littleton and his brother Fisher Littleton, can be accepted as correct, as a considerable collection of early Handel editions and manuscripts formerly belonging to them was sold in London a few years ago, some items of which are now in the possession of the present writer. Sir Edward Littleton died in 1812, and his brother, who became a barrister, was the "elderly gentleman" mentioned by Keith Milnes as having been personally acquainted with Handel.

Houbraken's plate, in the later and much worked over impressions, may be considered in some senses miserably engraved and open to criticism, but the earliest impressions have a softness, dignity and pleasing vitality which are not surprising when it is realized that the Houbraken portrait may be an original and not a copy. (See Plate No. 6.) The similarity in dress of the Houbraken portrait and the Kyte painting suggests that they represent Handel at the same time unless he wore the same coat for six or seven years, although this is not unlikely. The signature, date and painter's name are dealt with later on. Keith Milnes's statement about the existence of engraver's lines is correct, as an examination of the portrait shows, but as will be proved later on the lines could not have been made in connection with the Houbraken engraving. The size of the Kyte as compared with the Houbraken is roughly as indicated by Keith Milnes.

Sir Thomas Lawrence's opinion that Handel had sat for the

Kyte portrait is open to question although it cannot be denied.

The extract from Sir John Hawkins's *History* and Keith Milnes's commentary on it are interesting, but need qualification. Handel was abroad after 1736, namely in 1737, and it is most likely that the engraving by Grignion in Sir John Hawkins's *History* (1776) may have been taken from the extremely rare one by G. F. Schmidt, done in Paris not later than 1744. If this last assumption is correct, the Schmidt engraving and the painting on which it was based (the whereabouts of which is not known) present, according to Hawkins, the best likeness of Handel, and Keith Milnes is wrong in his criticism of Hawkins's statement as to the origin of the engraving by Grignion.

Moreover, although the Houbraken engraving has something in common with the Schmidt and the Grignion, the differences are such as to preclude the assumption that the last two works were derived from the former, although they all represent Handel at about the same time, wearing the same braided coat.

The Kyte portrait was rather badly reproduced in *The Musical Times*, special Handel number of December 14, 1893, but much better, in colour, in *Grove's Dictionary of Music and Musicians*, Third Edition, Volume II (1927). For the purpose of this study the writer has carefully re-examined the original picture in the National Portrait Gallery.

The portrait, painted on canvas mounted on wood, (approximately $6\frac{3}{4}'' \times 7\frac{1}{2}''$) is in good preservation, the signature and date, "F. Kyte pinxit 1742", not as given by Keith Milnes, being quite distinct, and the squared lines visible, particularly on the background. The only indication of subject is the name "Mr. Handel" in ink on the back of the wooden mount. (*See* Plate No. 7.)

Little has hitherto been known about Kyte, other than what can be derived from an examination of his works, and the brief references in the various authorities, which state that he was a mezzotint-engraver and portrait-painter, who worked in England from about 1710–45, was convicted of a bank-note forgery, was sentenced to stand in the pillory, and in consequence of this disgrace, afterwards used the Latin word Milvus [a kite] instead of his own name.

It is now possible, for the first time, to supplement these scanty details of Kyte, and also to give a fuller account of his criminal activities.

His holograph will is preserved at Somerset House. From the document, which is dated November 30, 1734, we learn that Kyte was then living in the Parish of St. Giles Cripplegate. He appointed his "Kinsman, George Wilding (of St. Giles Cripplegate, London, Chymist) to be my full and whole Executor". As the will was not witnessed, an affidavit was signed by John Wilford, Stationer of the Parish of St. Sepulchre's, London, and William Pardoe, Clothworker of the Parish of Christ Church [Newgate Street] London. Wilford and Pardoe testified that Kyte went to Bristol some ten years before his death, and the document dated March 22, 1745, records that Kyte was "six months dead", indicating, in the absence of a definite date of death, that it took place over six months before the date of probate. No details of Kyte's estate are given. Wilding presumably inherited what there was. It is evident that Kyte went to Bristol about 1734 and died there, probably in 1744. He was related, in what way we do not know, to George Wilding, and was well known to Wilford and Pardoe, the former being a popular bookseller and publisher. Presumably Kyte spent the last ten years of his life principally at Bristol, and if he painted the Kyte Handel in 1742, it was probably painted there. His characteristic signature occurs twice on the will, and can be compared with that on the painting of Handel.

The interesting account of Kyte's criminal activities, as recorded in the journals of the time and the official report of the Court proceedings, are made available here, and correct inaccuracies in some of the hitherto available statements, but establish the fact that the reputed portraitist of Handel was a crook.

The Daily Post, February 8, 1725, states:

> On Saturday last [February 6th] one Kite was apprehended at the Fountain Tavern in the Borough of Southwark, on suspicion of robbing the Chester Mail and other felonious practices, who being carried before three of His Majesty's Justices of the Peace, was by them committed to the new County Gaol in the said Borough. We

hear he is charg'd with erasing and altering a Bank Note from 20*l.* to 70*l.* and passing it for the latter Sum, and of altering one other Note of the like Value in the same manner", &c.

The Daily Post, February 26, 1725, gives the prisoner's name as Kyte, and on the following day the paper states: "Mr. Kyte, a Painter, who was lately apprehended", etc. The notice in *The Daily Post,* March 1, 1725, gives the full name:

> Francis Kyte convicted of a Misdemeanor, for uttering a Bank Note, eras'd and alter'd, receiv'd Sentence to stand once in the Pillory on Tower-Hill, to suffer six Months Impriso[n]ment, and to find Security for his good Behaviour for 12 months.

The Daily Post, March 2, 1725, states that Kyte was also fined twenty pounds.

The full official report of the Court proceedings suggests that Kyte was a man with some influence and important friends, judging from the penalty imposed on him in comparison with the much more serious ones of death or transportation on other prisoners, at the same Court, and also from the fact that he is only referred to by initials, and not under his full name. Moreover, some one must have given security for him. The report of the proceedings is as follows:

> B—— F, alias B——, of Aldgate, was indicted for a Misdemeanor, in publishing and uttering on the 26th of *Jan.* last, a Counterfeit Bank Note for 70*l.* payable to S—— B——, or Order, dated *Jan.* 23, 1724 [1725], he knowing the same to be False and Counterfeit. It appeared that on Saturday the 23rd of *Jan.* last, Twenty Pounds was paid into the Bank, for which a Bill, Numb. 107, payable to S—— B——, or Bearer, was taken out by the Person that brought the money; but none of the Witnesses were positive that the Person was the Prisoner. *Isaac Woodburn* depos'd thus. On *Tuesday* the 26th of *Jan.* about 8 at night, the Prisoner came to my House (the *Queen's Head* Tavern on *Tower-Hill*). He called for Wine, and ordered a Chicken to be broiled for Supper. When he had done eating, he asked me if I could change him a Bank Bill, for

he said he was obliged to go out of Town next Morning before the Bank would be open, and he should have Occasion for a little ready Money. The Bill was Numb. 10, dated the 23d of *Jan.* 1724 [1725] for 7*l.* payable to S—— B——, or Bearer. Not having so much Cash by me at the time, I sent my Drawer with the Bill to Mr. *Green*, a Goldsmith in the *Minories*, who returned Word, that he believed that the Bill was very good, and he would have changed it with all his Heart; but it happened that he had just before paid away a large Sum, and was unprovided. I shew'd it to a Club of Gentlemen that were then in my House; none of them could give me Money for it; but they all agreed that it was good. I carried the Bill again to the Prisoner, and told him I could not get it chang'd. He told me I need not be afraid, for the Bill was good; it was taken out in his own Name, which was S—— B——; that he had three new Houses in *Chiswell-Street*, and he lived in one of them, which was opposite the *Tobacco-Roll*: And then he asked me what Money I had in the House. I told him I could give him a 50*l.* Bank Bill, 10*l.* in Cash, and a Note on Demand for the other 10*l.* He told me that would do very well. I called my Drawer to be a Witness, and gave the Prisoner the 50*l.* Bill, and 10*l.* in Money. But he told me, that since what they did was before Witness, he would not give me the Trouble of writing a Note for the Remaining 10*l.* but he would take my Word, and call for it in two or three Days. He called for a Coach (N⁰. 370) and ordered the Coachman to drive him to *Chiswell-street*, I saw him no more till the 7th of Feb. when hearing that he was in the new Jail in *Southwark*, I went thither to pay him a Visit. On *Wednesday*, the Day after he was at my House, I sent my Servant to the Bank with the Prisoner's Bill, to receive 50*l.* of the 70*l.* which was readily paid him. And the next Day, I sent him again for the remaining 20*l.* which he also received. Most of this Evidence was confirm'd by *Sam. Clark*, the Drawer. *John Pin*, the Hackney Coachman, depos'd, that the Prisoner ordered him to drive opposite the *Tobacco-Roll* in *Chiswell-street*; but when he came to *Aldgate*, the Prisoner got out, gave him two or three hard Words, and a Shilling, and went away. *Mr. Legross* depos'd that he maid Enquiry at the *Tobacco-Roll*, the *Black Raven*, and several other places in Chiswell-Street, but could find nobody that knew, or had even heard of such a Man as S—— B——, or F—— K——, that had ever lived in the Parish; and much less been Owner of three new Houses there. *George Bromfield* depos'd, that the 50*l.* Bill which *Isaac Woodburn* delivered to the Prisoner, was paid at the Bank to a Woman, on the 27th of *Jan.* (which was the Day after the Prisoner took it of *Woodburn.*) This was mentioned as a Circumstance of the Prisoner's knowing the 70*l.* to be alter'd; for else he might have sent that as well as the other; and if he had gone a journey that Morning, he would have been as much hindered in waiting to receive the 50*l.* as in waiting to receive 70*l.* It appear'd that that Bill was so nicely alter'd, that it was not mistrusted even at the Bank, till they came to examine their Books, and then they found that there was no Bill payable to S—— B——, given out that day, but one for 20*l.* Numb. 107. The Head of the [T] was taken off, and the Body of it turned into an [S], the [W] was changed into [ev], and the [7] in the Number taken quite out. It appeared that the Prisoner went afterwards to the *Fountain* Tavern in the Borough. *Drawer*, says he, *I have been a Gaming, and have lost* 100*l. and have won* 70*l. for which I have taken a Bank Note; and if you'll get it off for me presently, I'll make you a handsome Amends, for I want a little ready Money just now.* The Drawer carry'd it to several Gentlemen in the House, but none of them could change it. The *Chester* mail being robb'd but a little before, and the Oddness of the Prisoner's offering a Gratuity to the Drawer, began at last to raise a Suspicion in some of them, that this Bill was taken from thence. Away the Drawer was sent to the Bank; but he came too late to receive the Money for it: However they told him it was good, and if he came the next day, they'd pay him. From thence he went to the Post-Office, but could make no discovery. In the meanwhile, the Prisoner appeared very uneasy, and ask'd Mr. *Parks* (the Master of the Tavern) if his Drawer was honest: and told him, that *if a Drawer proves a Rogue in such a Case, the Money will be expected from his Master.* The Prisoner still being suspected, he was taken into Custody till further Enquiry could be made. Guilty. Pillory. Fined 20*l.* six Months Imprisonment, and Security for 12 months.

In spite of the verdict, one must admit the possibility of a miscarriage of justice—but the evidence seems pretty conclusive that Kyte was guilty. The following notices which record his appearance in the pillory, give the name of his "alias", and report his attempted escape from Newgate:

> We hear that Francis Kyte, the Painter, who at the last Sessions at the Old Baily, was convicted of uttering a counterfeit Note for seventy Pounds payable to Sam. Brooks and is the same Persons describ'd in the printed Proceedings of that Sessions, by K—— F, alias B—— of Aldgate, will, on Friday next [March 19th] stand in the Pillory upon Little Tower Hill, pursuant to his Sentence; and that to prevent his undergoing that Punishment, he lately attempted to break out of Newgate." (*The Daily Journal*, March 16th, 1725.)
>
> Yesterday [March 19th] Francis Kite stood in the Pillory on Tower Hill pursuant to his Sentence at the Court in the Old Baily, for a Misdemeanor, in uttering a Bank Bill that was eras'd and alter'd, knowing it to be so: Some days ago he attempted an Escape out of Newgate, but was prevented by the Keepers, and thereupon confin'd in the Condemn'd Hold for better Security; and we hear the *Officers of the Bank* have not as yet done with him. (*The Daily Post*, March 20th, 1725.)

So much for the story of Kyte.

Recent research amongst eighteenth century records now shows to what extent the accepted views about the Kyte painting and engravings supposed to have been made from it are open to question, although some points remain in doubt and the story is still incomplete.

On March 26, 1737, *The Country Journal, or The Craftsman*, advertised number one of a work in parts entitled "The Heads of the most Illustrious Persons of Great Britain", etc. The notice continued:

> Specimens of the Work are to be seen at the Undertakers John and Paul Knapton at the Crown in Ludgate-street. N.B. This Collection will be engraven by Mr. George Vertue of London, Mr. Houbraken of Amsterdam, and some of the best Masters at Paris.

This very popular work is mentioned here because of Houbraken's association with it. In 1738 he executed what must surely be the most popular of all the early engraved portraits of Handel. This portrait formed no part of the series advertised on March 26, 1737, but is well-known as a frontispiece to volumes of Handel's works that were issued much later by Randall and his successors. It is now certain, as the following evidence will prove, that the engraving was made many years earlier than its appearance in the Randall volumes, and in consequence many of the previously accepted statements on the subject are incorrect.

On May 28, 1737, John Walsh, the Younger, advertised in *The Country Journal, or The Craftsman*:

> Just publish'd, Proposals for printing by Subscription, the New Opera of Berenice, and Alexander's Feast; an Ode, as they are perform'd at the Theatre-Royal in Covent-Garden. Composed by Mr. Handel. Subscriptions are taken in by John Walsh.

The proposals for printing *Alexander's Feast* continued to be advertised in *The Country Journal* of June 11, 18, 25 and July 2, etc. According to Chrysander the following notice of *Alexander's Feast* appeared in *The London Daily Post* of June 15, 1737:

> The work is in a great forwardness and will be carefully corrected and done with all expedition. Subscribers [sic] are taken in by the Author, in his house in Brook-street, Hanover Square; and also by John Walsh. . . . The price to Subscribers to be two Guineas, one Guinea to be paid at the time of subscribing, and the other on delivery of the book in sheets. A Print of the Author will be curiously engrav'd and given to the Subscribers and Encouragers of the work.

Chrysander says with regard to this advertisement of June 15, 1737, "Von Herrn Schölcher in einer mir nicht zugänglichen Zeitungsnummer gefunden und mir gütigst mitgetheilt". The present writer has also been unable to verify the advertisement, no copy of the paper mentioned being available, but the information in the notice can be accepted as it is not in conflict with the known facts.

Although *Alexander's Feast* was ultimately published in a fine full score, with the names of 124 subscribers to the first issue, the subscriptions must have been rather slow in coming in, as on January 27, 1738, and on subsequent dates in January and February, Walsh continued to advertise "In a short time will be publish'd *Alexander's Feast*".

The London Daily Post, March 2, 1738, announced:

> Next Week will be publish'd, And ready to be delivered to the Subscribers, by the Author at his House in Brook-street, Hanover-square; and by John Walsh in Catherine-street, Alexander's Feast. An Ode Wrote in Honour of St. Cecilia. By Mr. Dryden. Set to Musick by Mr. Handel. Note, Whereas a Print of the author is now engraving by an eminent Hand, and is very near finish'd; those Noblemen, Gentlemen and Ladies, who have done the author the Honour of Subscribing, may be assured as soon as it is finish'd, it shall be sent to their Houses, by John Walsh, the Undertaker of this Work for the Author.

Schœlcher, who quotes the latter part of this advertisement, wrongly stating that it is from *The London Gazette*, says: "It would be interesting to know what this print was. Being published under Handel's sanction, it may be presumed that it was a good likeness. Unfortunately, among the fifty-six engraved and lithographed portraits of him, which I have collected, I cannot find any belonging to 1738, or anything near that date."

Chrysander suggests that Hogarth may have been the artist responsible for the portrait, which, he remarks, does not exist in any known examples of *Alexander's Feast*.

Walsh was "the undertaker of this work for the author". In other words, he appears to have been the publisher and distributor of the print, having no doubt a business interest in it as he had in the edition of *Alexander's Feast*. What that interest was we do not exactly know, but it included some proprietary right which passed over to his successors, Walsh not using the print again apparently after its appearance in 1738.

On March 8, 1738, and subsequent dates *The London Daily Post and General Advertiser* contained Walsh's advertisement of published works including *Alexander's Feast*; and *The Country Journal* from March 11 onwards had advertisements that the work was ready and published. The most important notice of the period, however, is contained in *The Country Journal; or The Craftsman* of April 22, 1738. It reads:

> This Day is publish'd (And are ready to be deliver'd to the Subscribers for Alexander's Feast) A Print of Mr. Handel. Engraved by the celebrated Mr. Houbraken of Amsterdam. The Ornaments design'd by Mr. Gravelot. Printed for John Walsh in Catherine-Street in the Strand.

This advertisement, overlooked by all previous writers on the subject, is repeated in *The Country Journal* on subsequent dates. In *The London Daily Post* of April 24, 1738, and on later dates Walsh announced:

> Where may be had, To which is prefix'd a curious Print of the Author, Alexander's Feast, an Ode. Set by Mr. Handel.

It is perfectly certain from these advertisements that a Houbraken print of Handel, with ornaments by Gravelot was issued in April, 1738, either separately to subscribers to *Alexander's Feast*, who had already received the music, or prefixed as a frontispiece to copies of the music issued after the publication of the print. From some advertisements it seems probable that Walsh was prepared to issue copies of the print without the music. The queries of Chrysander and Schœlcher as to the origin of the print associated with *Alexander's Feast* are therefore answered. Houbraken, not Hogarth or another, was responsible for the engraved portrait and Gravelot did the ornamental design on the work.

The production as a whole can be accepted as having had the personal approval of the composer, and it is without question that the "print of Mr. Handel" from the plate with the engraved portrait by Houbraken and ornaments by Gravelot was the first issue of the one made popular through being used as a frontispiece to Randall's editions of Handel's works some thirty years later. The evidence for this conclusion is very strong, the main points being:

1. That copies of the print in the Randall volumes are of the right size to form a frontispiece to the early issues of *Alexander's*

Feast, which was one of the largest Handel volumes published by Walsh.

2. That the Randall prints are certainly by Houbraken, as they are signed at the bottom "I. Houbraken sculps. Amst."

3. That the Randall prints, although not signed by Gravelot were clearly ornamented by that artist, as an examination of his similar decorative work elsewhere will prove. Some of the pages of Bickham's *Musical Entertainer* issued in 1737–38 are signed by Gravelot and afford ample technical evidence on this point.

4. That the Gravelot pictorial design under the portrait in the Houbraken print represents without question the opening scene of *Alexander's Feast*. Alexander with Thais by his side, the "Valiant Peers", and "Timotheus plac'd on high, Amid the Tunefull Quire", striking the lyre.

Gravelot was also responsible for drawings after which the decorative ornament was engraved for some of the plates worked by Houbraken for "The Heads of the most Illustrious Persons of Great Britain", mentioned above.

Hubert François Gravelot, or rather Bourguignon-Gravelot, was born in Paris in 1699, died there in 1773, but worked in London from about 1732–45.

Jacobus Houbraken was born in Dordrecht in 1698 and died at Amsterdam in 1780. His work as an engraver of portraits is too well known to need further comment. Most of his plates are signed: "I. Houbraken sculps. Amst." and dated. There is no evidence that he visited London in connection with the Handel engraving, which is signed as above but not dated.

No copy of the Walsh edition of *Alexander's Feast* containing the Houbraken portrait has been traced by the present writer, although copies with Handel portraits (unnamed) have been listed in various sale catalogues. If, however, a copy of *Alexander's Feast* containing the Houbraken portrait came to light, it would be fairly conclusive evidence in support of the main argument of the present writer, but one must bear in mind the practice of putting portraits into works after publication as well as the more questionable one of taking them out.

It is now necessary to reconsider further the Kyte portrait, its date, authenticity and relationship, if any, to the Houbraken plate and prints. The painting has hitherto been accepted as the original portrait on which were based the Houbraken engraving published by Randall, as well as subsequent works by other engravers. Some of these are noticed later on, but Coopersmith's list should be consulted for further details. It is clear however that if the Kyte was painted in 1742, the Houbraken print preceded the painting by four years at least. If so, we are faced with two or three problems. Is the Kyte a spurious copy of an original work by Kyte, or by some other artist, preceding the Houbraken print (1738), or is the Kyte genuine but the date incorrect? Was Houbraken the portraitist for his own plate, or did he work to some unrecognized portrait-painter's original? Assuming the date to be correct, was the Kyte of 1742 painted from a copy of the Houbraken print? If so, it is not an original portrait of Handel.

The fine large scores of Handel's works issued from 1767 onwards by Randall and Abell or Randall alone, are well known, but the bibliographical information usually given about them is inaccurate or incomplete. It is unnecessary to deal in detail here with the various issues, but it must be pointed out that not all of the copies included the Houbraken print, which was probably used as a frontispiece for the first time in the Randall series for *Judas Maccabæus*, 1769.

After Randall's death probably early in 1776 the business with the stock of music, plates and prints passed to his widow Elizabeth Randall, and afterwards to Wright & Wilkinson, Wright & Co., and then to Thomas Preston. These, all in turn, continued to issue Handel volumes with the Houbraken frontispiece, and in course of time the plate became very poor and was frequently re-worked. This explains why most of the copies of the print offered to-day are such bad examples of the original. There must be very few prints about that date back to the Walsh issue with *Alexander's Feast* in 1738, and really fine early Randall copies are not common. Good impressions may be either part of the Walsh issue or of the early Randall period, but as many of the existing copies have been torn out of volumes the dates and particulars are uncertain. A critical examination of the paper might help towards the dating of some copies, and in those cases where the Randall volumes exist complete with the frontispiece there is not much difficulty in dating the work. What would be of extreme interest would be the discovery of an authenticated copy of Walsh's issue of the print, with or without *Alexander's Feast*.

A number of early engravings, in addition to Houbraken's, have also been described as having been taken from the Kyte portrait. Before examining these in chronological order it should be pointed out, that whether they owe their existence to one original portrait of Handel or not, they have enough in common to justify the conclusion that they represent Handel at the same period of his life, and wearing the similarly braided coat which is so conspicuous in Houbraken's engraving. As we have seen, until some earlier work in the same style is forthcoming, Houbraken's engraving, which was done in 1738, is probably the earliest of the group, and the portrait can therefore be reasonably accepted as representing Handel about that time.

Romain Rolland, in *A Musical Tour through the Land of the Past*, accepts the Houbraken as a "fine portrait" engraved "after the painting by F. Kyte in 1742", and adds that it represents Handel: "Under an exceptional aspect, after the serious illness which proved nearly fatal, traces of which are to be seen in his face. It is heavier, and fatigued, and the eye is dull; the figure is massive; his energies seem asleep; he is like a great cat slumbering with open eyes: but the old quizzical gleam still twinkles in his drowsy gaze." Apparently Rolland thought of the Kyte painting as portraying the composer soon after his illness in 1737.

It will be remembered that that year was a bad one for the composer. The opera season collapsed in ruin, and Handel, suffering from mental strain and physical weakness, went in the late summer to Aix-la-Chapelle for a cure. He returned to London in November, 1737, apparently quite recovered in health, and it is of particular interest to note that he passed through Flanders on his way home and is reported to have played the organ in one of the towns which he visited.

Is it unreasonable to suggest that it was when Handel was restored in health and still abroad in 1737 that his portrait was painted from life, and that this portrait which has since disappeared was the original of the Houbraken engraving and of the Kyte painting?

This suggestion is not at variance with the recorded facts,

and unless the Houbraken was an original portrait, the work on which it was based was certainly not the Kyte painting in the National Portrait Gallery, but a work still awaiting discovery.

An interesting question arises if the Houbraken is compared with the portrait of Handel supposed to have been by G. A. Wolffgang in London in 1737. The original, a miniature in pencil and sepia, on parchment, formerly in the possession of the *Musikbibliothek Peters*, Leipzig, has an inscription on the back in an old hand, "Georg Frideric Hendel. G. A. Wolffgang. Pinx. London 1737". If this information is correct and the portrait of Handel is a good one, we have to confess that his serious illness and financial worries of the period left no mark on his personal appearance, for as pointed out by Vogel (*Händel-Portraits. Jahrbuch der Musikbibliothek Peters für 1896*) the picture presents Handel "in der ganzen imponierenden Schönheit seiner Persönlichkeit".

The coat of the composer in the Wolffgang picture is different from that in the Houbraken, although wig and cravat are similar in each work. It is not unlikely that the date ascribed to the Wolffgang is a few years too late.

There is another miniature of Handel presumably by the same Georg Andreas Wolffgang (or Wolfgang) in Windsor Castle.

A larger portrait of Handel by "Wolfgang", the history of which is known up to 1879, cannot now be located. On May 8, 1789, *The Morning Post and Daily Advertiser* announced:

> To be disposed of, a very fine original half-length portrait of that much esteemed and celebrated musician, George Frederic Handel, Esq. Painted by Wolfgang, is in fine preservation and admirably well adapted to decorate an elegant Concert, Music or Ball-room &c.

This is presumed to refer to the portrait owned by Dr. Burney, the musician, mentioned in his will, purchased by James Bartleman at the Burney sale in 1814 for £12 1s. 6d., afterwards acquired by William Snoxell, and purchased at the sale of the Snoxell collection in London in 1879 by a M. W. Clark or Clarke. Little further is known of the picture. Vogel describes it as "Ein Seitenstück des Wolffgangschen Bildes soll

HANDEL

PAINTING BY F. KYTE, 1742

By courtesy of the National Portrait Gallery, London

GEORGES FREDERIC HANDEL
Seul Compositeur et Directeur Général
de L'Opera de Londres &
Né en Saxe.

La graces aux doctes veilles
D'un Artiste Laborieux.

ENGRAVING BY G. F. SCHMIDT, *c.* 1738-44

From a copy in the British Museum

PLATE NO. 8

sich in London in der Sammlung William Snoxells befunden haben."

In the 1814 sale catalogue the work was described as "A fine and original portrait of Handel, painted by Wolfgang, at Hanover, 1710 when at the Court of the Elector (afterwards George I) in [sic] his way from Italy to England." The date cannot be correct if the picture is similar to the Peters miniature supposed to have been painted in 1737. The probability is that both of the assigned dates are incorrect, but the whole question remains an open one until the Burney painting is found or authenticated reproductions of it. When sold in 1879, according to the sale catalogue, it was accompanied "with the Engraving".

Was this engraving the one known to have been made by J. G. Wolffgang (or Wolfgang) c. 1737–9, of which copies exist (see Frontispiece) and which was based on the G. A. Wolffgang (Peters) small portrait mentioned above. If so, it seems clear that the latter and the large Handel portrait sold in 1879 must have been similar portraits of Handel (as Vogel suggests) although so different in size. Perhaps the large painting was the earliest, and from this the engraving was made and the small Wolffgang (Peters) copied.

Little is known of Georg Andreas Wolffgang, one of a family of painters. He was born at Augsburg in 1703, therefore he could not have painted the Burney portrait in 1710. He is known to have worked in England for some time, and afterwards became Court Painter at Gotha. The engraving gives "G. A. Wolffgang Pinxit London", which makes more uncertain the connection, if any, with the Burney portrait, assuming that the statements about the latter are correct. Perhaps two members of the Wolffgang family provided original Handel portraits.

Of the engravings now to be described, some represent Handel looking to the right and some to the left. All of them show the braided coat, but some have in addition a loose coat or cloak over the shoulders. The earliest recorded engraving that has this outer cloak is the one by Georges Frederic Schmidt. This engraver, born in Germany in 1712, went to Paris in 1737 and remained there until 1743 or 1744. (See Plate No. 8.)

One of the most important contributions to the study of this subject is in the article already referred to, *Händel-Portraits*, by Emil Vogel. In keeping with other writers Vogel describes the Houbraken engraving as a copy of the Kyte painting, and although he does not date the Houbraken, he suggests that the Schmidt engraving was probably done from it and not from the Kyte original. This is an important point and might have been followed up by Vogel with advantage. As we know, Schmidt left Paris in 1743 or 1744, the latest possible dates for his work. Vogel points out that the sheet of manuscript music shown at the bottom right hand corner of the Schmidt print is the Allegro (Second movement) of Handel's Organ Concerto, Op. 4, No. 1. This work was first published by Walsh in 1738, and it is reasonable therefore to conclude that the Schmidt was done in the period 1738–44. As the Houbraken dates from 1738, it is not unlikely that the Schmidt and Houbraken were contemporary engravings worked from the same untraced original painting. The portraits in the two works are remarkably similar, although the clothing and positions are different. The Houbraken shows Handel looking half-right, the Schmidt half-left. In the latter, the composer is seated at an open window-like stone framing, wearing an outer cloak over the braided coat. The buttons of the coat in each case are on the right side, but in the Houbraken they appear partly covered by the left front of the coat. An important difference in the two prints is the sheet of music lying on the sill of the window-frame at the bottom right-hand corner of the Schmidt print.

At the bottom left-hand corner of the sill is the inscription "Georges Frederic Schmidt Sculp. á Paris". Below the sill the title:

> Georges Frederic Handel
> Seul Compositeur et Directeur General
> de l'Opera de Londrea
> Né en Saxe.

Below the print, on the edge of the paper, is the verse:

> Ici, graces aux doctes veilles
> D'un Artiste Laborieux.
> Ce lui qui fait tout le Charme des Oreilles
> Fait aussi le plaisir des yeux.

As the engraving could not have been done after Schmidt left Paris, it cannot be later than 1744. Copies of it are extremely rare, and the various authorities on Schmidt do not give any information as to the original painting on which the engraving was based.

L. D. Jacoby in *Schmidt's Werke*, published in Berlin, 1815, places the engraving at 1744, without any very definite evidence. As his description is inaccurate in some other particulars, his statements must be taken with reserve. A footnote, however, which he gives to his description of the portrait is of great interest, suggesting as it does, that the engraving was executed for a folio musical work which was not printed:

> Die Bestimmung dieses Bildnisses war, zu einem Werke in Folio über Musik, gebraucht zu werden. Der Druck des Werks kam nicht zu Stande, und die Platte soll abhänden gekommen seyn. Da nur ein paar Drucke davon abgezogen wurden, so ist es von der grössten Seltenheit. Sogar in des Künstlers eigenen Sammlung fand sich kein Abdruck, so wie schon bei einigen der Fall war. Bloss eine schriftliche Notiz fand sich darüber.

Jacoby's work is mainly a translation with corrections and additions, of A. Crayen's *Catalogue raisonné de l'Œuvre de feu George Frédéric Schmidt*, published in London in 1789. No copy of this work has been available for examination.

As the print includes an accurate extract from Handel's Concerto Op. 4, No. 1, it is not unreasonable to assume that the work was executed as a frontispiece to an intended French edition of the Concertos which was never carried out. As there is some circumstantial and technical evidence that the Houbraken and Schmidt engravings may have been issued about the same time and owe their existence probably to some common original, and as both were prepared in connection with musical works, one is tempted to make the fanciful suggestion that they were intended as rival productions, the Houbraken for Walsh's edition of *Alexander's Feast*, and the Schmidt to grace an issue of Handel's Concertos to be published in competition with Walsh's edition.

As against any technical evidence which may exist for assigning the Schmidt engraving to 1744, there is one reason at least for suggesting that it may have been executed earlier. The inscription underneath the portrait, referring to Handel as "Directeur General de l'Opera" would hardly apply in 1744, as the composer's association with the opera practically terminated 1737–38.

J. E. Wessely, in his work *Georg Friedrich Schmidt. Verzeichniss seiner Stiche und Radirungen*, Hamburg, 1887, mentions the engraving as existing in two states, the second with the top of the left sleeve of the cloak re-worked.

A fine reproduction is to be found in Dr. Woldemar von Seidlitz's *Allgemeines historisches Porträtwerk*, Serie VIII, Munich 1887.

The Schmidt engraving is also reproduced, with the title and verse cut off, in *The Magazine of Art*, Vol. VIII, 1885, in illustration of the article "Handel and his Portraits", by R. A. M. Stevenson, in which the writer says: "To Mr. Julian Marshall we are indebted for advice and liberty to copy the rare engraving by Schmidt, the head of which taken from this same portrait, was pronounced by Sir John Hawkins (who to be sure was not the wisest judge in the world) the best of all likenesses, but for the excessive prominence of the nose." This quotation does not report Hawkins correctly.

The engraving by C. Grignion, based on the Schmidt, and which appears in Hawkins's *History*, was taken, as stated above, from a print of a picture painted abroad, and which he considered to be a tolerable likeness. That the print he was referring to was the one by Schmidt cannot be seriously questioned when Grignion's engraving is compared with it. Moreover, Hawkins does not criticize the Schmidt likeness "for the excessive prominence of the nose". That is a misreading by Stevenson of Hawkins's remark, "In the Print of him by Houbraken, the features are too prominent," and this statement is clearly not intended to refer to the Schmidt print in any way. In the latter, Handel is portrayed looking to the left, but in Grignion's print to the right, showing the braided coat (buttons on the right side, partly covered) with the outer cloak.

Charles Grignion, the engraver, was born in 1717 and died in 1810. He was a pupil of Gravelot, who worked with Houbraken on the Handel plate. Grignion engraved the illustration, designed by Gravelot, for the title-page of *The Heads of the most Illustrious Persons of Great Britain*, to which Houbraken contributed so many of the engraved portraits. Although Grignion worked his plate for Hawkins, and apparently based it on the Schmidt, he no doubt had the Houbraken also in mind.

In March, 1784, there appeared in *The European Magazine* an engraving of Handel by W. Angus. The print shows the composer looking to the left, wearing the braided coat but without the cloak. Although the expression is rather different, it was probably founded on the Houbraken and Kyte portraits or reproductions of them. Vogel associates it with the Kyte and Schmidt.

We now come to an important work in this series of Handel portraits, namely, the engraving by Goldar issued in 1785 with Harrison's edition of Rapin (*History of England*), and it is of significant importance in a study of the Houbraken print and the Kyte painting. Obviously it owes its origin to the same source as the Houbraken, with which it is in general agreement, except that the figure is reversed, eyes looking half-left. The detail on the coat, braiding and buttons, follows that on the Houbraken most minutely, but changed over, right side to left, left side to right. This engraving may have been made from an original picture which antedated the Houbraken first issue of 1738 and the Kyte in 1742, or it may even be based upon a painting of which the Kyte is a copy. The reason for raising these queries is to be found on the copies of the Goldar engraving itself. In this work, the head and shoulders with the familiar braided coat, appear on an oval background framed with rectangular mount. Houbraken is not mentioned, but the following wording appears on the print:

> At the top above the frame: "London: Engrav'd for Harrison's Edition of Rapin. George Frideric Handel
> At the bottom below the frame: "In the Collection of the Honble John Spencer Esqr."
> Close to the bottom right hand corner of the frame: "Goldar sculp^t."

(See Plate No. 9.)

What was the picture owned by John Spencer? Was it the so-called Kyte of 1742, or the earliest Houbraken engraving, or an untraced original painting by Kyte or another on which the Houbraken may have been based and from which a spurious Kyte was painted in 1742?

An application by E. Croft-Murray to the present Earl Spencer as to any knowledge of the picture has produced the following statement: "I have never heard that my ancestor had a picture of Handel and none is mentioned in any old catalogue, so I do not know why the engraving is marked with his name unless the picture has been destroyed in some way."

It is not unreasonable to suggest that the Spencer picture referred to on the Goldar engraving was the Houbraken portrait issued with *Alexander's Feast* in 1738, either separate or as a frontispiece. Amongst the subscribers to that work was the Hon. John Spencer, and, presumably, he received his copy of the music and the portrait in its first fresh state. Few portraits of Handel could have been known by that time, and a Handel enthusiast would probably welcome the Houbraken, and have it framed and hung. As it was not an original picture, it could easily disappear in course of time without any record remaining of it.

In 1813 the print by Goldar was republished by Cornish & Co. Except for the addition of "Published by Cornish & Cº. 1813" at the bottom of the frame, the print appears to be exactly the same as the earlier issue in Rapin, with the same wording.

An engraving was issued in *The New London Magazine*, September 1, 1785, which is obviously a copy of Grignion's but reversed, showing Handel looking slightly to the left instead of to the right. It is in a small oval surround, coupled with an engraving of Corelli in similar style, and as a portrait is superior to the Angus engraving. According to Dr. Coopersmith the work is by Lowry.

Another engraving based on the Houbraken or Kyte portraits was made by [Cosmo?] Armstrong, and according to Coopersmith appeared in 1806 as one in a group of oval portraits forming a frontispiece to Volume IV of *The History of England* published by T. Cadell, London.

Dr. Coopersmith, to whose work the present writer is greatly indebted, also mentions prints based on the Houbraken or Kyte as follows:

H. Delius, undated, based on Kyte.
Houbraken, reduced by J. Caldwal, undated.
Ernest Ludwig Riepenhausen, 1820, on Houbraken.
Schertle, undated, on Kyte painting.

Copies of these works have not been examined by the present writer, but any further details of them would hardly add anything of importance to the major question of the relationship between the Houbraken and the Kyte.

In addition to the Angus print, mentioned above, Vogel states that the Schmidt was also the forerunner of the Schertle and Delius, but as Vogel described the Schmidt as based on the Kyte painting, through the Houbraken engraving, the statements of Coopersmith and Vogel about these works are not at variance.

J. Caldwal (i.e., James Caldwall) was a designer and engraver, born in London 1739, who is known to have been alive as late as 1789.

Keith Milnes issued in 1828 prints of an engraved portrait of Handel by F. C. Lewis, based on the Kyte of 1742. (See Plate No. 10.) The work is a lively reconstruction from two or three sources as described in the Keith Milnes *Memoir*. At the foot of the engraving are the inscriptions "Fr. Kyte, pinx^t. 1742. F. C. Lewis, sculp^t. 1828." Below is a reproduction of Handel's autograph, "George Frideric Handel", followed by the note:

> From an Original Portrait of the same size, by Francis Kyte, in the possession of Keith Milnes Esqr. which was formerly engraved by Houbraken. The Fac-simile of Handel's Signature is from an Original Letter to M^r. Jennens, dated 9th. Septr. 1742, in possession of The Right Honble. Earl Howe.

Keith Milnes gives the following description of the sources of the Lewis engraving: "In the course of the present engraving, although the Portrait by Kyte has been followed very closely and strictly, yet the two Statues by Roubiliac were also consulted; and—for some particulars of outline, more visibly or strongly marked upon that full sized scale than in the small Picture,—the large Portrait by Hudson in Windsor Castle.

When the Plate had advanced almost to its last stage of com-pletion, one of those lucky chances, which seem destined to attend the progress of this adventure, brought me into contact with Sir William Beechey. . . . Sir William's experienced eye as a Painter enabled him to suggest a few judicious improve-ments to the accurate and persevering Engraver, by whom they were at once appreciated and faithfully adopted."

In spite of the evidence brought forward by Keith Milnes, it cannot be conclusively proved that the picture he found was an original portrait of Handel drawn from life by Kyte, although the work described by Keith Milnes is without doubt the one now in the National Portrait Gallery.

Julian Marshall, who owned the picture before Dr. Cum-mings, possessed a copy of the Keith Milnes *Memoir*, which was sold in London in 1931 and passed into the possession of Dr. Coopersmith. The catalogue description of the work stated that it contained a manuscript note by Julian Marshall, lithographic portrait by F. C. Lewis after Kyte, seven original numbers of the *Spectator*, 1712, two autograph letters of Earl Spencer, views, facsimiles, etc.

This copy of the *Memoir* has the following notes in manu-script by Julian Marshall:

(a) "The portrait of Handel by Kyte described above, was bequeathed by Mr. Keith Milnes to Mr. Rolfe of Sandwich, a collector of antiquities and curiosities. At the death of Mr. Rolfe, his collection passed into the hands of his housekeeper, and were sold, with the exception of this picture and a few pieces of china, etc., which came at her death to her niece, the wife of a grocer of Sandwich, named Jacobs, of whom I bought this portrait, on the 29th Sept.ʳ 1874."

(b) "The print in Hawkins' Hist. Vol. V. is evidently a copy of one by G. F. Schmidt in which the drapery is the same."

The Spencer letters supposed to have been sold with the copy of the *Memoir* seem to have disappeared. If they came to light they might help considerably in this reconsideration of the Kyte painting and modify some of the conclusions arrived at and the suggestions offered.

Julian Marshall recorded in Grove's *Dictionary of Music*, that the "little picture signed "F. Kyte, 1742" . . . was the original of Houbraken's engraving and probably also of that by Schmidt, which is very rare". The accuracy of this statement must now be judged in the light of more recent evidence.

An eighteenth century portrait in oils of Handel, from the Arthur Hill collection, was purchased by the present writer at Sotheby's, June 18, 1947. It is described on the back by Hill as: "Portrait of Handel Painted by F. Kyte. The original of the engraving by Houbraken." This is incorrect, as the picture appears to be a copy of the Houbraken, with obvious differences, including the addition of a score of *Messiah*, opened at the "Hallelujah Chorus", and "I know that my Redeemer liveth". It is neither signed nor dated. The position of the head is the same as in the Houbraken, but the braiding on the coat is rather crudely worked, while the facial expression is very similar to that of the Kyte, with which it agrees roughly in size. It probably dates from about 1750–60, or at anyrate after the early performances of *Messiah* in London.

As already pointed out, Dr. Cummings acquired the Kyte portrait from Julian Marshall, and W. Barclay Squire bought the picture, and another portrait of Handel by Hermann Van der Myn, at the sale of Dr. Cummings's library in 1915. Both of these pictures were bequeathed to the National Portrait Gallery by Squire, who died in 1927. The Van der Myn is not very well known, and has been considered a poor portrait of Handel. It has no connection with the Houbraken or the Kyte, but has much in common with one of the Hudson portraits owned by the Royal Society of Musicians—the pose, wig, dress, and to an extent the expression, being similar in both pictures. (See Plate No. 11.) Van der Myn was in England in 1727, and perhaps for a few years afterwards. In 1737 he was in the Netherlands, and later on again in London. He is reported to have painted a picture of the Duke and Duchess of Chandos.

R. A. M. Stevenson, who wrote the article on "Handel and his Portraits" in *The Magazine of Art*, 1885, had as much to say about Handel's music and character as about his portraits, and following the quotation from the article given earlier, stated: "Neither the Kyte, however, nor any one of its adaptations, bears much resemblance to the Hudsons and Roubillacs: they give a sullen somewhat underhand view of Handel, and represent him as a man whose force of mind lay rather in a heavy, dogged power of resistance than in a fiery and agile impetuosity."

The present writer pretends to no particular knowledge of art or portraiture, but must question the idea that the Kyte and its adaptations all give a "sullen somewhat underhand view of Handel". There is a marked difference between the Houbraken prints and the Kyte painting, and the Houbraken prints differ one from another. It is without question, that a careful comparison of the best and earliest of the prints with the Kyte will show that they represent Handel, if not at different times, certainly in two different moods. The early prints suggest a sure, calm, healthy and vital personality; the Kyte, with the drooping mouth, heavy eyes and lifeless expression, depicts a sadder man, older in years and bearing the marks of strain if not of suffering. If the Houbraken engraving was from a portrait before Handel's illness in 1737, and it may have been, at any rate it is not later than 1737–38, and if the Kyte is rightly dated 1742, then the marked differences in the two works is not surprising. If however, we are to accept the Kyte as a contemporary portrait of Handel in 1742, rather than as a bad copy from a Houbraken print or other work, it does not seem to be a very convincing picture of the transcendant and sparkling genius who had rapidly composed *Messiah* a few months before, and had recently produced it in Ireland as the outstanding work in a series of triumphant performances.

Although there still remain a number of unanswered questions about the origin of the Houbraken engraving and the Kyte painting, some previously accepted statements and conclusions have now been corrected; and it is hoped that this study of a rather baffling Handel problem may encourage further investigation and lead to the discovery of other portraits of the composer including, perhaps, an original painting from which the Houbraken engraving was taken.

V

HANDEL'S FAILURE IN 1745
NEW LETTERS

HANDEL'S
FAILURE
IN
1745

NEW LETTERS

I T has been generally accepted by students of Handel's life, that the oratorio season of 1744–45 was a failure, ending, according to some authorities, in the composer's bankruptcy.

The contributory causes to this failure are said to have been the ill-health of Handel and the opposition of a society clique. While there is some evidence for these conclusions, such evidence is not overwhelming or consistent.

It is surprising that accurate contemporary records should be so frequently wanting in the story of a personality like Handel, who lived much in the public eye, and made many friendships. Authenticated statements of the composer, particularly letters are extremely rare, and therefore the two hitherto unnoticed letters of Handel on the 1744–45 season and other additional contemporary information reproduced in this chapter should be of interest.

There is no doubt that in endeavouring to popularize English oratorios amongst the eighteenth century opera-going public, Handel set himself a task, which at first was almost too big even for him. Making allowance for any society or professional opposition that he may have met with, probably the main reasons why he found it so difficult to succeed were, that many of the wealthy refused to subscribe in advance to the oratorios, and the prices at which the works were offered to the general public were too high in comparison with the prices for contemporary plays and other entertainments. Opera prices at the period were usually: Boxes, half a guinea; Pit, five shillings; First Gallery, three shillings; Second Gallery, two shillings. If, however, the subscribers were sufficient, and the composer could command the prices, the Pit and Boxes were combined at half a guinea a seat, the First Gallery was five shillings, and the Second Gallery, three shillings and sixpence, or three shillings, and in this case a number of the cheaper seats usually available to the general public were cut out. When this was done it was sometimes usual to apologize through the press, and from the tone of some of these notices, it looks as if the practice met with some opposition.

On April 8, 1741, when advertising his performance of *L'Allegro ed il Penseroso* at Lincoln's Inn Fields, the composer stated: "This being the last time of performing, many persons of quality and others are pleas'd to make great demands for Box Tickets, which encourages me (& hope will give no offence) to put the Pit & Boxes together at Half a Guinea each. Gall. 5s, 2nd Gall. 3s."

For the 1742–43 season at Covent Garden, the prices were; Pit and Boxes, half a guinea; First Gallery, five shillings; Upper Gallery, three shillings and sixpence; and each subscriber had to pay six guineas on taking out his subscription, which entitled him to three box tickets for every night of the first six performances, with the option of a further subscription at the same rate for the next six performances. In the 1744 season the subscribers to Handel's oratorios paid four guineas, which entitled them to one box ticket for each of the twelve performances.

Theatre tickets at the same period were usually five shillings, three shillings etc.; and at "Common Prices", Boxes, four shillings, Pit, two and six, First Gallery, one and six, Upper Gallery, one shilling.

While Handel was struggling to keep going at the King's Theatre, Defesch ran a short season of three subscription nights of his own oratorios *Love and Friendship*, and *Joseph*, at Covent

Garden in March and April, 1745, and advertised that the Boxes would be enclosed as usual at five shillings; Pit, three shillings; First Gallery, two shillings; Upper Gallery, one shilling.

Perhaps Handel at half a guinea was better than Defesch at five shillings; but art cannot always prevail over questions of cost.

From 1747 onwards, as pointed out by Streatfeild, "Handel abandoned subscription performances and threw his theatre open to all comers. This change of policy brought its own reward. Finding that his aristocratic patrons had failed him, Handel turned to the great middle class, who became his ardent supporters and brought him new fame and fortune." While this became true in the long run, the prices charged for seats in 1747 and till much later, were still the old rather prohibitive ones of half a guinea, five shillings and three shillings and sixpence.

The Theatrical Review (Vol. II., 1772, Appendix) has some very definite information on this point. Speaking of the Oratorios at Covent Garden (March, 1772) it says:

"The Oratorios performed at this Theatre, were conducted by Messrs. Arnold and Toms . . . It is worthy of remark, that these Gentlemen a few years since (1768) entered into Partnership, and opened Mr. Foote's Theatre in the Hay-market in Lent, where they performed Oratorio's at Play-house Prices, in opposition to Mess. Stanley and Smith, who at that time carried on their Oratorios at Covent-Garden on very high terms. To this bold attempt the Public owes the reduction of the terms of admission to Oratorios, which before were too exorbitant to be afforded by the generality of the Frequenters of Play-houses. This reduction has given many an opportunity of enjoying this noble Species of Entertainment, who were heretofore, excluded on account of the great expence."

The newspapers of the time give advertisements of the two series of oratorios referred to above, each of them including Handel items, Covent Garden prices being half a guinea, five shillings and three and sixpence, Haymarket prices, five shilling, three shillings, two shillings and one shilling.

The question of price has been dwelt with at length, because it deserves emphasis, as probably being a very important factor in Handel's struggle, and because it has hardly been noticed before.

It is not intended to reproduce in this chapter more than a selection of the most important references to the subject from the recognized authorities, and readers are especially advised to consult the most interesting article by the late W. Barclay Squire on "Handel in 1745" in the *Riemann-Festschrift* (Leipzig, 1909).

In the well known correspondence of Mrs. E. Carter, quoted by Streatfeild and others, there is a statement by Miss Catherine Talbot which is worth more than all the speculation on the matter. Writing on March 2, 1745, she says:

"Handel, once so crowded, plays to empty walls in that opera-house, where there used to be a constant *audience* as long as there were any dancers to be *seen*."

Mrs. Delany in her *Autobiography and Correspondence*, amongst many Handel references, gives evidence of opposition by all "the opera people" to *Semele* in the Lent of 1744, and the notorious Lady Brown was according to Burney "a persevering enemy to Handel, and a protectress of foreign musicians in general, of the new Italian style; and was one of the first persons of fashion who had the courage, at the risk of her windows, to have concerts of a Sunday Evening."

Burney does not date this lady's activities, but Horace Walpole refers to her in 1743 and she appears in 1748 in Martinelli's *Lettere familiari*.

The extent to which Handel lost his public to Lady Brown and her set is a matter for speculation, but there certainly was an opposition to the composer and his oratorios, although it is not clear how active it was in 1744-45. A hitherto unnoticed contemporary poem, quoted below, refers in veiled language to the opposition of some unnamed lady, who may have been Lady Brown.

Burney, who from 1745 onwards was in close touch with Handel, performed in his band, and attended rehearsals at his own house, says, (*General History of Music*), "In November, 1744, Handel finding the house unoccupied, engaged it for the performance of oratorios, which he began November 3d, and continued to his great loss, and the nation's disgrace, till the 23d of April."

In his *Sketch of the Life of Handel* published in *An Account of the Musical Performances . . . in Commemoration of Handel*, the same writer says:

"When he recommenced his Oratorios at Covent-Garden, the Lent following (1743) he found a general disposition in the public to countenance and support him. . . .

"But though the Oratorio of the Messiah increased in reputation every year, after his return from Ireland, and the crouds that flocked to the theatre were more considerable every time it was performed; yet, to some of his other Oratorios, the houses were so thin, as not nearly to defray his expences; which, as he always employed a very numerous band, and paid his performers liberally, so deranged his affairs, that in the year 1745, after two performances of *Hercules*, January 5th and 12th, before the Lent season, he stopped payment. He, however, resumed the performance of his Oratorios of *Samson*, *Saul*, *Joseph*, *Belshazzar*, and the *Messiah* in March; but I perfectly remember, that none were well attended, except *Samson*, and the *Messiah*.

"His late majesty king George the Second, was a steady patron of Handel during these times, and constantly attended his Oratorios, when they were abandoned by the rest of his Court."

It seems clear, then, that the extent to which Handel's oratorios failed was largely due to the fact that they did not appeal to the public. This conclusion is strongly supported by the newly-discovered letters of Handel, quoted below.

With regard to the question of the composer's health, the most valuable evidence is to be found in the *Malmesbury Papers* quoted by Streatfeild and others. The significant dates are March 13, August 29, and October 24, 1745.

The entries on the last two dates can be accepted as testifying to the composer's ill health, but the reference on March 13 is somewhat perplexing. Lady Shaftesbury in writing to her cousin James Harris says: "I went last Friday to *Alexander's Feast*, but it was such a melancholy pleasure as drew tears of sorrow to see the great though unhappy Handel, dejected wan and dark, sitting by, not playing on the harpsichord, and to think how his light had been spent by being overplied in music's cause. I was sorry, too, to find the audience so insipid and

L

tasteless (I may add unkind) not to give the poor man the comfort of applause; but affectation and conceit cannot discern or attend to merit."

No other record of this reported performance of *Alexander's Feast* can be traced. On the Friday referred to, March 8, *Samson* was given, not *Alexander's Feast*.

From the two later Malmesbury references, it is clear that in August, 1745, Handel was worried about his health, and that in October of the same year he was somewhat better, although he had been "a good deal disordered in his head."

An attempt will now be made to give a chronicle of events and notices during the season, embodying the most recent discoveries.

The composer's preliminary announcement, as given in *The Daily Advertiser*, October 20, 1744, and on subsequent dates, was as follows:

> By particular Desire.
>
> Mr. Handel proposes to perform, by Subscription. Twenty-Four Times, during the Winter Season, at the King's Theatre in the Hay-Market, and engages to exhibit two new Performances, and several of his former Oratorio's. The first Performance will be on Saturday the 3d of November, and continue every Saturday till Lent, and then on Wednesdays and Fridays. Each Subscriber is to pay Eight Guineas at the Time he subscribes, which entitles him to one Box Ticket for each Performance.
>
> Subscriptions are taken in at Mr. Handel's House in Brooke-Street, near Hanover-Square; at Mr. Walsh's, in Katherine-Street in the Strand; and at White's Chocolate-House in St. James's Street.
>
> Those Gentlemen and Ladies who have already favoured Mr. Handel in the Subscription, are desired to send for their Tickets at his House in Brooke-Street, where Attendance will be given every Day (Sundays excepted) from Nine o'clock in the Morning till Three in the Afternoon.

It will be noticed that Handel promised to "exhibit two new Performances." These two works were *Hercules* and *Belshazzar*, and when the promise was made Handel had already composed the oratorios, *Hercules* in July and August, *Belshazzar* in August and September, 1744, so they were not thrown together during the stress of the season. The principal singers were Mrs. Cibber, Miss Robinson, Signora Francesina, Beard and Reinhold.

On the first night, November 3, 1744 *Deborah* was given "With a Concerto on the Organ," and *The Daily Advertiser* of that date adds:

> Pit and Boxes to be put together and no Person to be admitted without tickets which will be delivered this Day, at the Opera-Office in the Hay-Market at Half a Guinea each. The Gallery Five Shillings. The Gallery to be opened at Four o'Clock, Pit and Boxes at Five. To begin at Six o'Clock.

The support must have been poor as *The Daily Advertiser* November 5, announced:

> As the greatest Part of Mr. Handel's Subscribers are not in Town, he is requested not to perform till Saturday the 24th instant; but the Subscription is still continued to be taken in at Mr. Handel's House in Brooke-Street, near Hanover-square, at Mr. Walsh's, in Katherine-Street in the Strand; and at White's Chocolate-House in St. James's Street.

Deborah, with a Concerto on the Organ, was repeated on November 24.

December 1. *Semele*, was given, with additions and alterations, and a Concerto on the Organ.

December 8. *Semele* repeated.

January 5, 1745, *Hercules* was produced as a "New Musical Drama."

The same day, the libretto was advertised (*General Advertiser*):

> This Day is Publish'd Price 1s. Hercules. A Musical Drama. As it is perform'd at the King's Theatre in the Hay-Market. The Music by Mr. Handel. Printed for J. and R. Tonson and S. Draper, in the Strand.

Subscribers to the musical score were asked for on January 8, and the work was published at half a guinea on February 9.

Mrs. Cibber probably failed to fulfil her engagement at the

production of *Hercules* on January 5, as the papers of January 9 announced that:

"Mrs. Cibber being perfectly recover'd of her late Indisposition will certainly perform on Saturday next (12th) in Hercules."

On January 12, *Hercules* was duly repeated, doubtless to a very poor house, and the result was that Handel decided to close down the season, and announced his intention through the press (*Daily Advertiser*, January 17, 1745) in the hitherto unnoticed and characteristic letter which follows:

Sir.

Having for a Series of Years received the greatest Obligations from the Nobility and Gentry of this Nation, I have always retained a deep Impression of their Goodness. As I perceived, that joining good Sense and significant Words to Musick, was the best Method of recommending *this* to an English Audience; I have directed my Studies that way, and endeavour'd to shew, that the English Language, which is so expressive of the sublimest Sentiments, is the best adapted of any to the full and solemn Kind of Musick. I have the Mortification now to find, that my Labours to please are become ineffectual, when my Expences are considerably greater. To what Cause I must impute the loss of the publick Favour, I am ignorant, but the Loss itself I shall always lament. In the mean time, I am assur'd that a Nation, whose Characteristick is Good Nature, would be affected with the Ruin of any Man, which was owing to his Endeavours to entertain them. I am likewise persuaded, that I shall have the Forgiveness of those noble Persons, who have honour'd me with their Patronage, and their Subscription this Winter, if I beg their Permission to stop short, before my Losses are too great to support, if I proceed no farther in my Undertaking; and if I intreat them to withdraw three Fourths of their Subscription, one Fourth Part only of my Proposal having been perform'd.

I am,
Sir,
Your very humble Servant,
G. F. Handel.

Attendance will be given at Mr. Handel's House in Brook's Street, near Hanover-Square, from Nine in the

Morning till Two in the Afternoon, on Monday, Tuesday, and Wednesday next, in Order to pay back the Subscription Money, on returning the Subscription Ticket.

This most interesting expression of the composer's own opinion on the situation is truly characteristic of Handel, and it will be noticed that no reference is made to his health or to any society opposition.

The letter met with a prompt response from an anonymous subscriber, published in *The Daily Advertiser*, January 18:

> To the Author.
> Sir,
> Upon Reading Mr. Handel's Letter in your Paper this Morning, I was sensibly touch'd with that great Master's Misfortunes, failing in his Endeavours to entertain the Publick; whose Neglect in not attending his admirable Performances can no otherwise be made up with Justice to the Character of the Nation, and the Merit of the Man, than by the Subscribers generously declining to withdraw the Remainder of their Subscriptions.
> I would lament the Loss of the Publick in Mr. Handel, in Strains equal to his if I was able, but our Concern will be best express'd by our Generosity.
> > We are,
> > > Sir,
> > > Your obedient Servants,
> > > > Subscribers.
> St. James's,
> Jan. 17. 1744–5.

Clearly the composer still had some staunch friends. On January 21, *The Daily Advertiser* published the following satirical poem, not recorded elsewhere, with the appended references to Ovid's *Metamorphoses*:

> To Mr. Handel.
> Tu ne cede malis, sed contra audentior ito.
>
> While you, Great Master of the Lyre;
> Our Breasts with various Passions fire;
> The Youth to Martial Glory move,
> Now melt to Pity, now to Love;

While distant Realms thy Pow'r confess,
Thy happy Compositions bless,
And Musical Omnipotence
In adding solemn Sounds to Sense;
How hard thy Fate! that here alone,
Where we can call thy Notes our own;
Ingratitude shou'd be thy Lot,
And all thy Harmony forgot!
Cou'd Malice, or Revenge, take Place,
Thou'dst feel, alas! the like Disgrace
Thy Father *Orpheus* felt in *Thrace*.
There, as dear *Ovid* does rehearse,
(And who shall question *Ovid's* Verse?)
The Bard's enchanting Harp and Voice
Made all the Savage Herd rejoice,
Grow tame, forget their Lust and Prey,
And dance obsequious to his Lay.
(a) The *Thracian* Women, 'tis wellknown,
Despis'd all Musick, but their own;
(b) But chiefly ONE, of envious Kind,
(c) With Skin of Tyger *capuchin'd*,
Was more implacable than all,
And strait resolv'd poor *Orpheus'* Fall;
Whene'er he play'd, she'd make (d) a *Drum*,
Invite her Neighbours all to come;
At other Times wou'd send about,
And dreg 'em to a Revel-*Rout*:
Then she: (e) Behold, that Head and Hand
Have brought to scorn the *Thracian* Band;
Nor ever can our Band revive,
While that Head, Hand, or Finger live.
She said: (f) The wild and frantic Crew
In Rage the sweet Musician slew:
(g) The Strains, which charm'd the fiercest Beasts,
Cou'd move no Pity in their Breasts.
Here *Ovid*, to the Sex most civil,
Says, in their Cups they did this Evil,
When nightly met to sacrifice
To *Bacchus*, as his Votaries:
The Deed the God so much provokes,
He turn'd the Wretches into Oaks.
But HANDEL, lo! a happier Fate
On thee, and on thy Lyre, shall wait;

The Nation shall redress thy Wrong
And joy to hear thy *Even Song*:
The Royal Pair shall deign to smile;
The Beauties of the British Isle,
The noble Youth, whom Virtue fires,
And Martial Harmony inspires,
Shall meet in crouded Audiences:
Thy Foes shall blush; and HERCULES
Avenge this National Disgrace,
And vanquish ev'ry Fiend of *Thrace*.

Ov. Met. L.11.

(a) Ecce Nurus Ciconum.—
(b) E quibus una, levem jactato crine per auram.—
(c) —Tectæ lymphata Ferinis
       Pectora velleribus.—
(d) Tympanaque plaususque, et Bacchei ululatus Ob-
       strepuere sono Citharæ.—
(e) En, ait, en, hic est nostri Contemptor.—
(f) —Tum denique Saxa
       Non exauditi rubuerunt sanguine Vatis.
(g) —Nec quicquam voce moventem
       Sacrilegæ perimunt.—

The references to the classical text are given as printed in the paper as it may be of interest for readers of this article to turn them up in the original text, (*Metamorphoses*. Book XI.)

The Latin quotation which prefaces the poem is from Virgil (*Aeneid*, Book VI, line 95) and is an appropriate encouragement to the composer to carry on.

The reference to the woman who "resolv'd poor Orpheus' Fall", by making a "Drum" or arranging a "Revel-Rout" whenever he played is particularly interesting. It is very strong corroborative evidence of the Lady Brown story.

In 1746 Smollett published a poetical satire "Advice". A passage on the Handel question is quoted from this poem by Streatfeild and other writers, but earlier in the work Smollett used the expression "rapt amidst the transports of a drum." To "Drum" he gives a footnote as follows: "This was a riotous assembly of fashionable people of both sexes, at a private house consisting of some hundreds, not inaptly styled a *drum*, from the noise and emptiness of the entertainment. There were also

155

drum-major, rout, tempest and hurricane; differing only in degrees of multitude and uproar, as the significant name of each declares."

In addition to the poem to Handel, *The Daily Advertiser* (January 21) also published the following:

> After reading Mr. Handel's Letter to the Public in this Paper of Thursday last.
>
> An Epigram
>
> Romans, to shew they Genius's wou'd Prize,
> Gave rich Support; and dead, did Bustos rise:
> But wiser we, the kindred arts to serve,
> First carve the Busts;* then bid the *Charmers* starve.

The statue referred to was the famous one by Roubiliac, erected in Vauxhall Gardens in 1738, and now adorning the premises of Messrs. Novello & Co., Wardour Street.

Handel's friends were evidently rallying round him and on January 25, 1745, he expressed in *The Daily Advertiser* his appreciation of their efforts in the following spirited letter, now reproduced for the first time:

> Sir,
>
> The new Proofs which I have receiv'd of the Generosity of my Subscribers, in refusing upon their own Motives to withdraw their Subscriptions call upon me for the earliest Return, and the warmest Expressions of my Gratitude; but natural as it is to feel, proper as it is to have, I find this extremely difficult to express. Indeed I ought not to content myself with bare Expressions of it; therefore, though I am not able to fulfil the whole of my Engagement, I shall think it my Duty to perform what Part of it I can, and shall in some Time proceed with the Oratorios, let the *Risque* which I may run be what it will.
> I am, Sir,
> Your very humble Servant,
> G. F. Handel.

On February 11, two days after the publication of the score of *Hercules*, the season was announced to re-open on February 16. The performance was however postponed until March 1, when *Samson* was given.

* Mr. Handel's elegant Marble Statue in Vaux-Hall Gardens.

This performance called forth the following letter in *The Daily Advertiser* of March 4:

> To Mr. Handel.
> Sir,
> It was with infinite Pleasure I read the Advertisement of your Intention to perform the Oratorio of Samson, and waited with Impatience till the Day came; but how great was my Disappointment to see the most delightful Songs in the whole Oratorio took from one, who, by her Manner of singing them charm'd all the Hearers; Was she once reinstated in the Part she always used to perform, your Samson would shine with the greatest Lustre, and be justly admir'd by all.
> I am, Sir,
> Your Friend and Well-Wisher,
> A. Z.

The writer was referring presumably to the substitution of Signora Francesina for Mrs. Cibber, who appears to have dropped out of the company about this time, as she was in *Hercules*, but not in *Belshazzar*. Mrs. Delany writing February 25, 1744, with reference to a visit to *Samson* the previous night, says "Francesina sings most of Mrs. Cibber's part and some of Mrs. Clive's." The last-named singer had created the original part of "Dalila" in *Samson* in 1743 (except for one number given to Signora Avoglio), but was not in Handel's company in the 1744–45 season.

One interesting piece of evidence showing that Handel was not without professional friends was the announcement in *The Daily Advertiser* (March 2 and 7) of performances of Arne's *Alfred*, at Drury Lane on Wednesday, March 20, and Wednesday, April 3, with the "Note, The above Days are fix'd on to avoid interfering with Mr. Handel."

Samson was repeated on March 8, *Saul* was given on March 13, and *Joseph* on March 15 and 22.

On March 27, Handel produced *Belshazzar*, his second new work of the season, which was repeated on March 29.

No announcement of the publication of the libretto of *Belshazzar* has been traced, but the work appeared with the following title-page:

157

Belshazzar. An Oratorio. As it is Perform'd at the
King's Theatre in the Hay-Market. The Musick by Mr.
Handel. . . . London: Printed by and for J. Watts . . .
And by B. Dod . . . 1745. [Price One Shilling.]

On April 9, Handel revived *Messiah* under the then accepted
title "The Sacred Oratorio", with a Concerto on the Organ.

A concert "For the Benefit and Increase of a Fund establish'd
for the Support of Decay'd Musicians or their Families" was
given at Covent Garden on April 10. This society, now
known as The Royal Society of Musicians of Great Britain,
was a cause in which Handel had always been interested since
its foundation in 1738, and on this occasion (April 10) as frequently, the music performed was chiefly by Handel, and in
cluded "Handel's Grand Sonata." The principal singers were
from the composer's company.

"The Sacred Oratorio" with a Concerto on the Organ, was
repeated on April 11, and the season closed on April 23 with
Belshazzar, with a Concerto on the Organ.

Handel had thus held out for sixteen performances, ten of
them subsequent to the interruption owing to the failure of the
first six.

Of this period in the Composer's career Streatfeild states:
"Only sixteen of the promised twenty-four concerts had been
given, but the performances did not cover their expenses, and
Handel's own funds, the proceeds of his successful visit to Ireland, were exhausted. His health forbade further efforts, and
once more he was declared a bankrupt."

There is no contemporary evidence that the later part of
the season was a failure, or if it was closed down owing to
Handel's health, and no public notice of his bankruptcy has
been traced.

On April 29 Miss Robinson had her benefit, Handel's singers
and his works again being in evidence. The programme included *The New Overture of Pastor Fido* and a Trio in *Acis and
Galatea*. The latter was sung by Miss Robinson, Beard and
Reinhold on April 29, and by Signora Francesina, Miss Robinson and Reinhold in the Concert on April 10.

Although the season had finished for Handel, he did not drop
out of public notice altogether.

On May 2, *The General Advertiser* announced the issue of "An Ode to Mr. Handel". This was a eulogistic poem on the composer's sacred works, beginning: "While you, great Author of the sacred song". It was published by R. Dodsley and is known to Handel students.

On May 10th, *The Daily Advertiser* announced:

> For the benefit of Miss Davis. A Child of eight Years of Age, lately arriv'd from Ireland. At Mr. Hickford's Room in Brewer-Street, this Day the 10th instant, will be perform'd a Concert of Vocal and Instrumental Music. Several favourite Organ Concertos and Overtures of Mr. Handels . . . with two remarkable Songs. Composed by Mr. Handel, entirely for the Harpsichord, accompanied by Miss Davis, with some select Songs to be perform'd by Mrs. Davis a Scholar of Bononcini's . . . Note. Miss Davis is to perform on a Harpsichord of Mr. Rutgerus Plenius's making, Inventor of the new deserv'd famous Lyrichord.

Plenius's Lyrichord, patented in 1741, is described in Grove "as being a harpischord strung with wire and catgut, made on the sostinente principle, and actuated by moving wheels instead of the usual quills, so that the bow of the violin and organ were imitated."

Walsh announced the publication of the score of *Belshazzar* in *The General Evening Post*, May 16–18.

On July 13, *The Daily Advertiser* advertised another Walsh work: "This day is publish'd (Price 5s.) A Grand Collection of English Songs set to Musick by Mr. Handel"; the same publication as that advertised on August 8 as "from the late Oratorios".

The Daily Advertiser, August 1, advertised: "To be Sold a Pennyworth At the Opera-House, Two Second-hand Chamber Organs. Inquire of Mr. Jordan in Budge-Row, near London-Stone." One wonders whether these were some of Handel's goods that he had to dispose of in order to meet his expenses, and which were now offered, in the language of the day, at bargain prices.

One of the references to Handel's health in the Malmesbury

Papers is a letter from William Harris to his sister-in-law, dated August 29. The composer was in London, and the correspondent who met him says, "He talked much of his precarious state of health, yet he looks well enough. I believe you will have him with you ere long."

Two days afterwards (August 31) Handel composed probably the last of his Italian Duets, "Ahi, nelle sorti umane", the dated autograph of which is in the Royal Music Library. (R.M.20.g.9.)

On September 10, Walsh advertised the first part of *Handel's celebrated Airs in the Oratorios of Belshazzar and Hercules, set for a German Flute and a Bass*, the second part being issued a little later.

Lord Shaftesbury recorded on October 24 that "Poor Handel looks something better. I hope he will entirely recover in due time, though he has been a good deal disordered in the head." (*Malmesbury Papers*.)

Presumably at some time in the late summer or early autumn Handel stayed at the Harris family mansion at Salisbury, where his health improved.

At Drury Lane, on November 14, and subsequent dates Lowe sang Handel's "Chorus Song, (Stand round my brave Boys) Set . . . for the Gentlemen Volunteers of the City of London." The subject was written up by Barclay Squire in the *Riemann-Festschrift*, but it seems to have escaped notice that the edition in sheet form was issued by "John Simpson, opposite the East Door of the Royal Exchange," on November 15.

This closes the record, as far as we know, of Handel's activities during 1745. Looking at the events as a whole, they present anything but a picture of failure, although it was obviously a period of struggle and difficulty, such as might have broken a lesser man. During the winter months he bided his time, still sure of his powers and not unmindful of what he owed to his friends.

His next public performance was on February 14, 1746, when he produced *The Occasional Oratorio*, repeating it on February 19 and 26. These three performances, according to a paragraph in *The General Advertiser*, January 31, were given by Handel "to make good to the subscribers that favoured him last season the number of performances he was not then able to complete."

Handel's own announcement in *The General Advertiser* of February 14, 1746, is given below, and forms a fitting conclusion to this attempt to tell the story of his difficulties in 1744-45 and the spirit in which he met them:

> At the Theatre-Royal in Covent Garden this Day, will be perform'd a New Occasional Oratorio. With a New Concerto on the Organ. Pit and Boxes to be put together, and no Person to be admitted without Tickets, which will be deliver'd this Day at the Office at Covent-Garden Theatre, at Half a Guinea each. First Gallery 5s. Second Gallery 3s. 6d. Galleries to be open'd at Half an Hour after Four o'Clock. Pit and Boxes at Five. To begin at Half an Hour after Six o'Clock.
>
> The Subscribers, who favour'd Mr. Handel last Season with their Subscription, are desired to send to the Office at Covent-Garden Theatre, on the Day of Performance, where Two Tickets shall be delivered to each Gratis, in Order to make good the Number of Performances subscrib'd to last Season.

VI

GUSTAVUS WALTZ
WAS HE HANDEL'S COOK?

IV

GUSTAVUS WALTZ

WAS HE HANDEL'S COOK?

GUSTAVUS
WALTZ
WAS HE
HANDEL'S
COOK?

Among the lesser known singers of Handel's day, Gustavus Waltz is best remembered, not because he was a singer, but because he is supposed to have been Handel's cook. Little has hitherto been known about him other than the brief, and in some cases inaccurate, references in Hawkins, Burney and later standard authorities.

Investigation of the subject shows, however, that he had a long and fairly distinguished career as a singer and actor in addition to being an instrumentalist. If he had ever served as Handel's cook, which is open to question, it could not have been for long, and at any rate, only in his younger days.

The story of his public career, as told here for the first time, not only records the many parts he played, but throws new light on the eighteenth century stage, supplies many fresh details and corrects a number of inaccuracies in the accepted works on the subject.

Handel is supposed to have settled at Brook Street, Hanover Square about 1720 at the earliest, certainly by 1725, and it was then probably that he found it necessary to have a household staff. Was Gustavus Waltz amongst the number? We do not know; but at any rate it is reasonable to assume that Waltz was not in the composer's service as a cook before 1720.

The dates of the birth and death of Waltz have not been traced. He is generally supposed to have been a German, although whether he was born in England or abroad is not stated. If he was German born and German speaking, it is strange that he made his earliest appearances in a number of English works, with almost entirely English casts, and which were given in competition with the Italian operas.

Hawkins in his *History of Music*, 1776 says, speaking presumably of the year 1734, "The contest between Handel and the nobility was carried on with so much disadvantage to the former, that he found himself the necessity of quitting the Haymarket Theatre at the time when his opponents were wishing to get possession of it; and in the issue each party shifted its ground by an exchange of situations. The nobility removed with Farinelli, Senesino and Montagnana, a bass singer, who had sung for Handel in Sosarmes and other of his operas; and Handel with Strada, Bertoli and Waltz, a bass singer, who had been his cook, went to Lincoln's Inn Fields. Here he continued but for a short time; for finding himself unable singly to continue the opposition, he removed to Covent Garden."

This is the first reference to Waltz as Handel's cook which we have, and the whole passage illustrates the importance of taking these early writers with a certain amount of reserve. Farinelli first came to England in 1734 and appeared at the opera of the nobility in *Artaserse*, (Hasse, etc.) at the King's Theatre, on October 29, with Montagnana, Senesino, Signora Cuzzoni, Signora Bertolli and Signora Maria Segatti. Hawkins quite inaccurately places Signora Bertolli in Handel's Company at this time, and the same writer, in following Mainwaring (1760) with regard to this supposed short season at Lincoln's Inn Fields Theatre, endorses a piece of fiction that has been copied by practically every subsequent biographer of Handel. Burney supplies further fictitious details. He says: "October 5th (1734), Handel having quitted the King's Theatre, began his campaign in Lincoln's Inn Fields, with the same auxiliaries as the preceding season. Here he performed *Ariadne* and *Pastor Fido*, till December 18th, when he removed to the new theatre in Covent-garden, where he brought out an opera called Orestes." It is quite certain that no such season took place at Lincoln's Inn Fields in the autumn of 1734. Two such glaring inaccuracies as the references to Bertolli and Lincoln's Inn Fields in Hawkins's short statement compel one to question the truth of his reference to Waltz as Handel's cook, although it must be allowed to stand in the absence of any definitely contradictory evidence.

Hawkins places Waltz as Handel's cook in 1734, or earlier, and from what has been said about Handel's house-keeping in 1720 the extreme dates of Waltz's service appear to be therefore 1720–34, but as is shown later on, he may have been known as a professional instrumentalist in 1709. He was on the stage as early as March 13, 1732, and his public career as an actor and singer continued until some time in 1759 at any rate.

The next early reference of importance is that in Burney's *Account of the Musical Performances in Westminster Abbey . . . in Commemoration of Handel, etc.*, published in 1785. In the *Sketch of the Life of Handel* in that work, Burney says: "When Gluck came first into England, in 1745, he was neither so great a composer, nor so high in reputation, as he afterwards mounted; and I remember when Mrs. Cibber, in my hearing, asked Handel what sort of a composer he was; his answer, prefaced by an oath . . . was 'he knows no more of contrapunto as mein cook, Waltz'."

If this statement is to be taken simply as it stands, and it is frequently misquoted, it infers that in 1745, or soon after, Waltz was Handel's cook. It must be remembered, however, that Burney is recording Handel's remark forty years or so after it was supposed to have been made, and the word "Waltz" at the end may have slipped unconsciously into Burney's mind, as he referred to or recalled Hawkins's statement that Waltz had been Handel's cook. Looking at Handel's reported words, the inclusion of Waltz's name seems a little open to question. Referring to a servant, an employer would be much more likely to say simply "my cook" without mentioning the name, although it is admitted that this line of argument is rather speculative. The remark of Handel as given by Burney has been dealt with by various writers, who have endeavoured to justify Handel's rather illiberal reference to Gluck by pointing out that

Waltz was an excellent singer and Gluck's operas at that time "slight and trivial specimens of the fashionable manner of the day" (Streatfeild.) If, however, Handel was referring merely to a cook and not Waltz in particular, his remark about Gluck was even less complimentary.

A very strong argument against the possibility of Handel mentioning Waltz in the discussion about Gluck in the way in which he is reported to have done, is the fact, that in 1744 Gustavus Waltz became a member of the Musical Fund, afterwards The Royal Society of Musicians, a rather exclusive professional organization of which Handel was a founder member, and in which he took very great interest. The records of the Society have been kindly placed at the disposal of the present writer and in the Admission Book the signature of Waltz appears on January 1, 1743–44, and against it the word "Dead", but unfortunately with no further date. It is to be regretted that most of the early records of the society are not in existence, but the writer has in his possession a printed list of the rules dated May 8, 1738 and a printed list of the subscribers of the year 1744. This list includes Waltz amongst the "Professors of Musick", and it seems apparent from the names of the non-professional members that they would hardly have welcomed a "cook". Handel must have known Waltz in 1745 as a fellow member of the Society and in the circumstances would not be likely to refer to him at that time as "mein cook", and speak deprecatingly of his musical knowledge.

Burney tells us in his *History*, that from 1745 onwards "there will be little occasion for my having recourse to tradition or books for information concerning the musical transactions of our own capital, as it has been the chief place of my residence ever since; except from 1751 to 1760", A confession which precludes the possibility of Burney having many personal recollections of Waltz before 1745.

Presuming, however, that Waltz was Handel's cook in 1745 or thereabouts, what can we make of Hawkins's statement with regard to the year 1734 when he says "Waltz, a bass singer, who *had been* his cook."

In 1789, four years later than Burney's *Account of the Musical Performances in Westminster Abbey*, he published the fourth volume of his *History of Music*. In this volume, speaking of the performances of Handel's *Ariadne* at the King's Theatre, January 26, 1734, he says: "Handel's singers were Carestini, Scalzi, and Waltz for the men's parts", and continuing, "The next air: Se ti condanno, was sang by Waltz, a German, with a coarse figure and a still coarser voice." Burney adds a footnote to Waltz in this passage: "It has been said that he was originally Handel's cook. He frequently sang in choruses and comic entertainments at Drury-lane, in my own memory; and as an actor, had a great deal of humour. It was imagined that his countryman Lampe had this song and singer in mind when he set 'Oh, oh, master Moor' in the Dragon of Wantley."

Leaving for the moment the reference to *The Dragon of Wantley*, it will be noticed that Burney is not quite so definite as he was in the earlier reference to Waltz. "It has been said", is hardly a convincing statement of historical fact.

It is difficult to see any connection between Waltz and the song, "Oh, oh, Master Moor". Moreover Lampe and Waltz were closely associated professionally from 1732–34, and on September 19, 1740, and on some later occasions, Waltz played Gubbins in *The Dragon of Wantley*, as indicated below. There is no evidence that Waltz and Lampe quarrelled, and the latter's song can hardly be considered a friendly gesture. The words are:

> Oh, oh, Master Moor
> You son of a whore,
> I wish I had known
> Your tricks before.

When Burney is discussing *Ariodante* (1735) he says: "The next air: *Volate amori* was a kind of *bravura* in its day. . . . This is, however, followed by an admirable bass song: *Voli colla sua tromba*; it was sung by Waltz, and accompanied by two French-horns, though the words called for a trumpet. This air deserves a better singer, for Waltz had but little voice, and his manner was coarse and unpleasant," and, continuing the same subject, "There is a light air: *Se l'inganno*, which was sung by the Negri; and another of a common cast, for Waltz."

It should be pointed out that the performances of Waltz in

Ariadne and *Ariodante* took place when Burney was less than ten years of age. By 1740, five years before Burney was living in London, Waltz's career as a singer in Italian opera and in Handel works was practically over, although he continued to act for some years, so that Burney may not have heard him sing at his best.

On May 12, 1736, Handel produced *Atalanta*, composed on the occasion of the marriage of the Prince of Wales to Princess Augusta of Saxe-Gotha. Waltz had the small part of Nicandro, and of his one song, Burney says (*History*) "Waltz's air: *Impara ingrata* has in it many passages and strokes of a great master." Burney adds a footnote to this statement: "Lampe has burlesqued a fine passage of this air in *Oh! Oh! master Moor* of the Dragon of Wantley, at the word *before*." This second reference of Burney to *The Dragon of Wantley* is as difficult to understand as the earlier one, as there does not appear to be much similarity between the music of "Impara ingrata" and "Oh, oh, Master Moor."

So much for what Hawkins and Burney tell us about Waltz. One further piece of information must be considered as important circumstantial evidence on the question as to whether he was Handel's cook. The composer was accustomed to write the names of the singers on some of his manuscripts. On the three occasions when he mentioned Waltz on autographs in the Royal Collection he spelled the name incorrectly. On *Alcina* and *Arianna* it is given as "Walls" and on *Israel in Egypt* as "Wals". On the autograph of *Alceste* (British Museum, Add. MSS. 30310) Handel in 1750 gave the singer's name as "Mr. Walz". These would be pardonable errors if Handel did not know the person well, but to make such mistakes about a man who was or had been his cook, and was a fellow countryman, is rather strange. Moreover, Handel, as a rule spelled his singers' names correctly.

Although not a very important point, Handel did not mention Waltz in his will or codicils, as he might have done had the singer been in his employment at the time these documents were executed.

There is in existence a portrait in oils of Waltz. (See Plate No. 12.) Formerly owned by T. W. Taphouse of Oxford, it was exhibited at the Loan Collection of the International

Inventions Exhibition, London, 1885, and at the Music Loan Exhibition (Worshipful Company of Musicians), 1904. The portrait, attributed to Friedrich Ludwig Hauck, is not signed, but bears on the frame: "Gustavus Waltz—Handel's Cook. Hauck—Pinx^t." A mezzotint, with the caption: "Cantores amant Humores dicit. Gustavus Waltz", gives the artist as I. M. Hauck and the engraver as I. S. Müller. This mezzotint was reproduced in *The Musical Times*, December, 1893, and elsewhere, but it is not a good copy of the original painting. In this, Waltz appears as a 'cellist with a harpsichord in the background. The present writer has traced one other piece of contemporary evidence which may refer to Waltz's activities as an instrumentalist—the reference in the Thomas Coke papers, given in detail later on. Neither Hawkins nor Burney mention him in this capacity. One of the songs represented in the painting begins: "Wine is a Mistress". This taken in conjunction with the other details and the caption may have been meant to indicate Waltz's enjoyment of other things besides music.

It may be of interest to record that he was a subscriber to W. De Fesch's *Sonata's for Two German Flutes or Two Violins with a Through Bass. Opera Settima*, published for the author by Benjamin Cooke in 1733.

On the evidence presented up to this point, readers must come to their own conclusions as to Waltz's career in Handel's kitchen. The remainder of this chapter is concerned with the professional life of Waltz as singer and actor over a period of may-be fifty years, with comments by the way on some of the works in which he played.

What may be the earliest reference to Waltz is in the Thomas Coke (Vice Chamberlain) papers connected with the London Theatres, 1700–40, as published in the *Proceedings of the Musical Association*, 1913–14. In this collection there is a list, in Heidegger's handwriting, of instrumentalists who signed a petition for certain rates of pay "for every night they are to play." Amongst these is the entry "Waltzer, £1 0s. 0d." There is no proof that the person mentioned was Gustavus Waltz. The list is not dated, but may be placed at about 1709–10, and if the reference was to Gustavus Waltz, he must have had a very long public career as instrumentalist and singer, and we know nothing about him between c. 1710 and 1732.

The earliest appearance of Waltz which some of the authorities record is as Polyphemus in *Acis and Galatea*, at the New (Little) Theatre, Haymarket, May 17, 1732. This production is dealt with later on, because Waltz appeared as a singer two months earlier.

A preliminary announcement of interest appeared in *The Daily Post*, February 26, 1731–32: "At the New Theatre in the Haymarket on Monday, the 13th day of March next, will be perform'd (by subscription) a new English Opera, call'd *Amelia*, after the Italian Manner. By a Set of Performers who never yet appear'd in publick. Subscriptions are taken in at the following Places, at One Guinea, to be paid by each Subscriber at the Delivery of the Ticket, which will admit the Person so subscribing into the Boxes four Nights, viz., at St. James's Coffee-House by Palace Gate; at Mr. Fribourg's, Maker of Rapee Snuff at the Play-house Gate; at Tom's Coffee-House in Russel-street, Covent-Garden; at Nando's Coffee-House by Temple-Bar; at Garraway's Coffee-House in Exchange-Alley; and by the Author at the Golden Heart in King-street, St. Anne's."

The cast of the production was:

Osmyn, Grand Vizier, Commander of the Turks	*Waltz*
Casimir, Prince and General of the Hungarian Army	*Kelly*
Rodulpho, his friend	*Snider*
Amelia, wife of Casimir	*Miss Arne*
Augusta, sister to Casimir	*Mrs. Mason*

It is worthy of notice that Miss Arne, afterwards Mrs. Cibber and one of Handel's greatest oratorio singers and a personal friend, made her debut in *Amelia*. If Handel included the name of Waltz in his remarks to Mrs. Cibber about Gluck, recorded above, it is a pity that we do not know what Mrs. Cibber thought about the matter. She could hardly have forgotten her early appearance with Waltz, and he was probably still in her circle of professional acquaintances. *Amelia* was written by Henry Carey, with music by J. F. Lampe. The work was given eleven times in March and April, 1732, including a benefit for Snider and Waltz on April 24. In the character of Osmyn, a prominent part, Waltz, opened the work and had the following songs:

> What toil, what danger and what care.
> I'll destroy the proud foe in his glory.
> The eagle with its prey.
> Lovely creature! While I'm gazing.
> All my glories I resign.

Waltz and Miss Arne (Amelia) appeared in the duet: "To one so fair and kind", and in addition, Miss Arne had several songs.

The libretto of *Amelia* was published by J. Watts in 1732. Unfortunately no copy of the complete music, if published, has been traced.

On May 17, 1732, Thomas Arne, the father of the well-known composer, produced Handel's *Acis and Galatea* at the New Theatre (Little Theatre) Haymarket, a second performance being given on May 19. Whether these performances were with Handel's permission or not is unknown, although it has been customary to say that the work was pirated and that Waltz was guilty of having played Handel, his master, a rather scurvy trick in appearing in the production. The cast included:

Polyphemus	.	.	*Mr. Waltz*
Acis	.	.	*Mr. Mountier*
Damon	.	.	*Mrs. Mason*
Galatea	.	.	*Miss Arne*

Waltz's part indicates the range of his voice at that time.

On November 16, 1732, Waltz took the two parts of Mars and Honour in *Britannia*, an English opera, text by Lediard, music by Lampe, at the Haymarket Theatre. The work was repeated on November 20, 23 and 27. The production offered something new in stage decoration: "A transparent theatre, illuminated and adorn'd with a great number of emblems, mottoes, devices, and inscriptions, and embellish'd with machines, in a manner entirely new " In addition to his part in the dialogue of *Britannia*, Waltz had the following songs:

> Cupid, God of soft desire.
> Tho' Goddess still you fly me.
> Goddess, majestic, awful, great.

This opera with a "transparent theatre", a large design of which was given as a frontispiece to the libretto, was evidently looked upon as something original and likely to have a continued success. The following notice is taken from *The Daily Post* of November 15, 1732: "We hear that yesterday there was a Rehearsal of the English Opera Britannia, at the New Theatre in the Haymarket. The Musick (set by Mr. Lampe) gave great Satisfaction to the Audience, who were no less pleased with the Vocal and Instrumental Performers; so that when the whole is exhibited with the Transparent Theatre, 'tis not doubted but it will meet with Applause from the Town. Miss Cæcilia Young was particularly admired, which gave Occasion to the following Lines, alluding to the famous St. Cæcilia:

> No more shall Italy its Warblers send,
> To charm our Ears with Handel's heav'nly Strains;
> For dumb his rapt'rous* Lyre, their Fame must end.
> And hark! Cæcilia! from th' Ætherial Plains,
> Her Sounds once call'd a Seraph from the Skies:
> To sing like Accents see! she hither flies.

This tribute to Miss Young, who became the wife of T. A. Arne in 1736, does not appear to be generally known. The reference to *Cato* is explained by the fact that up to November 15, the date of the extract, only one opera, an anonymous work called *Cato*, had been produced at Handel's Opera House that season, which opened November 4, 1732.

Handel, however, was not entirely "dumb" as the poem suggests. He revived *Alessandro* on November 25, followed by performances of *Acis and Galatea* and *Tolomeo* until January 27, 1733, when he produced *Orlando*, one of his finest works. On March 3, he revived *Floridante*, on March 17 produced *Deborah*, on April 14 revived *Esther*, and the season was continued until

* The Opera of Cato is not Mr. Handel's.

June 9 with these works and *Griselda* by G. B. Bononcini. The date of the production of *Orlando* is usually given as January 23, but it is incorrect.

On June 13, 1733, a paragraph appeared in the press announcing a meeting at Hickford's Great Room on June 15 of "The Subscribers to the Opera in which Signor Senesino and Signora Cuzzoni are to perform," etc. This meeting, noticed more fully in some of the biographies of Handel, is supposed to have been a significant move in the quarrel between Handel and what became known as the opera of the nobility. The matter is referred to again later on.

John Christopher Smith the younger produced his first operatic work, *Teraminta*, at the age of twenty, in 1732, and his second work *Ulysses*, an opera with words by Samuel Humphreys at, Lincoln's Inn Fields Theatre, on April 16, 1733. This was a benefit performance for the composer and the cast as given in the libretto was:

Ulysses	. . .	*Mrs. Barbier*
Penelope	. .	*Miss Cecilia Young*
Telemachus	. . .	*Mr. Kelly*
Antinous	. . .	*Mr. Waltz*
Antigone	. . .	*Mrs. Wright*

In addition to his part in the dialogue Waltz had the following numbers:

> Songs: Thou know'st not the treasure.
> With noble derision.
> Trio, with Miss Young and Mr. Kelly:
> O cease thy soft anguish.

The work appears to have been played only once.

The *Opera of Operas*, an adaptation of Fielding's *Tragedy of Tragedies*, was a popular work of the period. Two versions were apparently used in competition in rival theatres, one with music by T. A. Arne and the other with music by J. F. Lampe, and Waltz appeared in both of them.

Arne's production, presumably in three acts, was given at the Haymarket Theatre on May 31, 1733, and had at least six performances that season. The work was advertised as "never acted before" and set to "Musick after the Italian manner". Waltz, sometimes given as Watts and Walts, took the parts of Lord Grizzle and the Ghost of Gaffer Thumb. Arne's version was revived at the Haymarket Theatre on October 29, 1733, as an "Entertainment of one Act . . . Set to Musick by Mr. T. Arne, Jun.," and was played at least seventeen times during the season, the last performance being on January 28, 1734. For this production, a number of changes were made in the cast. Waltz was not in the company and the part of Lord Grizzle was taken by "Mr. Charke".

Waltz probably appeared in *Athalia* and other works (*Esther, Deborah, Acis and Galatea*, etc.) given by Handel at Oxford in July, 1733, but the evidence on the matter is conflicting, and it is not quite certain whether Montagnana had left Handel's company by this time or not. Montagnana's name appears on the autograph score of *Athalia*, and the part was clearly intended for him, but Waltz's name appears on the first edition of the work, published in 1735, in which year he certainly took the part of Abner, formerly allotted to Montagnana. Various references are given in Chrysander and elsewhere that seem to prove that Waltz and not Montagnana was in the Oxford production.

On November 7, 1733, one of the dates on which Arne's version of *The Opera of Operas* was playing at The Haymarket, Lampe's edition of the work was produced at Drury Lane as "never acted there before". This version was in three acts "set to Musick after the Italian manner by Mr. John Fredk. Lampe". It was repeated on November 9 and December 13. Waltz played in these performances his former parts of Lord Grizzle and the Ghost of Gaffer Thumb, and Mountier, another of Arne's players in his version of May 31, 1733, was also in Lampe's company. There is no evidence as to whether Lampe and Arne were having a friendly rivalry or a business competition. It is interesting to remember that the rivals subsequently married sisters—Arne, Cecilia Young in 1736, and Lampe, Isabella Young in 1738 or 1739, this approximate date not being generally known hitherto.

The librettos of these 1733–34 versions are not available, so that it is impossible to compare them, or to say exactly what Waltz's part consisted of. There is, however, a libretto of a production by Arne in Dublin in 1743, in which Lord Grizzle has the following songs:

> The spaniel when bid does obey.
> I'll roar, I'll rant, I'll rave.
> No, no, I will no rival bear.
> My body's like a bankrupt's shop.

As a specimen, the words of the first of these numbers is given here:

> The spaniel, when bid, does obey,
> And twenty fine tricks show with all;
> The soldier's observant as Tray
> And both will come to at a call.
>
> The lover's more fawning than these,
> Or any court-sycophant spark,
> He'll shout, fetch and carry to please,
> And all for a touch in the dark.

Benjamin Cooke published the music of Arne's 1733 version of *The Opera of Operas* as *the Most Celebrated Aires in the Opera of Tom Thumb*. It includes two of Waltz's songs: "The spaniel, when bid does obey", in the Bass Clef, and "My body's like a bankrupt's shop", in the Treble Clef.

The Opera of Operas has been dealt with here at some length as the existing references are incomplete or inaccurate.

So far as can be discovered, Waltz made his first appearance in Italian Opera in Handel's *Ottone*, on November 13th, 1733, at the King's Theatre, but before continuing with the details of Waltz's career it is necessary to give some attention to Handel's work at that time.

Because Burney, who is the last word to many subsequent writers, has little to say on the early part of the 1733–34 season, most of the later authorities give no additional information and simply repeat Burney's inaccuracies. It is impossible to do more than summarize here the previously known facts as they have been verified and supplemented by the present writer.

Handel's season opened at the King's Theatre on October 30, 1733, with *Semiramis* (*Semiramide riconosciuta*), based on

Metastasio with music probably by Vivaldi. This work was given also on November 3, 6, and 10. The singers were Margherita Durastanti, Anna Strada del Po, Carlo Scalzi, Maria Catterina Negri, Maria Rosa Negri and Giovanni Carestini, one of the greatest Italian singers of the day. All the important writers on this subject following Burney say without question that Carestini made his London debut in *Caio Fabrizio* (Caius Fabricius) on December 4, 1733. It can now be shown, however, that Carestini was certainly in some, most probably all of the four performances of *Semiramide*, and four of Handel's *Ottone* given prior to December 4, as his name is in the two contemporary librettos of the works.

Ottone was given on November 13, 17, 20, and 24. The libretto is in existence and raises an interesting question. It is dated on the title-page 1733, and as *Ottone* was not played between April, 1727, and November, 1733, the libretto must refer to the latter season.

The strange thing about the libretto is that it has two entirely different casts printed in it. The first cast includes Senesino, Signora Strada, Montagnana, Signora Celeste, Mr. Montier (Mountier) and Signora Bertolli. All except Strada went over from Handel's company to the rival opera of the nobility, which opened up at Lincoln's Inn Fields on December 29, 1733, and which will be dealt with later on. The second cast in the *Ottone* libretto includes Giovanni Caristino (Carestini), Signora Strada, Signora Margherita Durastanti, Carlo Scalzi, Signora Maria Catterina Negri and Mr. Walz (Waltz). This cast is on the first of two extra leaves which contain also the text of the following additional songs: (a) "Bel labbro formato". (b) "Tu puoi straziarmi". (These two numbers are in the original libretto of 1723, but are omitted from the body of the text of the 1733 edition.) (c) "Sino che ti vedrò." (This number does not appear in the 1723 libretto, which has in its place "Lascia, che nel suo viso".) (d) "D'instabile fortuna". (Presumably from *Lotario*.) (e) "Pupille sdegnose". (A modification of the text and presumably of the music from *Muzio Scevola*.) It is not clear whether this number is to precede or displace "D'inalzar i flutti al Ciel", which is given to Emireno in the 1733 libretto, but to Adelberto in the 1723 libretto and in the *Händel-Gesellschaft* edition. The last three additional songs are not associated with *Ottone* in the *Händel-Gesellschaft* edition. All of the extra numbers were added to the 1733 libretto, as originally planned, for the character of Adelberto. This role was taken by Carlo Scalzi, one of Handel's new singers, and the amplification of the part suggests that the composer had no mean opinion of Scalzi's qualities. It is of interest also to point out that Margherita Durastanti as Gismonda played the same part in Handel's original production of *Ottone* in 1723.

The significance of these two casts in the one book is that they throw a new light on the story of the rival Italian operas of this season. It has generally been accepted, that the idea of giving operas in opposition to Handel was hatched in the summer of 1733, and that the sponsors of this scheme were accomplished strategists and seduced the greater part of Handel's company from him. This may be true, but in reading the accounts of the story, it is as well to accept only those statements that are documented, as some of the reports bear evidence of having been dictated by prejudice and personal spite.

From the first cast printed in the *Ottone* libretto, it looks as if Handel had intended to produce this opera in the autumn of 1733, mainly with the principal singers of the previous season, but that they left him, or he quarrelled with them, after preparations for the production of *Ottone* were fairly advanced. Whatever the facts are, Handel was able to provide an alternative company at short notice, including Carestini, and to put on *Semiramide* followed by *Ottone*, and on December 4 *Caio Fabrizio*, a pasticcio. This work was performed four times. Handel, therefore, gave in all twelve performances before his rivals got going on December 29 at Lincoln's Inn Fields with Porpora's *Ariadne*. It has also been asserted that the King and the Prince of Wales were in opposition over the rival companies, the Prince of Wales supporting Handel's competitors. Although there is evidence that the Prince was interested in the opera at Lincoln's Inn Fields, it certainly was not the case that the King and Prince were entirely at variance, as the following details of royal attendances at the two houses prove.

On November 10, 1733, the King, Queen and Prince of Wales were at Handel's performance of *Semiramide*, on November 13, they saw *Ottone*, on December 22 the King heard *Caio Fabrizio*, on January 5, 1734, according to one account "Their

Majesties and the Royal Family" went to the Haymarket to hear *Arbaces* and according to another account only "Their Majesties and the elder Princesses", while the Prince of Wales was at the Lincoln's Inn Fields' performance of *Ariadne*. On January 8, in company with Their Majesties and the three eldest Princesses, the Prince of Wales visited Handel's house and saw "the new Opera called *Arbaces*". On January 24, His Majesty and the Prince of Wales were at a ball at the Opera House. The King, Queen, Prince and the three eldest Princesses attended Handel's *Ariadne* at the Haymarket on February 12. The same royal party patronized *Ariadne* again on March 5, and on March 13 they attended the performance of Handel's *Parnasso in Festa*. It is quite natural to think that in spite of any family quarrel, the Prince was compelled to appear at times in company with the King, but this brief list of selected notices hardly leaves the impression of the King in splendid isolation supporting Handel, and the Prince encouraging the rival company.

A brilliant satirical pamphlet in defence of Handel and entitled "Harmony in an Uproar" appeared in February, 1734. It has been ascribed to John Arbuthnot, and by some writers wrongly placed as appearing in 1733, as it bears that date for 1734. It is quoted almost in full by Chrysander, but as the English writers only give extracts, it is worth further attention. All the allusions in the pamphlet which can be checked show that it has the value of a historical document, and for that reason excerpts are given here which endorse the conclusions already arrived at concerning some aspects of the quarrel between the rival opera companies. The pamphlet is in the form of a letter addressed to 'F—d—k H—d—l, Esq., M—r of the O—a H—e in the Hay-Market, from Hurlothrumbo Johnson, Esq; Composer Extraordinary to all the Theatres in G—T B—N, Excepting that of the Hay-Market.' The names of the singers, etc. are suggested by first and last letters only or by pseudonyms. The particular passages of special interest (the names in brackets not occurring in the original) are as follows:

"I am sensible you wou'd have it believ'd in your Favour, that you are no way to blame in the whole of this Affair; but that when S—no (Senesino) had declared he would leave England, you thought yourself oblig'd in Honour, to proceed with your Contract, and provide for yourself elsewhere; and that as for C—oni (Cuzzoni), you had no Thoughts of her, no Hopes of her, nor no want of her, S—da (Strada) being in all respects infinitely superior, in any Excellency requir'd for a Stage; as for Singers in the under Parts, you had provided the best Set we ever had yet; tho' basely deserted by Mon—na (Montagnana), after having sign'd a formal Contract to serve you the whole of this Season; which you might still force him to do, where (sic) you not more afraid of W—r H—ll (Westminster Hall) than ten thousand D—rs (Doctors), or ten thousand D—ls (Devils)."

"I (Handel) was prodigiously caress'd at Court, the Royal Family (as in all other polite Arts and Sciences) being not only Lovers, but perfect Judges of Musick; but more particularly the divine Princess Urania (Princess Anne), who condescended to be my Scholar, and made that Proficiency, as seemed almost miraculous to me her Master; nay to that exquisite Degree, that the Amusement only carried it to as great a Height in her, as in the most Ingenious, who made it their Profession: This Favour so far from diminishing, created me fresh Foes . . . determin'd to oppose my Scheme, and have an O—a (Opera) of their own . . . Nay, they went so far as to give out, that they received some Encouragement from Monseigneur, the K—g's (King's) eldest Son, who only laugh'd at them in his Sleeve. I had then in Pay a perfect set of Performers, particularly Angelo Carrioli (Carestini) and Cœleste Vocale (Strada); the Unprejudic'd were amaz'd at the Vastness of their Judgment and Justice as well as Beauty of their Execution. My opponents were obliged to make use of all their Interest and Industry, not only to get Company to their House, but to keep those who could not suffer their low Entertainments from coming to mine; nor did they spare entering into the most indirect Means to ruin me; having not only decoy'd a noted Performer (Montagnana), from me, after having for a Term formally bound himself to serve me, but by some underhand Slight, they spirited away two very remarkable Monsters, the first Night of a new O—a (Opera), who had for a considerable Time been trained up, to the Stage; but by good Luck, I had some more Monsters in another Den, tho' not so expert at their Business." (This apparently refers to the two *Ottone* casts.)

"For some Time I played gently with these charming Gudgeons, and, maugre all their pitiful Efforts kept my Head above Water; but at last I came slap-dash upon them with a new O—a (*Ariadne*) of my own Composition; which answer'd to my Profit, and the Pleasure of the Town; their Weakness was made manifest, they were defeated and I triumph'd."

To return to Waltz, the part he had in the 1733 *Ottone* was Emireno, taken by Boschi in the 1723 production of the opera. In this character Waltz had the following songs, "Del minacciar del vento", "Le profonde vie dell'onde", "D'inalzar i flutti al Ciel" (given to Adelberto in the 1723 production) and "No, non temere o bella".

Carestini of course took the title role of *Ottone* in 1733, and with this famous singer in the cast, Waltz was in good company when he made his debut in Italian opera.

One further question may arise in the reader's mind about *Ottone*. A work advertised in the papers as *Otho*, without any indication of composer or singers, was performed on December 10, 14, 17, 21 and 23, 1734, by Handel's rivals, who were then in possession of the King's Theatre. It has been suggested that the 1733 libretto of Handel's *Ottone* described above was connected with the 1734 season, hence the cast containing Senesino, Montagnana, etc. But this suggestion is groundless, as the libretto of the performances in 1734 was published by Charles Bennet, the publisher of other librettos of the opera of the nobility. Unfortunately no copy is available, but from what is known no composer's name was given, so that we are left with Burney's remark "it is most probable that the music was Handel's." Burney is wrong in saying that it was performed on December 28 and 31 in addition to the five other occasions, because on these two later dates *Artaserse* (music mainly by J. A. Hasse and Riccardo Broschi) was given.

On November 26, 1733, and most likely at nine or ten subsequent performances at Drury Lane in November and December, 1733, and in January and May, 1734, Waltz played the

Earthy Spirit in *A Dramatic Opera, call'd The Tempest; or The Enchanted Island*. The only mention of the music in the notice is, "The part of Dorinda by Mrs. Clive, with the song of 'Dear pretty Youth', compos'd by the late Mr Henry Purcel." The following criticism from the *Daily Journal* of November 27, 1733, is of interest: "We hear from the Theatre Royal in Drury-Lane, that the Play of the *Tempest*, was perform'd there last night, to a numerous Audience, with great applause, the Dances, Airs and Chorus's being esteem'd more compleat and perfect than they have been in that Entertainment for many Years past; Miss Young particularly, in the Character of Amphitrite, was receiv'd with the highest marks of Approbation, tho' the first time of her Appearance on any stage." Miss Young was probably Isabella Young who afterwards became the wife of J. F. Lampe.

On December 4, 8, 15 and 22, 1733, Waltz was back again in Handel's Company playing Caio Fabrizio in the work of that name with Carestini as Pyrrhus, which as pointed out above has hitherto been considered his first part on the London stage. In this work Waltz had only one song, "Quella è mia figlia," in addition to a speaking part in the third act. In the libretto of this work Waltz is given as "Signor Walz".

Caio Fabrizio was a pasticcio to which Handel wrote the recitatives. Hasse composed a work of the same name, the libretto of which was the foundation of Handel's production. Waltz's song "Quella è mia figlia" is in both librettos and the music of this number by Hasse is in the British Museum (Add. MSS. 31592). Presumably Hasse's setting was used by Handel. Reference to the score at Hamburg would probably clear up this point.

On January 26, 1734, Handel produced *Ariadne* which had at least sixteen performances that season at the King's Theatre and five in the following season at Covent Garden. The cast as given in the libretto, dated 1733, was as follows:

Ariadne	.	.	*Signora Strada*
Theseus	.	.	*Giovanni Carestino*
Alcestes	.	.	*Carlo Scalzi*
Carilda	.	*Signora Maria Catterina Negri*	
Minos	.	.	*Signor Waltz*
Tauris	.	.	*Signora Margherita Durastante*

The instrumental movement generally known as the Minuet, although not so described by Handel, follows the stage directions for Scene 1 in the autograph, and was therefore played (as Rockstro and others have pointed out) after the curtain went up, displaying Minos seated in state surrounded by other characters. The *Händel-Gesellschaft* edition gives the minuet as part of the overture, which is incorrect. This minuet, which became very popular, must have been associated with Waltz in the minds of those who saw the original production. Waltz had in addition to his speaking part only one song, "Se ti condanno", and a part in the final chorus. The song must have been impressive as it was sung when Minos (Waltz) was sentencing Ariadne, his unrecognized daughter, to death. The English version in the libretto is:

> If I condemn you it is sure
> The judgment is most just and pure,
> And not a cruel tyrant's doom,
> But does from rigid virtue come.

Burney's reference to this song has already been quoted.

The autograph of *Ariadne* (*Arianna*) is dated by Handel October 5, 1733, and in the manuscript the composer gave Waltz as "Mr. Walls". This is the earliest Handel work on which the singer's name appears.

On February 4, 1734 at Drury Lane, Waltz created the parts of Bacchus and Mynheer Bassoon in a new Pantomime Entertainment *Cupid and Psyche or Columbine Courtezan*, which was played about twenty times during the season. Presumably Lampe wrote the music, some of which appeared in "A Collection of all the Aires, Pastorells, Chacoons, Entre, Jiggs, Minuets and Musette's in Columbine Courtezan and all the late Entertainments, Compos'd by Mr. John Frederick Lampe. To which is Prefix'd the Original Medley Overture. . . . London. Printed for and sold by I. Walsh", etc. This overture contains a number of Handel's melodies.

Handel's *Parnasso in Festa* was produced on March 13, 1734, at the King's Theatre, in honour of the marriage of the Princess Royal and the Prince of Orange. Waltz was most probably in the cast as Proteo and had one song, "Del Nume Lieo quel sacro liquor." The work was given four times in the month of March.

On March 21, 1734, Arne, not to be outdone by Handel's loyal tribute of *Parnasso in Festa*, produced at Drury Lane "*Love and Glory*. A Serenade composed on the present joyous occasion of the Royal Nuptials. The words by Mr. Thos. Phillips. The music by Mr. Arne." In this Waltz took the part of one of the followers of Mars. In an adapatation from this work, a masque entitled *Britannia*, on April 29, Waltz as Mars, had a speaking and singing part with the song "Swift as lightning from above."

Handel's *Deborah*, first produced on March 17, 1733, with Senesino (Sisera) and Montagnana (Abinoam) in the cast, was revived at the King's Theatre on April 2, 1734 and repeated on April 6, and 9, with Waltz as The Chief Priest of Baal, a small part; Thomas Reinhold probably taking Abinoam and The Chief Priest of the Israelites, although Waltz may have taken either of these latter roles. The work was given in the following March on three evenings at Covent Garden, and as Waltz was in Handel's company, it is presumed that he was in these performances. The first edition of the work, consisting of only a few songs, was issued in 1735, a very imperfect publication, with two numbers from *Esther* and two from *Athalia*. One of latter, "To darkness eternal", is a soprano aria sung by Athalia in that work, but in this early edition of *Deborah* it is given to Waltz, which is strange, as Waltz took the part of Abner, a bass rôle, in *Athalia*.

Handel's opera, *Sosarme*, was revived at the King's Theatre, on April 27, 1734, but no evidence is forthcoming as to whether Waltz had a part or not. The same uncertainty exists about the performance of *Acis and Galatea* on May 7, 1734.

Il Pastor Fido, originally produced in November, 1712, had no performance after that season until May 18, 1734. The work was given thirteen times at the King's Theatre, the details of the cast not being available, but as Waltz was in the Covent Garden version on November 9, 1734, and subsequent evenings, he may have been in the May production. The revival on November 9, was the edition of the work which had as prologue the ballet *Terpsichore*, in which Mlle Sallé was the star dancer. In this version of *Il Pastor Fido*, which was given five times,

Waltz appeared in the last act as Tirenius, having one song, "Dell' empia frode il velo".

On January 8, 1735, Handel produced *Ariodante* at Covent Garden. The work was given eleven times that season, and Waltz was in the cast as Il Re di Scozia. Besides the aria, "Voli colla sua tromba la fama", which has been mentioned above in connection with Burney's discussion of *Ariodante*, the *Händel-Gesellschaft* edition gives three other numbers to Il Re di Scozia, one of them an alternative song not in the autograph manuscript. Incidentally it may be pointed out that copies of Walsh's edition of the "Songs" in this opera are extremely rare.

Athalia, produced at Oxford in July, 1733, was revived at Covent Garden on April 1, 1735, and ran for five performances. Waltz, who, as already mentioned, may have appeared in the Oxford production, took the part of Abner at Covent Garden originally created by Montagnana, who had left Handel's company. The other singers of the cast were Signora Strada, Carestini, Beard, The Boy and Miss Young. Waltz had three numbers:

> When storms the proud to terrors doom.
> Ah, cans't thou but prove me.
> Oppression, no longer I dread thee.

Handel's *Alcina* was given at Covent Garden, on April 16, 1735, and had eighteen performances that season, a testimony to its popularity. Waltz as Melisso had one song, "Pensa a chi geme d'amor piagata", and a part in the final chorus. It is on the autograph, against this last number that Handel spelt Waltz as "Walls".

Atalanta was produced at Covent Garden on May 12, 1736, and ran eight times that season. As Nicandro, Waltz had one song, "Impara, ingrata, ad esser men crudele", sung in the opera to Nicandro's daughter. Burney's remarks on this song have already been quoted. The contemporary translation of the number is:

> Learn silly maid to be more kind
> To one who asks your love;
> One whom you always faithful find,
> Tho' you so cruel prove:

> And while he strives your heart to gain,
> Take pleasure in his pain.

Atalanta appears to have been the last of Handel's operas in which Waltz took part. He seems to have left the company at the end of that season, although he appeared for the composer later on in oratorios, and continued his career on the stage for a number of years. For the season 1737–38 Handel had back his old Basso, Montagnana, as the company with Farinelli dispersed in the summer of 1737. Although the composer had no rivals at this time, in spite of Heidegger's management and the production of *Faramondo* and *Serse* the season finished up so badly that Heidegger was unable to make arrangements for opera in the ensuing season.

Burney's comment on "Ombra mai fù", the "Largo", or as Handel marked it "Larghetto e Piano", in *Serse* is of interest. He says, "The first act opens with a short recitative, and a charming slow cavatina for Caffarelli: *Ombra mai fù*, in a clear and majestic style, out of the reach of time and fashion". A shrewd and prophetic criticism.

Although Handel gave no regular season of operas in 1738–39, he had possession of the Opera House mainly for oratorios. He produced *Saul* and *Israel in Egypt*, and gave performances of *Alexander's Feast* and *Il Trionfo del Tempo*. It is not known whether Waltz performed in all of these works or not, but without question he was in *Saul* and *Israel in Egypt*. If he had been a poor singer, as some have suggested, he seems to have been particularly lucky in having been chosen for the first performances of some of Handel's most famous works.

Saul was produced on January 16, 1739, and had at least six performances. Waltz, whose career since his appearance in *Atalanta*, in 1736, is unknown, returned to Handel in the part of Saul, Beard playing Jonathan.

Israel in Egypt, produced on April 4, 1739, was given three times that season, twice in a shortened form "intermixed with songs". On the autograph score Handel has written in pencil "Mr Wals, Mr Reinhold" over the bass duet, "The Lord is a man of war", so it is reasonable to assume that Waltz was in the original production.

Between the performances of *Saul* and *Israel in Egypt*, Waltz was engaged to Play Orlando in Pescetti's pastoral opera, *Angelica e Medoro*, at Covent Garden, on March 10. The work was given four times, and Waltz had three arias. The company included Mrs. Arne, Reinhold and Rochetti.

From 1739 onwards, Waltz's appearances in musical parts seem to have been few and his roles as an actor mostly unimportant. He was in the Covent Garden company 1739–41, and appeared in the following works during that period.

On December 10, 1739 he had the small part of one of the Bacchanals in a work advertised as "*A Masque of Musick call'd Cupid and Bacchus*, written by Mr. Dryden and compos'd by Mr. Hy. Purcell", and introduced into *A Dramatic Opera, The Island Princess or The Generous Portuguese*, music by Daniel Purcell. Mrs. Lampe and Miss Young were both in the cast of this work, which was given again on December 11.

On February 12, 1740, a new dramatic entertainment of music was given called "*Orpheus and Eurydice*, intermix'd with a new Pantomime called *The Metamorphoses of Harlequin*, music by J. F. Lampe, text by Lewis Theobald". Waltz appeared as one of the villagers. The work was immensely successful, playing forty-five times that season, and many times the next, with Waltz still in the company.

On April 30, 1740, Lampe's earlier production, *The Opera of Operas*, was revived for the benefit of Mrs. Lampe and Miss Young, and Waltz had his old part of Lord Grizzle.

Carey's burlesque *The Dragon of Wantley* with music by Lampe, was one of the most popular works of the period. It was first produced at Covent Garden on October 26, 1737, and Burney's reference to the work and its connection with Waltz has already been quoted. Waltz appeared in the work at Covent Garden on September 19, 1740, in the small speaking part of Gubbins, probably also singing in the choruses. The work was given nine times or more during the season.

On May 15, 1741 Waltz performed at Covent Garden in a work advertised with the queer title "*An Interlude in two comick scenes in Music betwixt Signor Capoccio, a Director from the Canary Islands and Signora Dorinna, a Virtuosa.* The part of Capocchio by Mr. Waltz, Dorinna—Miss Hillier." This was probably the same work as that which had been given at the Haymarket on April 16, 1741, words by Lewis Theobald, music by Galliard.

It was a skit on the Italian opera, and the same text was incorporated into Arne's comic opera, *The Temple of Dullness*, which is referred to later on. On September 30 and October 22, 1741, Waltz appeared again as Gubbins in *The Dragon of Wantley*. These were his last appearances at Covent Garden for some years, his movements between 1742–43 being unknown.

A musical entertainment was given at the Haymarket on January 19, 1744, entitled *The Queen of Spain: or Farinelli at Madrid*. This was a skit on the famous singer who had gone to Spain in 1737, where he remained in court favour for many years. The work was by James Worsdale, with music perhaps by Lampe, and was played at least four times during the season. Mrs. Lampe was the Queen of Spain and Waltz the King of Spain.

On April 16, 1744, a new work was given at the Haymarket entitled *The Kiss accepted and returned*. It was advertised as "An Operetta never performed before. The words by Mr. Ayre (James Ayres) and the Musick by Mr. Lampe." Waltz was in the cast as Colin and Mrs. Lampe as Phoebe, Colin's wife. The work was given twice.

Waltz's next advertised public performances were in May, 1744, as a singer at "Ruckholt-House near Low-Layton" (Leyton) in Essex. This house, formerly the residence of the Hickes family, stood a mile or so south of the church, and had been opened for a year or two as a place of public amusement during the summer for breakfasts and afternoon concerts, when oratorios were sometimes performed. Lowe, Baildon and Brett were the advertised singers for 1743, and amongst the works given that year were Boyce's *Solomon* and Handel's *Alexander's Feast*. Waltz was not in these performances. The opening of the 1744 season was advertised on May 7 (*General Advertiser*) as follows: "Ruckholt-House in Essex. The Breakfasting at this place will open this Day and be continued every Monday during the Season, with a select Band of Musick. The Vocal Parts to be perform'd by Miss Young, Signora Avolio, Mr. Waltz, etc. Tickets Two Shillings, which will entitle each Person to a Breakfast. The same will be continued in the Afternoon, each Person to pay (after Two o'clock) One Shilling Admittance, excepting those who Dine there. As desired by several Gentlemen the last Season, not one of those who perform'd there will be engaged this. Proper Cooks are provided every Day in the Week and Plenty of Fish."

The identity of Miss Young is not certain. She may have been Esther Young, sister to Mrs. Arne and Mrs. Lampe. Other members added to the company on May 14, were Miss Molly Turner, singer, and Burk Thumoth who played "Concerto's on the German Flute."

On May 21, 28, and June 4, 1744, Boyce's *Solomon* was given with Waltz among the soloists, and on June 11, 18 and 25, *Alexander's Feast*, with the "vocal Parts by Mr. Brett, Signiora Avolio, Mr. Waltz, Mr. Barrow, etc." Waltz may have performed in the miscellaneous concerts which continued the season until August 27, but his name is not mentioned in the notices.

The history of the performances at Ruckholt-House seems to have escaped the notice of the writers on the period.

Waltz was in the Drury Lane company in the season 1744–45. On January 17, 1745, he appeared as Signor Capochio in "A new Comic Opera called *The Temple of Dullness*. With the humours of Signor Capochio and Signora Dorinna. . . . With a new Overture founded on some favourite Irish Tunes. The musick compos'd by Mr. Arne." Mrs. Arne played Signora Dorinna. Arne and his wife had recently returned from Ireland, and doubtless the Irish Overture was one result of their visit. *The Temple of Dullness* was given seven times at least during the season. Reference has already been made to Waltz's appearance in an Interlude in two comic scenes on May 15, 1741, the text of which was incorporated in *The Temple of Dullness*. The libretto of this work gives "The music by Mr. Arne".

In 1733 T. A. Arne took Addison's libretto of *Rosamond*, to which Thomas Clayton had set music in 1707, and put his own music to the text. This work was played on various occasions, but Waltz did not appear in the cast until January 31st, 1745, at Drury Lane, where he played the part of Sir Trusty on thirteen or fourteen occasions.

The Dragon of Wantley was revived on February 15, 1745, at Drury Lane with Waltz in his old part of Gubbins, which he played six times that season.

At Drury Lane on April 15, 1745, Waltz had a speaking and singing part as "Puff, a degraded Field Marshall" in *King*

190

Pepin's Campaign, a burlesque opera in two acts, words by William Shirley, music by T. A. Arne. Mrs. Arne, Lowe and Mrs. Sybella were in the advertised cast, although Mrs. Clive appears in the libretto and not Mrs. Sybella. The work was given three times.

References to Waltz between 1745 and 1748 have not been traced. On January 29, 1748 he appeared "For the benefit of Mr. Troas. At the New Theatre in the Haymarket in a Concert of Vocal and Instrumental Musick. The Vocal Parts by Signiora Pirker and Mr. Waltz. The First Violin by Mr. Collet. And the rest of the Instruments by the best Masters." Mr. Troas was evidently Christopher Troas, one of the foundation members of the Royal Society of Musicians.

On December 9, 1748, Waltz had a benefit concert announced in the papers as follows: "For the Benefit of Mr. Waltz. At the New Theatre in the Haymarket, this Day, will be perform'd a Concert of Vocal and Instrumental Musick. The Vocal Parts by Signora Sybilla, Miss Young, Mr. Waltz, Mr. Hague and Mr. Messing, jun. The first Violin by Mr. Freak. And the rest of the Instrumentalists by the best Masters." The programme commenced with "The Overture in *Otho*" and concluded with "*The Water Musick* of Mr. Handel's, accompanied with Four Kettle-Drummers." The first half of the programme was miscellaneous and the second part included "*The Musick on the Thanksgiving Day*, compos'd by Mr. John Frederick Lampe as it was performed'd on Thursday the 9th Day of October 1746, in the Savoy." This was originally performed by the "Churchwardens and all the Gentlemen belonging to the German Lutheran Church in the Savoy . . . in their native language" to celebrate the suppression of the Stuart rebellion.

Waltz was in the Covent Garden company, in the season 1749–50, playing many times from November 23 onwards the part of one of the Infernals in *Perseus and Andromeda*, a dramatic entertainment with Lowe as Perseus and Leveridge as Cepheus.

We know from Handel's dated autograph (January 8, 1750) of some of the numbers in *Alceste* (British Museum Add. MSS. 30310) that Waltz was cast for the character of Charon in that projected work. Handel spelt his name as "Mr. Walz" on the bass song "Ye fleeting shades", a number afterwards used as a basis for the alto song "Lead Goddess, lead the way" given to Hercules in the *Choice of Hercules*, produced in March, 1751. There is no evidence that Waltz was in the *Choice of Hercules*, although it embodied much of the music of *Alceste*.

On April 16, 1750 *The General Advertiser* announced at Covent Garden "For the Benefit of Mr. Bencraft. A Tragedy call'd *Macbeth*. Macbeth, Mr. Quin. . . . With the original musick. The Vocal Parts by Mr. Leveridge, Mr. Lowe, Mr. Waltz, Mr. Wilder. . . . To which will be added *Perseus and Andromeda*". Waltz appeared again at Covent Garden in the music of *Macbeth* on November 8, 1750.

On October 29, 1750, *Perseus and Andromeda* was revived and Waltz took the part of Cepheus on several occasions between then and the end of the season.

It is a matter of speculation as to what Waltz was doing when not performing on the public stage. As pointed out he is credited with having been an instrumentalist, but there is no evidence to this effect other than the Hauck portrait, and the uncertain reference in the Thomas Coke papers.

From an advertisement in *The General Advertiser*, March 18, 1751, we hear of him in a new role. "At the Desire of several Ladies of Quality. For the Benefit of Miss Isabella Young, a Scholar of Mr. Waltz, who never appeared before in Publick, At the New Theatre in the Haymarket, This Day the 18th of March will be perform'd a Concert of Vocal and Instrumental Musick. The Vocal Parts to be performed by Mr. Waltz and Miss Isabella Young; and the Instrumental by the best Masters." Isabella Young is not to be confused with the singer of the same name who became the wife of J. F. Lampe, but is assumed to have been a niece of Mrs. Arne's and Mrs. Lampe's and daughter of Charles Young (1715–55). We know from another notice on March 2, 1752, that Mr. Young, presumably the father of Waltz's pupil, lived at King Street, Westminster. The writer owns a copy of the *Ode for St. Cecilia's Day* with her name on the cover and also a copy of *The Choice of Hercules*, a gift to her niece, "C.M.B. (now Henslowe)". She made her debut as a singer, but, as will be seen later, she was also an instrumentalist. Whether Waltz taught her to play as well as to sing is not known.

In the spring of 1751 Waltz reappeared at Covent Garden in several of his old parts, these being probably amongst his last professional engagements as an actor, although the matter is uncertain. On April 20, 22, 23 and 29 he played Gubbins in *The Dragon of Wantley* for several benefit performances, and on May 3 and on two or three other occasions, Lord Grizzle in *Tom Thumb*, or as it is recorded above (1733) *The Opera of Operas*. This was Arne's version and the performance of May 3 was for the benefit of Mrs. Arne and Miss Young, presumably Waltz's pupil.

The next reference to Waltz in the papers is a year later. On March 2, the following notice appeared: "For the benefit of Miss Isabella Young, Scholar of Mr. Waltz. At the New Theatre in the Haymarket this Day the 2nd of March will be performed a Concert of Vocal and Instrumental Musick. The Vocal Part by Miss Young and the Instrumental Parts by the best Masters. And one of Mr. Handel's Organ Concertos will be also performed by Miss Young."

The Public Advertiser announced on April 30, 1753: "For the Benefit of Miss Isabella Young, Scholar to Mr. Waltz. At the New Theatre in the Haymarket This Day April 30th, will be perform'd a Concert of Vocal and Instrumental Musick. The Vocal Parts by Miss Young; and the Instrumental Parts by several of the best Masters: and (by particular Desire) several of Mr. Handel's Concertos will be performed by Miss Young." On the same day the same paper announced a benefit for Mrs. Lampe and Miss Young at Covent Garden on May 2, so there were clearly two Miss Young's at the time on the public stage. The various persons of the name, descendants of Charles Young (d. 1758) are not easily identified from the newspaper notices. Mrs. Delany writing to her sister on August 8, 1758 said: "Mrs. Arne and Miss Bayly sing, and a girl of nine years old accompanies them on the harpsichord most surprisingly— she is a niece of Mrs. Arne's; the race of the Youngs are *born* songsters and musicians."

The last reference to Waltz that the present writer has been able to trace is in the list of singers taking part in the Foundling Hospital annual performance of *Messiah*, May 3, 1759, which was to have been directed as usual by Handel, but in consequence of his death, was given by Christopher Smith. In the list of singers Waltz appears as "Mr. Walz, 10. 6." It is interesting to recall that fifty years earlier, probably the same person was asking for £1 per night as an instrumentalist.

Waltz apparently dropped out of public life about this time and may have died a little later.

The date of his death has not been traced, and as pointed out above, the records of The Royal Society of Musicians only bear the word "Dead" against his name in the register.

The reader is now, however, in possession for the first time of the main details of the life of one who played many parts on the London stage during a long period. None of the available records other than Burney and Hawkins provide evidence to show when, or if ever, Waltz was Handel's cook, and as it has been pointed out, the statements of Burney and Hawkins are open to question.

It is hoped that in this attempt to sketch the career of Waltz, something of importance has been added to the previously known history of the eighteenth century stage in London, its plays and players, and new light thrown on some of Handel's productions.

VII

ACIS AND GALATEA
IN THE
EIGHTEENTH CENTURY

ACIS AND GALATEA

IN THE

EIGHTEENTH

CENTURY

I T is remarkable that the period in Handel's life (1718–20) during which he produced four different types of work, each of them significant in his own career and of importance in English musical history, should be a period about which little is really known.

The works in question, *Acis and Galatea, Esther*, the *Chandos Anthems* and *Te Deum*, and the *Suites de Pieces*, are generally ascribed to the time when the composer is supposed to have been associated with James Brydges, Earl of Carnarvon, afterwards Duke of Chandos. The Duke was no insignificant figure, and the story of the wealthy state in which he lived is well authenticated, even to the details of the contents of his mansion near Edgware, with its collection of pictures and comprehensive library. The extent to which Handel accepted the Duke's patronage, and lived at Cannons or at his London residences in Albemarle Street or St. James's Square, is not clear. Although much has been written on the subject, the terms and conditions under which the composer worked during this period are still shrouded in mystery. What may be considered the most reasonable evidence on the matter is briefly reviewed here.

That Handel as a musician had some personal association with the Duke cannot be doubted, as there are too many early references for the subject to be in dispute. Handel's earliest English biographer, Mainwaring, who is said to have written his work, published in 1760, from information partly supplied by J. C. Smith, gives the following details of the composer's works of the period in question:

> Acis and Galatea, for the Duke of Chandois about the year 1721. (The words of this piece wrote by Mr. Gay.) Several Anthems made for the Duke of Chandois between 1717 and 1720.
> Esther. [Without place or date.]
> Harpsichord-Lessons.

These bald statements of a writer who was very inaccurate at times cannot be hastily dismissed, and they are much nearer the truth than some of the fantastic and imaginary stories that grew up later on about Handel, Cannons, the Harmonious Blacksmith and the Chandos circle.

Dr. Cummings, who did much valuable Handel research, cleared away a good deal of the fiction that had gathered round some of the facts. His guarded statement in *The Musical Times*, January 1, 1885, on the question of Handel and Cannons reads as follows: "Handel resided in London from 1715 to 1720; he became chapel-master and director of music to the Earl of Carnarvon (afterwards Duke of Chandos) in 1718, who then resided in Cavendish Square. It is not probable that Handel visited Cannons until he went there in 1720 to produce his Oratorio *Esther* for his patron, who had been created Duke of Chandos in April, 1719." The statement, which is partly in accord with opinions expressed elsewhere, is unsupported by definite evidence on some points, and the writer is wrong in stating that the Earl lived at Cavendish Square in 1718. At that time he was living at Albemarle Street.

Among the very few Handel letters which have been traced, there is no reference to the Duke or to Handel's association with his household.

A report in *The Weekly Journal or British Gazetteer* (*Read's*), September 3, 1720, is as follows:

His Grace the Duke of Chandois's Domestick Chappel at his Seat at Cannons, Edgworth [sic!], is Curiously adorned with Painting on the Windows and Ceiling, had divine Worship perform'd in it with an Anthem on Monday last, (August 29th) it being the first time of its being opened.

This vague statement has been accepted by some writers as a proof of Handel's life at Cannons, and the performance of the Anthem on August 29 identified as the production of *Esther*. No other newspaper reports giving any help have been traced.

Some interesting evidence exists in a letter of May 15, 1721, of Humphrey Wanley, Librarian to the Earl of Oxford, quoted by J. R. Robinson (*The Princely Chandos*) as from the "Strawberry Hill Collection". Wanley wrote to his patron: "Mr. Kaeyscht (at the Duke of Chandos') has kindly promised to lend me the score of Mr. Handel's 'Te Deum', being his second which he composed for the Duke of Chandos, who can likewise procure the scores of all his services and anthems." Cummings in quoting this passage (*Handel, The Duke of Chandos*, etc.) adds: "Kaeyscht, variously spelt Keitch, Keutsh, had been a bassoon player at the opera in the King's Theatre. He played the *obbligato* part in Handel's *Rinaldo* in 1711", etc. Probably "Kaeyscht" was the same person as Kytch, an oboe player, whose name is commemorated in connection with the foundation of The Royal Society of Musicians. Burney refers to a "Solo and concerto by Mr. Kytch on the German-flute and Hautbois" at a "consort" at Hickford's room in February, 1720. The reference in Wanley's letter to the *Te Deum* as the "second" which Handel composed for the Duke of Chandos, needs some explanation. Authorities only know of the *Te Deum in B flat* written for performance at Cannons, afterwards modified, shortened, and issued in the Key of A. The *Te Deum in D* which is generally attributed to about 1714 is not usually associated with the Duke of Chandos.

There is in existence a volume of Handel's Church Music (1718–20?) described as probably written in order of composition by J. C. Schmidt and his son J. C. Smith about 1726–30. This handsome volume contains eight "Anthems", *Utrecht Jubilate* and *Te Deum in B flat* and was formerly in the library of the Duke of Chandos. It was also owned by Dr. Cummings, who described it in his pamphlet *Handel, The Duke of Chandos*, etc. A list of the contents and a reproduction of the binding appeared in Quaritch's Catalogue No. 355, October, 1919.

The Duke of Chandos died in 1744 and his library was sold in March, 1747. The catalogue of the sale contains over four thousand items, ranging over a wide field of literature, but there does not appear to be a single musical work amongst the number, and no reference to any printed editions or manuscripts of Handel's works. If a separate catalogue of music was issued, no copy has been traced.

In the preface to the second edition (1774) of the oratorio *Omnipotence*, the music of which was selected from Handel's compositions by Dr. Arnold and words selected by Dr. Arnold and Edward Toms, the editor (Dr. Arnold) says: "No part of Mr. Handel's works are held in higher estimation by the best judges, than his compositions for the Duke of Chandos. They are difficult to attain, and the collection from which this performance is selected, hath been the attentive pursuit of several years, at Sales and Auctions; in the progress of which, I made discoveries of some I had never heard of; and got information of others, which I have not been able to trace. A complete collection cannot well be expected, as some of the original scores have been exposed to public sale."

None of the autograph manuscripts of Handel's works of the Chandos period, which are in the King's Music Library and the British Museum collections, bear any evidence of place of production, but singers' names occur on some of the *Acis and Galatea* manuscripts, and of these, RM.20.a.2. may have been used for the Cannons performance. Particulars of other manuscripts and singers are given later on.

It is worthy of note in connection with the problem of Handel's association with the Duke of Chandos, that the edition of the music described below as Number 2, has on the title-page "made and perform'd for his Grace the Duke of Chandos".

Handel produced no new operas between *Amadigi* (May 25, 1715) and *Radamisto* (April 27, 1720) his first work for the Royal Academy of Music; a reasonable explanation of his operatic inactivity being that he was otherwise engaged and had no time or opportunity for that type of composition.

According to *The Original Weekly Journal* (*Applebee's*) of February 21, 1719, "Mr. Hendel, a famous Master of Musick, is gone beyond Sea, by Order of his Majesty, to Collect a Company of the choicest Singers in Europe, for the Opera in the Hay-market." This statement has been accepted without qualification by some writers, who have also recorded the composer's return to London about November, 1719. From the only two existing letters that Handel wrote between 1716 and 1725 we know that his departure must have been delayed for some time after February 21. Both of these letters were addressed from London, one on February 20, 1719 to M. D. Michaëlsen his brother-in-law, and the other on February 24, 1719, to Johann Mattheson. Percy Robinson, whose intimate knowledge of the Handel period is beyond question, suggests that the composer left England as late as August, 1719, and did not return until February, 1720, but from what has been said in Chapter II, it seems perfectly certain that in July, 1719, Handel was engaged on business abroad, after some pressing affairs at home, and could not have been at Cannons at the same time.

It has been assumed that it was during the period of Handel's supposed residence at Cannons that he was appointed musicmaster to the daughters of Caroline, Princess of Wales. In 1720 he published the first volume of the *Suites de Pieces*, a collection, which according to some writers, came into existence as lessons for the composer's royal pupils.

This is not the place to discuss the history of the *Suites*, but the association of the collection as we know it with the Princesses is shadowy and vague. No official evidence of Handel's appointment as music-master is available earlier than 1728. Princess Anne was born in 1709, Princess Amelia in 1711 and Princess Caroline in 1713. References in the press show that as early as 1724 at least the Princesses Anne and Caroline attended St. Paul's to hear their master (Handel) perform upon the Organ.

While there is nothing to contradict the story of Handel's association with the Duke of Chandos, it seems reasonably clear that he was not in permanent residence as a member of the Duke's household. As Streatfeild says, he "lived a busy life at this time. He had duties in London as well as at Canons", and again, in referring to *Esther* and *Acis and*

Galatea, the same writer says, "It is very much to be regretted that so little is known of the circumstances in which two works of such exceptional importance in the history of Handel's musical development were written and produced."

The suggestion that Handel succeeded Pepusch as the Duke's "Kapellmeister" in 1718 is equally without convincing evidence, as Pepusch dedicated his *Six English Cantatas* (Book II) in 1720 to the Duke of Chandos, signing himself "his Grace's most devoted and most obedient Servant" and a letter of Pepusch's dated from "Canons," January 3, 1722, exists in the British Museum. (Egerton, 2159.)

A critical examination of the statements put forth by Burney and the many other writers who have dealt with the subject leads one to no definite conclusion as to the date and place of production of *Acis and Galatea*. None of the evidence at present forthcoming is strong enough to be accepted as conclusive, and we are left to assume that the association of the work with the Duke of Chandos may be reasonably placed about the period 1718–20.

The libretto of *Acis and Galatea* is generally referred to as being by Gay, although the earliest edition issued as by that writer is one advertised by Watts, December 13, 1739, and in a list of libretti published by Watts, and advertised in 1733 (*Grub Street Journal*, May 17), *The Beggar's Opera* and *Achilles* are mentioned as being by Gay, while *Acis and Galatea* is given without any author's name.

Streatfeild in his interesting pamphlet *Handel, Canons and the Duke of Chandos*, points out that Gay seems to have compiled his work from any source that offered. "From Dryden's translation of Ovid's *Metamorphoses* he borrowed:

A hundred reeds of a prodigious growth
Scarce made a pipe proportion'd to his mouth.

"and the dying cry of Acis:

Help, Galatea! Help my parent gods
And take me dying to your deep abodes.

"He fashioned a passage in the trio from some lines out of Pope's *Pastorals*:

> Not bubbling fountains to the thirsty swain,
> Not balmy sleep to labourers faint with pain,
> Not showers to larks, or sunshine to the bee,
> Are half so charming as thy sight to me.

"And from the same poet's translation of Homer's *Iliad* he borrowed the splendid description of the wrathful Neptune and adapted it to the monster Polypheme:

> At Jove incens'd, with Grief and Fury strung,
> Prone down the rocky Steep he rushed along.
> Fierce as he past, the lofty Mountains nod,
> The Forests shake! Earth trembled as he trod,
> And felt the footsteps of th' immortal God.
> From Realm to Realm three ample strides he took,
> And at the fourth the distant Aegae shook.

"Another of the songs in *Acis*, 'Would you gain the tender creature', was contributed by the poet John Hughes."

Streatfeild also points out that as Pope's *Iliad* was first published in 1718, and Hughes died in February, 1720, and Handel was absent from England nearly the whole of 1719, "the natural conclusion is that *Acis* saw the light in 1718."

Before dealing with the early editions and performances of the work, it may be useful to point out that autograph scores and contemporary manuscript copies of *Aci, Galatea e Polifemo* and *Acis and Galatea* exist in the King's Music Library, the British Museum, the Fitzwilliam Museum, the Royal College of Music, and elsewhere in other public and private collections. These manuscripts cannot be listed here, but in any detailed study or reconstruction of the works these early records are of importance for comparison with the printed versions.

In the following attempt to describe the early editions of *Acis and Galatea* (music and libretti) and to relate them to the contemporary productions, it will be noticed how the form and description of the work changed from time to time. The record is incomplete, and accurate details are wanting in some cases, but it contains all that modern research has been able to discover on the early history of this ever-popular work. It must be borne in mind, however, that the descriptions of the Editions

of the Music as No. 1, No. 2, etc. are provided by the present
writer on the available information, and they may need correction as copies of other early issues come to light. Moreover, it
is very difficult, in some instances, to gather from the newspaper advertisements whether a reference is to a new edition or
not, and in compiling the information it has been necessary, in
some cases, to rely on advertisements that cannot be clearly
associated with any identifiable issue of the work.

MUSIC—Edition No. 1. [1722.]

No newspaper notice of this edition has been traced earlier
than the one in *The Post-Boy*, October 16–18, 1722, when Walsh
advertised after a list of "New Musick" as "Also lately publish'd, great Variety of Vocal Musick, as the Favourite Songs
in the Opera's of Crispus, Muzio Scævola, and Acis and Galatea
. . . Printed for John Walsh . . . in Katharine-street in the
Strand, and John and Joseph Hare at the Viol and Flute," etc.

The title-page of this edition reads as follows:

> The favourite Songs in the Opera call'd Acis and Galatea.
> London Printed for & sold by I: Walsh Servt. to his
> Majesty at the Harp & Hoboy in Catherine Street in the
> Strand: & In^o. & Ioseph Hare at the Viol and Flute in
> Cornhill near the Royal Exchange.

(See Plate No. 13.)

Copies may have been issued with a very similar title-page,
but with the information differently engraved and set out. If
so, the copy described here, may be a little later in date than
1722, but in the absence of definite evidence to the contrary, it
can be considered a first edition.

The title-page was adapted from one used by Walsh for
Muzio Scævola and other works, *Acis and Galatea* replacing the
original title. For this reason the use of the word "Opera"
must not be taken too seriously as an accurate description
of *Acis and Galatea*, which is called a "Mask" inside the work.
The volume consists of thirty-eight leaves ($8\frac{3}{4}'' \times 13\frac{3}{4}''$ in the
copy examined), printed on one side only, containing title-page,
then "A Table of the Songs in the Mask call'd Acis and Galatea" (fifteen items), followed on the same page by a list of

forty-nine advertised publications, in forty-seven lines, described as "Vocal Musick of the best Editions which may be had where these are sold". This list includes three works by Handel, who is not mentioned: *Floridant*, *Rinaldo* and *Favourite Songs in Muzio Scævola*. Following the leaf with the "Table" are thirty-six pages of music, paginated from one to thirty-six at the top centre. There are variations in the style of the engraving, and separate numbers may have been done by different hands. Some of the sheets were probably issued and sold separately before being brought together in one work; at any rate single sheet issues were made after the volume appeared. and four of the numbers: "Lo here my Love", "Stay shepherd, stay", "Cease to beauty", and "Consider fond shepherd", had previously appeared in *The Monthly Mask of Vocal Music*, April–July, 1722, published by J. Walsh and J. Hare, the same plates being used for these numbers in the first edition of *The favourite Songs in the Opera call'd Acis and Galatea*; with the pagination of that work added. The interesting point about this early edition is that Handel's name does not appear anywhere on the work, but most of the songs are described in turn as: "A Song by an Eminent Master", or "A Song Set by an Eminent Master".

The "Table of the Songs" as given on the leaf after the title-page is as follows:

Ye verdant plains	1
Where shall I seek	4
Stay Shepherd stay	5
Lo here my Love	7
As when the Dove	9
Happy, happy pair Duet	12
I rage I melt I burn	16
O ruddier than the Cherry	17
Whither fairest art thou runing	20
Cease to beauty to be sueing	21
Wou'd you gain the tender creature	23
Love sounds th' alarm	25
Consider fond Shepherd	28
The flocks the Mountains Duet	30
'Tis done thus I exert	34

As this "Table" (giving Recitatives in some cases and Arias in others) does not clearly indicate all the numbers in the work, a complete list of the contents taken from the items themselves is appended:

Recitative:	Ye verdant Plains.
Air:	Hush hush ye pretty warbling Quire.
Air:	Where shall I seek the charming fair.
Recitative:	Stay Shepherd stay.
Air:	Shepherd what art thou pursuing.
Recitative	Lo here my Love.
Air:	Love in her eyes sits playing.
Recitative:	O did'st thou know the pains of absent love.
Air:	As when the Dove.
"A Song for 2 Voices":	Happy happy Pair.
Recitative:	I rage, I melt, I burn.
Air:	O ruddier than the Cherry.

Recitatives:	Whither fairest.	Described as
	The Lyon calls not.	"A song by
	Thee Poliphemus.	an Eminent
	Of Infant limbs.	Master."

Air:	Cease to beauty to be suing.
Air:	Woud you gain the tender Creature.
Air:	Love sounds th' alarm.
Air:	Consider fond Shepherd.
"A three part Song":	The Flocks shall leave the Mountains.
Recitative:	'Tis done, thus I exert my Pow'r Divine.
Air:	Heart, the seat of soft delight. Described as "A Song by an Eminent Master."

The numbers are printed in two, three, or four stave score, with unfigured bass. "Hush ye pretty warbling quire" and "Wou'd you gain the tender creature" have a separate Flute part at the end of the number.

Copies of this edition are of the utmost rarity, and the above details are taken from a fine example in the possession of the writer. The fact that the work appeared anonymously raises the perplexing question of Handel's dealings with Walsh, and whether the issue was pirated or not. The question cannot be conclusively answered, but the following points are of interest. Prior to *Acis and Galatea* Walsh had published editions of *Rinaldo* for Handel, from 1711 onwards. *Radamisto* and the *Suites de Pieces* were issued by Handel in 1720 through Christopher Smith and Richard Meares, and on June 14 of the same year Handel was granted by royal licence the sole right of printing and publishing his *Vocal and Instrumental Musick*. In virtue of that right he employed Walsh, in conjunction with John and Joseph Hare, to issue the fine scores of *Floridante* (1722), *Ottone* (1723) and *Flavio* (1723). It is hardly conceivable, therefore, that after the publication of *Floridante*, early in 1722, Walsh would steal Handel's *Acis and Galatea* in the same year and issue it without authority, but the facts about music publishing at the time are anything but clear, and rightly or wrongly, Walsh has been looked upon by some writers as a rather discreditable business man.

MUSIC. Edition No. 1. (Another issue.) [1725?]

It is on record that an issue of the anonymous edition (No. 1) of *Acis and Galatea* was made with "J. Walsh and Joseph Hare" only in the imprint. No copy is available for examination, and if one existed it was probably issued with the altered imprint after the death of John Hare in 1725.

In *The Post-Boy*, February 28– March 2, 1723, following an announcement by Walsh and John and Joseph Hare of *The Monthly Masque of Vocal Musick* and *Twelve Cantato's in English*, is the additional advertisement *Also the Masque of Acis and Galatea*, etc. It will be noticed that the work is called a "Masque", Handel's name is not mentioned, and John and Joseph Hare are associated as publishers. It is impossible, however, in the absence of other evidence, to say whether the advertisement refers to:

    a. Edition, No. 1;
        or
    b. A new issue of No. 1 (anonymous) with Masque or Mask on the title-page;
        or
    c. An earlier issue of Edition No. 2 with a different imprint.

An edition of *Acis and Galatea* for the Flute, was published about 1724 by J. Walsh, John and Joseph Hare. Details are given later on after the descriptions of the fuller editions.

A copy of an unidentified edition was advertised by Grant, Edinburgh (December, 1921) as "*Acis and Galatea, Songs from the Opera of.* Folio, original paper covers, uncut. Walsh. [1725.]" This may have referred to a copy of the work described above as No. 1, or to some other issue of it, with the early description "opera" still on the title-page, published by Walsh alone, 1730 or after.

MUSIC. Edition No. 2. [1725–30?]

The title-page of this edition reads:

> The Songs and Symphony's in the Masque of Acis and Galatea made and perform'd for his Grace the Duke of Chandos Compos'd by M^r: Handel Fairly Engraven and carefully corrected London Printed for J: Walsh Servant in Ordinary to his Britanick Majesty, at ye Harp & Hoboy in Katherine street, near Somerset House in ye Strand, & J: Hare at ye Viol & Flute in Cornhill near the Royall Exchange.

The size, table, advertisement of music, and contents of this edition are the same as in Edition No. 1, with the music, consisting of thirty-six pages, on both sides of the paper, except the last leaf, the verso of which is blank. The title-page is not plain and undecorated like that of the earlier edition, but the finely illustrated canopied title-page which Walsh had already made good use of in *Rinaldo*, etc. Significant features are, the use of Handel's name as composer, the description "Masque", and the reference to the work as having been "made and perform'd for his Grace the Duke of Chandos". Why Walsh put out the earlier edition anonymously will probably never be known, but the fact that the edition with Handel's name was practically a duplicate of the first, stamps each of them with some sort of authority. Although Handel had left the Duke's service before either of the editions were issued, the mention of the Duke's title on the second edition was probably with the consent of the composer. If so, it is an additional reason for accepting the traditional story of the Chandos association, and even if Walsh was entirely responsible for the title-page, he must have been sufficiently well informed of the generally accepted knowledge as to how and where the work came into existence. Moreover, he would hardly be guilty of making a false statement about such a prominent and important public figure as his Grace the Duke.

No advertisement of *Acis and Galatea* agreeing with the particulars of the title-page (Edition No. 2) has been traced. If the J. Hare in the imprint stands for Joseph Hare, as is most likely, the issue was made after September, 1725 when John Hare died, and not later than 1730.

No copies of libretti of the early editions (Nos. 1 and 2) have been traced, or any newspaper notices of contemporary performances.

Between 1725 and 1731, in addition to the major issue of the work (No. 2) certain numbers of *Acis and Galatea* in single sheets, the Overture in parts and for the Harpsichord, and other extracts, appeared in various collections. Details of some of these issues are mentioned later on, although it is impossible to record all of them.[1]

The work as a whole came to public notice in March, 1731. The revival at this time has been well recorded by Handel's biographers, but some important details given here have not been noticed hitherto. *The Daily Journal* of March 13, 1731, has the following announcement:

> At the Desire of several Persons of Quality. For the Benefit of Mr. Rochetti. At the Theatre-Royal in Lincoln's-Inn-Fields, on Friday, being the 26th Day of

[1]In the Schœlcher manuscript catalogue at King's College, Cambridge, Dr. Mann has inserted the following notice under "Acis and Galatea":
> On June 17, 1723, was performed at the King's Arms Playhouse, "The Country Wedding", taken out of the fam'd Musick of Acis and Galatea.

This reference has not been traced elsewhere, but it is reasonable to suppose that it had nothing to do with Handel's work, but referred to Motteux's "Acis and Galatea" (1701 etc.) with music by John Eccles, the comic part of which was renamed *The Country Wedding*. (1714 etc., Allardyce Nicoll.) A libretto of the Drury-Lane performances of Motteux's *Acis and Galatea* was issued in 1723.

March, will be presented, A Pastoral, call'd, Acis and Galatea. Compos'd by Mr. Handel. Acis by Mr. Rochetti; Galatea, Mrs. Wright; Polypheme, Mr. Leveridge; and the other Parts by Mr. Legar, Mr. Salway, Mrs. Carter, and Mr. Papillion. Tickets may be had at the Theatre. Boxes 5s. Pit 3s. First Gallery 2s. Upper Gallery 1s. N.B. The Tickets deliver'd out for the 17th, will be taken on the 26th Instant.

The advertisement was repeated in *The Daily Journal*, March 15, with variations, the cast being given as follows: "Acis by Mr. Rochetti; Galatea, Mrs. Wright; Polypheme, Mr. Leveridge; Coridon, Mr. Legar; Damon, Mr. Salway." Mrs. Carter and Mr. Papillion are not mentioned.

A further advertisement in *The Daily Journal*, March 24, adds to the notice of March 15 the following: "With additional Performances, as will be expressed in the Great 'Bills', and after the prices *Multa Pauca faciunt Unum satis*."

This announcement was repeated again on March 25, and on the day of performance, March 26, *The Daily Journal* has the further addition to the previous notices: "Likewise Mr. Rochetti will sing the Song, Son Confusa Pastorella, being the Favourite Hornpipe in the Opera of Porus."

The production of March 26 was described as a "Pastoral", and evidently a number of performances, presumably with Handel's consent, were planned, but only the first appears to have been given, and this was postponed apparently from March 17 to 26. The King's Music Library manuscript copy of Handel's 1732 version of *Acis and Galatea* (R.M.19.f.7.) has "Sig^r Rochetti" pencilled in Handel's writing above the Recitative and Aria, "Un sospiretto d'un labro pallido." Little is known of this singer. He was a member of the Lincoln's Inn Fields company 1731–32, and appeared in a number of productions of the period. Philip Rochetti's name occurs in the 1744 list of subscribers to the "Fund for Decayed Musicians", afterwards "The Royal Society of Musicians". The item from Handel's *Poro* was evidently popular. English words, "When fearful Pastorella," were set to it by Th. Brerewood, Junior, who also put English words, "Return fair maid", to "Caro vieni", from *Poro*. The other performers named in the advertisements were all members of the Lincoln's Inn Fields company of Comedians;

and Legar sometimes' appeared in the bills as Laguerre. Leveridge is too well known to need special notice. In discussing musicians of about 1731, Burney (*History*) says, "The favourite playhouse singer was Salway". Mrs. Wright's name appears on manuscripts of *Athalia* and a song for *Admetus*, and she took part in other Handel works. Mrs. Carter and Mrs. Papillion, whose names only appear in the *Acis and Galatea* advertisement of March 13, could have had only minor parts, probably in the choruses. There is little reason for thinking, as some writers have stated, that the work was done without choruses. It is true that they are not mentioned as they are in the next recorded production, but until there is definite evidence to the contrary, it must be assumed that the work was given as a whole, and with Handel's consent if not his co-operation.

One interesting feature of the Rochetti production on March 26 was the introduction of a new character "Coridon". The name does not appear on Handel's manuscripts, and it has hitherto been a matter for speculation as to what this character's part consisted of. Chrysander suggested, as pointed out by Squire, that Corydon's part was introduced to fill up the blanks left by the omission of the choruses. This explanation cannot be accepted however. No copy of the libretto of the 1731 production has been traced. The present writer recently acquired three later libretti of *Acis and Galatea* which include "Corydon" among the Dramatis Personæ, and it is reasonable to suppose that the name of the character and the part were taken over from the Rochetti production. These later libretti will be described in due course, but at this point it is of interest to state, that in them "Corydon" is given one number only, Damon's air, "Would you gain the tender creature". This lyric, it will be remembered, was supplied to Gay's text by John Hughes the poet, a friend and admirer of Handel's, and who provided the words of *Venus and Adonis*, a cantata for which Handel composed the music.[1]

On November 27, 1731, Walsh was still advertising (*Daily Journal*) *The Mask of Acis and Galatea*, but whether this was a new edition or just an announcement of the earlier editions is not

---

[1] Discovered in the British Museum by the writer and published by Augener & Co., London, 1938.

clear. Similar advertisements appeared in the papers on February 9, May 18, June 7 and June 14, 1732.

The next recorded production of *Acis and Galatea* was that on May 17, 1732, at the New (or Little) Theatre, Haymarket. The work was repeated on May 19, a fact not generally known, although the performance on May 17 has been well written up and accepted as an act of piracy by Thomas Arne, the father of the better known Dr. Arne. There is, however, little evidence to support this opinion, as will be seen later on. The New (or Little) Theatre in the Haymarket, almost opposite the King's Theatre, or Opera House, was occupied during the season 1731-32 by a number of theatrical adventurers in turn, who presented very mixed performances, as they were able to rent the building for a night or two. Amongst these companies was that of Thomas Arne, an upholsterer by trade, who in association with J. F. Lampe and Henry Carey, produced a series of English Operas. The first work sponsored by Arne was *Amelia*, March 13, 1732. This was announced as "A New English Opera, after the Italian Manner, call'd Amelia. By a Set of Performers who never yet appear'd in publick," etc. The text was by Henry Carey, with music by J. F. Lampe, and it is of interest to Handel students because Miss Arne, afterwards Mrs. Cibber, made her debut in the title role of Amelia, in company with Gustavus Waltz who played the part of Osmyn, Grand Vizier, Commander of the Turks. Waltz has been frequently referred to by various writers as Handel's cook, and his performance in *Acis and Galatea* on May 17, 1732, inaccurately recorded as his first stage appearance. By taking part in Arne's "pirated" version of Handel's work he has been accused of having played his master a scurvy trick. The evidence that Waltz was Handel's cook is, however, very meagre and unconvincing and has been dealt with in Chapter V.

A preliminary notice of the Arne production of *Acis and Galatea* appeared in *The Daily Post*, May 2, 1732, as follows:

> We hear that the Proprietors of the English Opera will very shortly perform a celebrated Pastoral Opera call'd Acis and Galatea, compos'd by Mr. Handel, with all the

In the Collection of the Hon.ble John Spencer Esq.r

ENGRAVING BY GOLDAR, 1785

From a copy in the possession of Wm. C. Smith

PLATE NO. 9

George Frideric Handel

ENGRAVING BY F. C. LEWIS, AFTER THE PAINTING BY KYTE, 1828

From a copy in the possession of Wm. C. Smith

Grand Chorus's and other Decorations, as it was perform'd before his Grace the Duke of Chandos, at Cannons; and that it is now in Rehearsal.

A similar notice appeared in *The Daily Journal*, May 3.

On May 6, 8 and 10 the performance was advertised for
May 11, but on that date and on May 12, it was announced as
put off until May 17, "it being impossible to get ready the
Decorations before that time". Further advertisements of the
performances on May 17 appeared on May 15 and 16.

The reference in the notices of May 2 (*Daily Post*) and May 3
(*Daily Journal* etc.) "with all the Grand Chorus's and other
Decorations, as it was perform'd before his Grace the Duke of
Chandos" is modified in the notices of May 6, etc., and of May
17, the date of production, when *The Daily Post* announcement
was as follows:

> At the New Theatre in the Hay-market this present
> Wednesday being the 17th Day of May, will be per-
> form'd in English, a Pastoral Opera, call'd Acis and
> Galatea. Composed by Mr. Handel. With all the Grand
> Chorus's, Scenes, Machines, and other Decorations:
> being the first Time it ever was perform'd in a Theatrical
> Way. The Part of Acis by Mr. Mountier, being the first
> Time of his appearing in Character on any Stage;
> Galatea, Miss Arne. Pit and Boxes to be laid together at
> 5s. Gallery 2s. 6d. Tickets may be had, and Places taken,
> at Mr. Fribourg's, Maker of Rappee Snuff, at the Play-
> house Gate. To begin exactly at Seven o'Clock. N.B.
> Tickets deliver'd out for Thursday the 11th will be taken
> this Day.

There has been much speculation as to the nature of the
early performances of *Acis and Galatea* and to what extent the
work was "acted". As already pointed out, details of the
Cannons performance are wanting.

The advertisement of the Rochetti production as a "Pastoral"
and that of Arne's as a "Pastoral Opera" suggest that there
was a difference in the nature of the performances. The Arne
libretto gives entrances and a few acting instructions.

It is significant that Arne's notice of May 2 stated "with all
the Grand Chorus's and other Decorations, "as it was per-

form'd before his Grace the Duke of Chandos", but the modified notices of May 6, etc., and of May 17 read, "With all the Grand Chorus's, Scenes, Machines and other Decorations; being the first Time it ever was performed in a Theatrical Way."

It would be interesting to know why this change in the notices took place and who was responsible for it. It is quite clear that Arne's version was a "dramatic" performance in the ordinary sense of the word. As Handel announced his performance of June 10, 1732, with "no action on the stage", it suggests that he was drawing a clear distinction between his own adapted *Acis and Galatea* and the preceding productions.

It will be noticed that Handel was given full credit as composer of the *Pastoral Opera* performed on May 17, 1732, while at the same time Walsh was still advertising the work as a "Mask". The libretto of Arne's production, advertised *Daily Post*, May 11 and 17, was printed in good style, with the following title-page and cast:

Acis and Galatea: An English Pastoral Opera. In Three Acts. As it is Perform'd at the New Theatre in the Hay-Market, Set to Musick By Mr. Handel. [Ornament.] London: Printed for J Watts at the Printing-Office in Wild-Court near Lincoln's-Inn Fields. MDCCXXXII. [Price Six Pence.]

Dramatis Personæ.
Men.
Acis. Mr. Mountier.
Polyphemus. Mr. Waltz.
Damon. Mrs. Mason.
Women.
Galatea. Miss Arne.
Chorus of Shepherds and Shepherdesses.

The volume is octavo, ten leaves, paginated 8–11, 13–16, 18–21.

The second act commences with "Wretched Lovers", the third with the air, "Consider, fond Shepherd".

Apart from slight variations in text and the omission of a couple of lines, the edition follows the autograph manuscript of the music fairly well. "Wou'd you gain the tender creature", given to Damon, follows "Cease to beauty", and the chorus "Happy we" existing in later editions at the end of Part II is not included.

The extent to which unofficial pirated editions of libretti were issued for performances during the eighteenth century is not clear. Sometimes more than one publisher was advertising the same edition of the work. In some cases the "publisher" may have been acting simply as selling agent. An edition of *Acis and Galatea*, issued apparently in competition with Watts's edition for Arne's production, is mentioned amongst the list of new publications in *The London Magazine*, May, 1732 as follows:

> Acis and Galatea: An English Pastoral Opera. In three Acts. Set to Musick by Mr. Handel. Sold by J. Roberts. Price 6d.

As Roberts was a printer and bookseller who issued a number of contemporary works, including the libretto of John Eccles's *Acis and Galatea* in 1723, there is no reason for supposing that the above-quoted advertisement may not have referred to an issue by Roberts, but it is much more likely that Roberts was only announcing Watts's edition, as in *The Daily Post*, May 17, 1732, the work was advertised as "Printed for J. Watts . . . and sold by J. Roberts", etc. It has been asserted that Dr. Arne, son of the producer, conducted the performance of May 17, 1732.

In the absence of definite evidence, it is difficult to say just how Arne acquired the work for production, and whether he used it with or without Handel's permission. The music must have been available as well as the text, and as Walsh did not publish the choruses in his early editions, some of the music must have been obtained from manuscripts probably in Handel's possession. At any rate, there is little reason for assuming that the production was rank piracy, and that Arne even engaged Handel's own servant Waltz to assist in a mean robbery of his master. After all, Handel's name was fully advertised in connection with the performance. No special edition of the music for Arne's version can be identified.

It would be interesting to know what prompted Handel to undertake the revival of *Acis and Galatea* in an entirely new form on June 10, 1732. Arne's version was reasonably faithful to the original Cannons work, and we know, from the revivals and editions of 1739 and after, that the composer must have retained a permanent affection for this early version, which with few changes became the popular and accepted one for all time. Amongst the attempted explanations for the performances of the work in a new form, is that of W. Barclay Squire (*Musical Times*, October 1, 1921). He says: "The inartistic character of the performances has much exercised Handel's biographers, who have found considerable difficulty in defending it. But, clearly, the real reason for Handel's procedure is that things were going badly with the opera, and the success of Arne's production showed a chance of reimbursement for the season's losses at the King's Theatre. Handel's company there included Italian singers who could not sing English, and to make use of them he hit upon the plan of interlarding the English *Acis and Galatea* with parts of the old Italian Serenata. The result was certainly inartistic, but it answered its purpose. The polyglot work was performed at Oxford in 1733, and was frequently repeated during the following years until about 1740, when it was replaced by *Acts and Galatea* as we now know it."

Streatfeild, however, gives an explanatory reference from the Shaftesbury papers stating that the production of June, 1732 was designed to compensate opera subscribers for the fact that only forty-nine performances instead of the promised fifty had been given during the preceding season. This statement, however, is at variance with the advertisements of June 10 etc., from which one gathers that the full number of operas agreed upon had been given. Streatfeild does not agree with Squire that the opera season of 1731–32 had been going badly, and from contemporary records it seems clear that it was quite successful.

The newspapers give no help as to the origin of the production. If Handel was intending to show what he could do against unauthorized performances of his own work, he seems to have succeeded, as his new version advertised June 5, 6, 7, 8, and 9, was given on June 10, 13, 17 and 20, 1732, and on December 5, 9, 12 and 16 of the same year as part of the subscription series of operas at the King's Theatre. Members of the Royal Family attended the performances on June 20, December 5 and 16. The announcement in *The Daily Journal*, June 10, the day of the first performance was as follows:

> At the King's Theatre in the Hay-Market, this present Saturday, being the 10th of June, will be perform'd, A Serenata, call'd Acis and Galatea. Formerly composed by Mr. Handel, and now revised by him, with several Additions, and to be perform'd by a great Number of the best Voices and Instruments.
>
> There will be no Action on the Stage, but the Scene will represent, in a Picturesque Manner, a Rural Prospect, with Rocks, Groves, Fountains, and Grotto's, amongst which will be disposed a Chorus of Nymphs and Shepherds, the Habits and every other Decoration suited to the Subject. Pit and Boxes to be put together, and no Persons to be admitted without Tickets, which will be deliver'd This Day, at the Office in the Hay-Market, at Half a Guinea each. Gallery Five Shillings. By His Majesty's Command. No person whatever to be admitted behind the Scenes. To begin at 7 o'Clock. N.B. The full Number of Opera's agreed for in the Subscription being Compleated, the Silver Tickets will not be admitted, but only the Subscribers themselves in Person.

The *Serenata* was a combination of Handel's Cantata or Serenata, *Aci, Galatea e Polifemo*, written in Naples in 1708, with some numbers and adaptations from the Cannons version of *Acis and Galatea*, arias, etc., from other works, and some entirely new material. It was mostly in Italian with a few numbers in English. Copies of the libretto are extremely rare and the details given here are from the *Händel-Gesellschaft* edition, Vol. LIII, where the work is set out in full with introduction by Chrysander. Schœlcher states that the libretto was printed for J. Watts, but the title-page as given by Chrysander reads:

> Acis and Galatea a Serenata. As it is Perform'd at the King's Theatre in the Hay-Market. Formerly Compos'd by Mr. Handel, and now Revis'd by him, with several Additions. London. Printed for T. Wood in Little Britain, and are to be sold at the King's Theatre in the Hay-Market. 1732.

The "interlocutori" are given, without singers' names:

Acis . .	Contralto. (Soprano.)
Galatea .	Soprano
Clori . .	Soprano
Polifemo .	Basso
Sylvio .	Tenore
Filli .	Alto
Dorinda .	Alto
Eurilla .	Soprano
Damone .	Alto
Coro	

The volume is octavo, sixteen leaves, paginated 4–5, 7–31.

The work is in three parts, and according to the *Händel-Gesellschaft* edition only the following numbers were in English, although two others had an English translation:

Chorus: O the pleasures of the plains.
Chloris: Hush ye pretty warbling choir.
Eurilla: Would you gain the tender creature.
Chorus: Smiling Venus.
Chloris: Love ever vanquishing.
Clori: Consider fond Shepherd.
Chorus: Galatea, dry thy tears.

It is unnecessary to transcribe here the full list of numbers as given in Chrysander's version of the work (H.G. Vol. LIII), to which the reader is referred. Barclay Squire's article in *The Musical Times*, October, 1921, should also be consulted. Rockstro's attempt at a reconstruction in his life of Handel, is obviously inaccurate in the light of later research.

In the examination of the problem of singers which follows, it will be noticed that Miss Robinson (Clori) and Mrs. Davis (Eurilla) were the only two English singers in the cast. This may explain the existence of the English numbers in the work, which apart from the choruses are for Clori or Eurilla. Perhaps Handel would have produced an entirely Italian work had there been available an entirely Italian cast, a speculation in opposition to that of Barclay Squire's already quoted, but equally reasonable.

In the absence of a complete contemporary list of the cast of this production, Rockstro and other writers have supplied names from various manuscripts and other sources. The following particulars are offered as being the most authoritative:

Galatea	. . .	*Signora Strada*
Acis	. . .	*Senesino*
Damon	. . .	*Campioli*
Polifemo	. . .	*Montagnana*
Clori	. . .	*Miss Robinson*
Filli	. . .	*Signora Bagnolesi*
Dorinda	. . .	*Signora Bertolli*
Eurilla	. . .	*Mrs. Davis*
Silvio	. . .	*Pinacci*
Coro		

All of the above singers' names except that of Campioli appear, mostly in abbreviated forms, on the King's Music manuscripts R.M.20.d.2. and R.M.19.f.7. the latter of which also includes the names of Rochetti, Powel, Francesina, Jones, Kelly, Aedwin (or Aldwin) and Savage.

Handel advertised his work as a "Serenata", although no edition of the music with this title appears to have been published at the time, but advertisements of November 25 (*Daily Journal*) and November 28 (*Daily Post*) 1732, refer to "New Musick . . . The Mask of Acis and Galatea" and "The Masque of Acis and Galatea". December announcements mention the work again, which may be identified as the following (Edition No. 3), issued not earlier than 1732 or later than 1739. In the absence of conclusive evidence it is dated here provisionally as 1732.

MUSIC. Edition No. 3. [1732 or later.]

The title-page, of this edition, a modification of the canopied form of the previous issue, reads as follows:

> The Songs and Symphony's in the Masque of Acis and Galatea made and perform'd for his Grace the Duke of Chandos Compos'd by M^r: Handel with the Additional Songs London Printed for J: Walsh Servant in Ordinary to his Britanick Majesty, at ye Harp & Hoboy in Katherine street, near Somerset House in ye Strand, N°. 287.

The title-page is from a very much worn plate, Hare's name having been removed from the imprint, and Nᵒ. 287 added at the end. This is the issue number of the work in accordance with Walsh's practice of so enumerating many of his publications. The work consists of title-page, table and thirty-eight pages of music. The previous editions have thirty-six pages of music. This edition has the thirty-six pages from the plates of the previous editions, with the headings "A Song by an Eminent Master, "etc.,erased, and with two additional pages at the end containing one additional song. This number, "De l'aquila l'artigli" (Dell' aquila gli artigli) is headed "An Additional Song Sung by Sigʳ. Senesino in Acis and Galatea". This song was in the second part of Handel's 1732 production and has no connection with the Cannons version. It is the only number from "Aci, Galatea e Polifemo" printed at this time.

It has been pointed out that Hare's name was removed from the plate of the title-page for this edition, and it has been assumed hitherto that as Joseph Hare died in 1733, works without his name in the imprint are all 1733 or afterwards. This is not the case, however, because from towards the end of 1730 Joseph Hare's name was absent from Walsh's publications. It is therefore not unreasonable to assign the Edition No. 3 to 1732, some time after Handel's production of that year. It was the last edition of the work by John Walsh the elder, who died in March, 1736.

The next performance to be noticed, is one given by Handel at Oxford, probably on July 11, 1733, as part of "The Oxford Act", the details of which are incomplete and conflicting. Rockstro says: "We have arrived at the conclusion that *Acis and Galatea* was represented, at the King's Theatre, on the 10th June, 1732, at the Theatre in Oxford, in July, 1733, and in London and Dublin on some later occasions, with the well-known Airs and Choruses of the English Serenata interspersed among the Italian pieces enumerated in the following scheme."

There is no definite evidence to upset Rockstro, but very little to support him, although Barclay Squire, as already pointed out, is in agreement with him on this point. The libretto of the

Oxford production is not available for examination, but Chrysander (H.G. Vol. III.) gives the detail of title-page as follows:

> Acis and Galatea. a Serenata : or Pastoral Entertainment. As Perform'd at the Theatre in Oxford. At the time of the publick Act, in July, 1733. Formerly Compos'd by Mr. Handel, and now Revised by him, with several Additions. London: Printed for John Watts at the Printing-Office in Wild-Court near Lincoln's-Inn Fields: And are to be had at the Theatre in Oxford. 1733. [Price One Shilling.]

This was presumably an octavo.

The use of the expression "with several Additions" favours the assumption that the production was on the lines of the June, 1732, performances. Some authorities give "Wood" as the publisher of the libretto for Oxford, and definitely relate the work to the Italian-English version. It has also been suggested that the production consisted of the first act up to and inclusive of the air "As when the dove", from the original Cannons and Arne versions, followed by "Come la rondinella" and the rest of the June, 1732, work. It will be noticed that Watts published Arne's libretto and Wood published Handel's 1732 libretto. According to the H.G. Vol. III transcript of the title of the Oxford libretto given above, Watts was the publisher, and it might be concluded therefore that this version was related to Arne's version because the publisher of that libretto was also Watts. This is not a very sound assumption, however, when it is remembered that Watts and Wood probably produced rival editions of the libretti for Arne, 1732, for Handel, 1732, and for the Oxford production. In the absence of further evidence little more can be said, except to point out that the description "Serenata or Pastoral Entertainment", given on the title-page of Watts's Oxford libretto, is a bit of both Watts's and Wood's earlier descriptions, with the substitution of the word "Entertainment" for "Opera", which may have been meant to indicate that the nature of the performance was not operatic.

The details of the singers in Handel's Oxford company are anything but certain. Signora Strada, Mrs. Wright, Salway, Rochetti, Waltz, Montagnana, Powell and Roe (Row?) are all mentioned in one authority or another, but the probability is that Waltz and not Montagnana took the part of *Polyphemus* in *Acis and Galatea*.

In this survey, it is impossible to trace every performance of *Acis and Galatea* during the period under review. A certain number of isolated performances of no particular significance are noted, but more detailed attention is given to those of special interest.

A revival was given at the King's Theatre, May 7, 1734, when the work was announced as a "Serenata". Handel's name was not mentioned. No libretto can be identified and no special edition of the music appears to have been published, although Walsh on December 7 of the same year was still advertising the *Mask of Acis and Galatea*. (*Country Journal.*)

W. J. Lawrence (*Musical Quarterly*, July, 1922) records a performance at Aungier Street Theatre, Dublin, 1735, and the work is said to have been given also in Dublin in May, 1734.

Two performances on March 24 and 31, 1736, were advertised (*London Daily Post and General Advertiser*) as follows:

> At the Theatre-Royal in Covent-Garden, this Day, March 24, will be reviv'd a Serenata, call'd Acis and Galatea. There will be no Action on the Stage, but the Scene will represent a Rural Prospect of Rocks, Grotto's, &c. amongst which will be dispos'd a Chorus of Nymphs and Shepherds. The Habits and other Decorations suited to the Subject. The Pit and Boxes will be laid together at Half a Guinea. First Gallery 4s. Upper Gallery 2s. 6d.

These performances, followed by two of *Esther* on April 7 and 14, although mentioned in Husk's "Account of the Musical Celebrations on St. Cecilia's Day" are not generally known, and although two libretti of *Acis and Galatea* were produced by rival publishers as no copies are available the details are obscure. Walsh the younger does not appear to have produced a special edition of the music at the time. The advertisements of the libretti were as follows:

> Now publish'd, Price stitch'd 6d. As it will be perform'd To-morrow at the Theatre in Covent Garden.

222

> Acis and Galatea, an English Pastoral Opera, in three
> Acts. Set to Musick by Mr. Handel. Printed for John
> Osborn, at the Golden Ball in Pater-noster Row. (*London
> Daily Post and General Advertiser*, March 23, 1736.)

This advertisement of what may have been an unauthorised
issue of the libretto was repeated on the following day, when
the paper also announced:

> This Day is publish'd, Price 1s. With several Additions
> and Alterations. Acis and Galatea, a Serenata, as it is
> perform'd at the Theatre-Royal in Covent Garden. Set
> to Musick by Mr. Handel. Printed and sold by Tho.
> Wood in Little-Britain, and at the Theatre in Covent
> Garden.

This was perhaps the authoritative issue, and it is interesting
to note the different descriptions of *Acis and Galatea* in each
case. The Osborn libretto uses the description "English Pastoral Opera, in three Acts", which agrees with Watts's libretto
published for Arne's production in May, 1732. The Wood
libretto appears from the announcement to have been somewhat similar to the issue for Handel's performance, June, 1732.
The London Magazine Monthly Catalogue of Books, March, 1736,
also announces the Osborn and Wood libretti, and definitely
describes the first as "An English Pastoral Opera" and the
second as "in Italian and English". Clearly two forms of *Acis
and Galatea* were on sale at the same time, which does not help
towards deciding which form was used in the contemporary
performances, although the Wood version "in Italian and
English" may have been the more authoritative.

Another issue of the libretto in 1736, without publisher's
name or place of publication, is in possession of the present
writer. The title-page reads:

> The Masque of Acis and Galatea. [Ornament.] Printed
> in the Year, MDCCXXXVI.

The work is octavo, eight leaves, with paper cover, paginated
4–8. It is in two parts, the first finishing with the duet, "Happy
we", but does not include the chorus "Happy we". Dramatis
Personæ are given as:

Galatea.

Damon.

Acis and Galatea.

Corydon.

Polypheme and Acis.

To Corydon is given the air, "Would you gain the tender creature".

This extremely interesting libretto is evidence of the reversion to an entirely English text of the work divided into two parts, three years before the date given by some authorities. The libretto may have been issued for a performance not given in London, and it was probably based on the Rochetti production of 1731. The division of the work into two parts is not indicated in the original manuscript, or in the first full score (1743).

Reference has already been made to Rockstro's remarks on the performances in 1732 and 1733; continuing the same subject he says: "There is abundant evidence to prove that fresh changes were introduced, as often as a new Singer took part in the performance. . . . On the 13th of September, 1739, Handel once more returned to the pure English version, as it had originally been performed at Cannons; but divided, as now, into two Acts, the first of which ended with the Chorus added to 'Happy we'."

No contemporary evidence of a performance on September 13, 1739, has been traced, but the papers record performances on December 13 and 20 of the same year, at Lincoln's Inn Fields. As late as September 6, 1739, Walsh was still advertising the earlier editions of the music as a "Masque", but the edition of December 13, 1739 (described below) was called a "Serenade", although in December, 1743, the publisher reverted to the description "Mask".

The London Daily Post and General Advertiser of December 13, 1739, announced:

> At the Theatre-Royal in Lincoln's-Inn Fields, this Day, will be perform'd Acis and Galatea, A Serenata. With two new Concerto's for several Instruments, never perform'd before. To which will be added, The last New Ode of Mr. Dryden's, And a Concerto on the Organ. Boxes Half a

Guinea. Pit 5s. First Gallery 3s. Upper Gallery 2s. Pit and Gallery Doors will be open'd at Four, the Boxes at Five. Box Tickets will be sold this Day at the Stage-Door. Particular care will be taken to have Guards plac'd to keep all the Passages clear from the Mob. To begin at Six o'Clock.

The libretto of this performance was also announced in *The London Daily Post and General Advertiser* of December 13:

> This Day is published, Acis and Galatea. A Serenata or Pastoral Entertainment. Written by Mr. Gay. To which is added, A Song for St. Cæcilia's Day. Written by Mr. Dryden. Both set to Musick by Mr. Handel. Printed for John Watts at the Printing-Office in Wild-Court near Lincoln's-Inn Fields. The Price to Gentlemen and Ladies in the Theatre is One Shillings; if more is ask'd, it is an Imposition.

This libretto appears to be the first to give the author's name, and has something therefore of authority about it, as it can hardly be imagined that Handel had no interest at all in the form in which *Acis and Galatea* was given. The description "Serenata or Pastoral Entertainment" was the same as Watts had used on his libretto for the Oxford production in 1733.

The *Ode for St. Cecilia's Day*, was first performed on November 22, 1739 (St. Cecilia's Day), with *Alexander's Feast*, two new Concertos for several Instruments and one for the Organ. As the *Ode* was given on December 13, 1739 and other occasions with *Acis and Galatea*, Walsh advertised and sold these two works together as one item, which explains why they are sometimes found together in collections of works of the period.

MUSIC. Edition, No. 4. [1739.]

It was in connection with the performance of December 13, 1739, that a new edition of *Acis and Galatea* was probably issued. Walsh's advertisement in *The London Daily Post and General Advertiser* on the above and later dates was:

> This Day is Published,
> 1. The Songs in the New Ode of Mr. Dryden's for St. Cecilia's Day, set to Musick by Mr. Handel. Price 3s.

2. Acis and Galatea, a Serenade (as it is now perform'd) Pr. 4s.

3. The Favourite Songs in Alexander's Feast. Price 5s.

Printed for John Walsh in Catherine-street in the Strand. At the same Place may be had the Original Score of Alexander's Feast, with the Chorus's, &c. Where may be had, Proposals for Printing by Subscription; Twelve Grand Concerto's, in 7 Parts. Composed by Mr. Handel. The Price to Subscribers is Two Guineas, One Guinea to be paid at the Time of Subscribing, and the other on the Delivery of the work, which will be in April next.

N.B. Two of the above Concerto's will be perform'd this Evening, at the Theatre-Royal in Lincoln's-Inn Fields. Subscriptions are taken by the Author, at his House in Brook's-street, Hanover-square; and John Walsh in Catherine-street in the Strand.

A repeat of the advertisement on December 15 states: "Four of the above Concerto's have been perform'd at the Theatre-Royal in Lincoln's-Inn Fields." The set of "Twelve Grand Concertos in 7 Parts" was issued by subscription in 1740.

The title-page of the music of Edition No. 4, advertised on December 13, 1739, reads as follows:

Acis and Galatea A Serenade. with the Recitatives Songs & Symphonys Compos'd by M^r. Handel. London Printed for J: Walsh Servant in Ordinary to his Britanick Majesty, at ye Harp & Hoboy in Katherine street, near Somerset House in ye Strand,

This was a further use of the canopied style of title-page, as used in Edition, No. 3, with different wording, Hare's name and "N°. 287" being omitted. Copies exist (a) with thirty-six pages of music, with the "Table" and advertisements of "Vocal Musick" on the verso of page thirty-six; (b) with thirty-eight pages of music, including the additional song "De l'aquila" at the end, with no "Table" or advertisements. As by December, 1739, Handel had apparently given up performances of the mixed English and Italian form of the work, it looks as if the authoritative issue of Edition No. 4, was the one with thirty-six pages and without the Italian song at the end, but that Walsh with his rather careless practice of putting new title-pages to

226

existing stock sheets, issued some copies of this edition with the additional song at the end, as it had appeared in Edition, No. 3. It is therefore impossible to date these two issues accurately, but they are assumed to be contemporary with or soon after the advertisement of December 13, 1739. It should be noticed, that all editions and issues up to and including those of 1739 contain the same music from the original plates of the first edition, except for the inclusion or omission of the additional song "De l'aquila", and these copies are all without Overture or Choruses.

It was the performance of December 13, 1739, that started the practice of giving *Acis and Galatea* with other items, vocal or instrumental; and probably it was simply to make a balanced programme that where the work was divided into two parts, other items (Concertos, etc.) were introduced between the two parts, and the chorus "Happy we" was subsequently inserted to round off the first part.

Referring to the production of June, 1732, Schœlcher says: "Handel afterwards returned to the simplicity of his English version of *Acis* which he gave, divided into two acts, in 1739, with Dryden's *Ode on St. Cecilia's Day*. It was then only that he added, as a termination to the first act, the delicious chorus, 'Happy, happy, happy we.'"

This chorus, however, does not appear in any editions of the music before 1743, and the earliest dated copy of the libretto containing the number, known to the present writer, is the British Museum copy (M.K.8.d.4.(2.)) issued in Dublin? 1742, and referred to again later on.

Chrysander (H.G. Vol. III.) says: "Handel . . . certainly as early as 1740, returned to the Masque as composed and performed at Cannons. The single alteration made was dividing it into two parts instead of performing it as an unbroken whole. To give the first part a more natural close, he added the chorus 'Happy we'. (H.G. Vol. III, pp. 47–50.) The original manuscript gives us nothing in relation to this beyond the direction at the close of the duet, 'il Coro, la seconda volta', written by Handel apparently between 1735–40, at which time doubtless the chorus was composed. Not much earlier—judging from the handwriting about 1735—he composed that longer chorus upon the themes of the duet, which we have given in the appendix.

(H.G. Vol. III, pp. 123-132.) The original, very hastily written and full of errors both in text and music, is now in the Fitzwilliam Museum at Cambridge. It seems hardly probable that Handel could have intended the chorus in this form for public performance; it was no doubt written for some friend who found a charm in the Welsh melody, 'The rising sun' which appears in it. Upon dividing the work into two parts the chorus, remodelled and reduced to the form in which we now have it, made a natural close for the first part."

The note in the "Catalogue of the Music in the Fitzwilliam Museum, Cambridge", referring to the autograph manuscript of "Happy we" is as follows: "The chorus 'Happy we' as printed on p. 123, H.-G., signed at the end 'Fine dell Atto 1 mo'. In pencil Handel has added 'end', as if the work at one time finished with this number".

The idea that Handel used a Welsh melody in his chorus "Happy we" was subsequently discredited by Chrysander in his life of Handel because of the existence of a similar melody elsewhere; a view supported by Leichtentritt and other authorities.

It is interesting to note that the chorus, "Happy we" is the only number in the work that includes the "Viola" in the orchestration.

The cast for the production of December, 1739, appears to have been:

Galatea	.	*Signora Francesina*
Acis	.	. *Beard*
Polyphemus	.	. *Reinhold*
Damon	. *The Boy*	(*presumably Robinson*)

These names appear in Handel's hand on his autograph manuscript. (The King's Music Library, R.M.20.a.2.)

A performance of *Acis and Galatea* advertised (*The London Daily Post and General Advertiser*) for February 7, 1740, at Lincoln's Inn Fields was postponed "for a few Nights" owing to the cold weather, re-announced for February 14 and again postponed owing to the "Two chief singers being taken ill". The work was then advertised for February 21, when, presumably it was performed:

HANDEL

PAINTING BY H. VAN DER MYN *c.* 1740

By courtesy of the National Portrait Gallery, London

GUSTAVUS WALTZ
PAINTING ATTRIBUTED TO HAUCK

From the original in the possession of Mrs. A. D. Taphouse

> At the Theatre-Royal in Lincoln's-Inn Fields, this Day, will be perform'd Acis and Galatea, A Serenata. (Being the last Time of performing it this Season.) With two new Concerto's for several Instruments, never perform'd but twice. To which will be added The last New Ode of Mr. Dryden's, And a Concerto on the Organ . . . Particular Care has been taken to have the House survey'd and secur'd against the Cold, by having Curtains plac'd before every Door, and constant Fires will be kept in the House 'till the Time of Performance.

On March 28, 1740, *The London Daily Post and General Advertiser* announced for that day a performance at Lincoln's Inn Fields of:

> Acis and Galatea. A Serenata. With the two new Concertos, performed in the same this Season for several Instruments. To which will be added, The last new Ode of Mr. Dryden's, and the Concerto on the Organ, that was composed by Mr. Handel on the same Occasion this Season.

This performance was "For the benefit and Increase of a Fund established for the Support of Decayed Musicians and their Families". Burney (*History*) says of this performance "Handel, though never nearer ruin himself, benevolently gave *Acis and |Galatea*, with his own performance of two new concertos at Lincoln's-Inn Fields, for the benefit of the Musical Fund". Handel's support of this charity, afterwards known as "The Royal Society of Musicians", was continued throughout his lifetime, and in the last codicil to his will, just before his death he bequeathed to the Fund one thousand pounds.

Acis and Galatea, A Serenata was performed with *Dryden's Last New Ode* at Lincoln's Inn Fields on February 28 and March 11, 1741, and during 1740 and 1741 Walsh was still advertising the work as a "Serenade". On February 28th, 1741 and other dates the Walsh announcements include *Acis and Galatea; and the Songs in Dryden's New Ode.*"

As already pointed out, a complete list of the early performances is impossible, and details of many editions of the libretto are wanting. The particulars of issues that follow are considered of sufficient importance to be mentioned as they

were doubtless related to contemporay performances and help
to show changes in the work.

A libretto exists (British Museum, 1344.m.13.) which cannot
be accurately dated. It is described on page one as:

> Acis and Galatea. A Masque. Set to Music by Mr.
> Handel.

The work is octavo, four leaves, and paginated 2–8. The title-
page is missing, supposing one was issued, and the text, eight
pages, not divided into parts, follows with few exceptions the
Arne version. The edition contains, however, the indication,
"Chorus, Happy we, etc." after the duet "Happy we". The
words of the chorus are not given, but if, as Chrysander has
maintained, this chorus was introduced as early as 1740, or as
others have stated in 1739, then the date of this libretto can be
assumed to be about 1740. The text agrees with the score of the
music issued in 1743.

Handel went to Dublin in November, 1741, and gave a
series of performances between December, 1741, and his
return to London in August, 1742. The visit is of supreme
importance because *Messiah* was produced on April 13, 1742,
after a rehearsal performance on April 8. During the visit,
Handel gave *Acis and Galatea*, with Dryden's *Ode for St. Cecilia's
Day* and Concertos, on January 20 and 27, 1742. A libretto in
the British Museum (M.K.8.d.4 (2.)) appears to be the one
issued for the Dublin performances. No publisher's name is
given, the title reading:

> The Masque of Acis and Galatea. The Musick by Mr.
> Handell. Printed in the Year MDCCXLII.

It is a quarto, eleven leaves, paginated 3-21.

The text of *Acis and Galatea*, in two parts, is followed by "*A
Song for St. Cecilia's Day*. Written by Mr. Dryden." At the end
of the First Part of *Acis and Galatea* are the words "A Concerto
on the Organ", and at the end of the Second Part, "A Concerto
on the Organ for several Instruments". The characters are

Acis, Galatea, Polyphemus, Damon, Shepherds and Shepherdesses. The text agrees with the edition described above (British Museum, 1344.m.13.) with the following principal exceptions: The Chorus, "Happy we" is written out in full; "Wou'd you gain the tender creature" is given to a Shepherd, not Damon; "Wretched Lovers", "Cease to beauty", and "Must I my Acis still bemoan", are omitted, "A Concerto for Several Instruments" being inserted in place of the last named; the Chorus ("Cease Galatea") which should follow is made a Recitative and given to Damon. The libretto may have been published by Faulkner, Dublin.

The following particulars of a performance in Dublin, after the introduction of the work to the Irish people by Handel earlier in 1742 are recorded by Townsend. (*Account of the Visit of Handel to Dublin*):

"The Charitable Musical Society opened their concerts for the winter, with a performance of *Acis and Galatea* in their Music-Hall, on the evening of December 17th, 1742. The Coronation Anthem, *Zadok the Priest*, was also performed; and Dubourg played a new solo. Both the choirs assisted, together with Mrs. Arne and other singers."

The two choirs referred to were those of the Cathedral Churches of Christ Church and St. Patrick's.

MUSIC. Edition, No. 5. [1743.]

The first complete edition of *Acis and Galatea* appeared in 1743. It was published in ten separate parts, and afterwards sold complete in one volume. *The Daily Advertiser* announced the appearance of the parts from August 24 to November 19, and *The London Evening Post* from September 1–3 to November 24–26.

The first announcement in *The Daily Advertiser*, August 24, 1743, was as follows:

> Musick. This Day is publish'd, (Price 1s.) Number I. of The entire Masque of Acis and Galatea, in Score, as it was originally compos'd, with the Overture, Recitativos, Songs, Duets, and Chorusses, for Voices and Instruments. Set to Musick by Mr. Handel.
> I. This Work will be printed in a neat and correct

Manner, and the Price to Subscribers is Half a Guinea.
II. A Number will be publish'd every Fortnight, at
One Shilling, till the whole is finish'd.

N.B. This is the only Dramatic Work of Mr. Handel
which has yet been publish'd entire.

Subscriptions are taken in by J. Walsh in Katherine-
Street in the Strand; Simpson, and Hare, in Cornhill;
Johnson, in Cheapside; Barret, and Wamsley, in Picca-
dilly; Mr. Cross, at Oxford; and Mr. Hopkins, at
Cambridge.

Just publish'd, The Oratorio of Samson, in Score.

The first notice in *The London Evening Post* of September 1–3
was slightly different from the above, stating: "The Work will
be printed compleat, in a neat and correct Manner for Half a
Guinea . . . Subscriptions are taken in and the Numbers
deliver'd, by J. Walsh in Catherine-Street in the Strand, and
all the Musick-Shops in Town."

No. II was advertised, *London Evening Post*, September
6–8; *Daily Advertiser*, September 7. Price 1s.

No. III. *London Evening Post*, September 17–20; *Daily
Advertiser*, September 21. Price 1s.

No. IV. *Daily Advertiser*, October 5. Price 1s. No. III
wrongly advertised for No. IV *London Evening Post*,
September 29–October 1.

No. V. *London Evening Post*, October 11–13; *Daily
Advertiser*, October 17. Price 1s.

No. VI. *Daily Advertiser*, October 21. Price 1s.

No. VII. *London Evening Post*, October 27–29; *Daily
Advertiser*, October 27. Price 1s.

No. VIII. *London Evening Post*, November 3–5; *Daily
Advertiser*, November 3. Price 1s.

No. IX. *London Evening Post*, November 15–17; *Daily
Advertiser*, November 10. Price 1s.

No. X. *London Evening Post*, November 24–26; *Daily
Advertiser*, November 19. Price 1s. 6d.

These details have been given rather fully as they are interesting for two or three reasons. Rarely did Walsh publish
Handel works in parts, and co-operation between himself and
the other music dealers named was quite exceptional. The

complete edition in one volume was announced, November 28, 1743 (*Daily Advertiser*) as just published "The entire Masque of Acis and Galatea in Score." The title-page reads:

> Acis and Galatea A Mask As it was Originally Compos'd with the Overture, Recitativo's, Songs, Duets & Choruses, for Voices and Instruments. Set to Musick by M^r. Handel London. Printed for I. Walsh, in Catharine Street, in the Strand.

(See Plate No. 13)

The title-page, plainly engraved in square border lining, verso blank, is followed by "A Table of the Songs, etc.", twenty numbers, with a list of "Musick Just Publish'd by I. Walsh Compos'd by Mr. Handel". The verso of this leaf is blank, then follow pp. 1–89 of music, the verso of p. 89 being blank. This is an entirely new edition, with figured bass throughout, no use being made of the old Walsh plates of the earlier editions. The work is not divided into acts or parts, and it includes the overture and choruses, with the short version of the chorus "Happy we" as in H.G. Vol. III, pp. 47–50.

There is one interesting feature about the 1743 complete edition. It is the assignment of the number "Consider fond Shepherd" to Clori and not to Damon, as in all of the earlier editions of the music. This was one of the English numbers retained by Handel in his mixed Italian and English version of 1732, and was sung by Clori, but why Walsh put Clori in his edition of 1743 is not clear as the rest of that edition has no particular connection with the 1732 production. Moreover Clori was retained instead of Damon in the Randall editions (1768 etc.) following Walsh, and in Arnold's edition of 1788, which was a new one. All except two of the libretti up to the end of the eighteenth century, that have been available for examination, give Damon. In H.G. Vol. LIII (1732 Italian and English version), the number is given to Clori, and in "The Words of such Pieces . . . performed by the Academy of Ancient Music" (1761, 1768) it is given to Cloris.

Reference is made later on to the introduction of a new character, "Chloris", with additional airs. (1762 etc.)

One method of attempting to arrive at the date of the various libretti, is an examination of the variations in the text. It is surely reasonable to suppose that the first full score of the entire work (1743) had Handel's approval. The text agrees in the main with that in the libretto described above (British Museum, 1344.m.13.) dated approximately 1740 or a little later. Neither this libretto nor the score is divided into parts, each has the chorus "Happy we" indicated or in full, and even an alteration in text ("The Floods the Turtle Dove" to "The Woods", etc.) is made in each case in manuscript. This edition was advertised from time to time by Walsh, who put out later impressions of the work, one at least with the table and list of works on the verso of the title-page. It is not easy to distinguish in point of time and order the various issues, but the condition of the plates, and the watermarks in the paper are some help. The edition of 1743, as reprinted from time to time, and advertised 1747, 1754, 1757 etc., had no rival until William Randall's editions of 1768 etc. (Nos. 7 and 8 below), and it was the Walsh edition of 1743 that Randall and Abell advertised on the Full Score of *Messiah* in 1767.

The work was given on February 9, 1744:

> For the benefit of Mr. Edmund Larken At Stationers-Hall in Ludgate-street . . . The Masque of Acis and Galatea. With all the Chorus's composed by Mr. Handel. The Songs of Galatea to be perform'd by a celebrated *Young Lady*, being the first time of her appearing in any Publick Concert. The other Parts . . . by the most eminent Performers. The First Violin by Mr. Brown. A Concerto on the German Flute by Mr. Burk Thumoth. An English and an Italian Song by the Sister of the above Lady (A Child of Nine Years of Age). The whole to conclude with the Coronation Anthem, God save the King. The Trumpet by Mr. Valentine Snow. Tickets to be had at the Mourning-Bush, Aldersgate. Books of the Masque will be given Gratis at the Place of Performance, &c. (*London Daily Post and General Advertiser*, Feb. 9th, 1744.)

According to Townsend (*An Account of the Visit of Handel to Dublin*) "The Philharmonic Society of Dublin" was advertised to give "at their Musick-Room in Fishamble street" performances of various Handel works, including *Acis and Galatea*, during the winter season 1744–45. No further particulars are available. Another Dublin performance was that of February 7, 1749, at Neal's Music Hall, Fishamble Street, when *Acis and Galatea* was given at a benefit concert for Mrs. Arne, and "Mrs. Arne and Mrs. Lampe introduced several favourite Songs and Duets".

No copy has been traced of a libretto the only recorded details of which are:

> The words of the Pastoral or the Masque of Acis and Galatea. Printed in the year, 1745.

An octavo edition of the libretto published in Dublin about 1745 or later has been recorded with the following title:

> The celebrated Masque of Acis and Galatea. J. Hoey: Dublin.

No copy is available for verification, and the particulars given may refer to the one mentioned by Chrysander (H.G. Vol. III. Preface p. 3) as "Composed by Mr. Handel for his Grace the Duke of Chandois", or to a later one, probably issued for a Dublin performance, December, 1757.

Eighteenth century performances of *Acis and Galatea* or selections from it, are recorded in Lyson's *History of the Origin and Progress of the Meeting of the Three Choirs of Gloucester, Worcester and Hereford*, from 1745 onwards, as follows:

1745 Gloucester; 1757 Gloucester; 1764 Worcester; 1765 Hereford; 1780 Hereford; 1790 Gloucester; 1791 Worcester; 1797 Worcester; 1800 Worcester.

A musical society afterwards known as the Castle Society was established in the early part of the eighteenth century at the house of John Young, music publisher and instrument seller, who lived at the sign of the Dolphin and Crown, London House Yard, St. Paul's Church Yard. Talbot Young, the son of John Young, established meetings for the practice of music which developed into popular concerts supported by subscription. The Society moved to the Queen's Head Tavern in Paternoster Row and in 1724 to the Castle, Paternoster Row. By

1755 it had moved again to Haberdashers' Hall in Gresham Street, where it continued until removal to the King's Arms, Cornhill, 1764 or after.

Three libretti used at the Castle Society performances 1747 1755 and 1764, are recorded.

The title-page of the first of these (British Museum, 11775.e.3.(1.)) reads as follows:

> Acis and Galatea. A Serenata. As Perform'd at the Musical Society at the Castle in Pater-Noster Row. The Music by Mr. Handel. [Ornament] London: Printed for J. Watts at the Printing-Office in Wild-Court near Lincoln's-Inn Fields. MDCCXLVII.

There is an outer half-title reading: "Acis and Galatea. A Serenata. [Price Sixpence.]" The work is octavo, eleven leaves paginated 6–10, 12–21. The text is very similar to the British Museum libretto, 1344.m.13. c. 1740, including the indication of the chorus "Happy we", but the work is divided into two parts. The second part opens with "A Concerto on the Organ", preceding "Wretched Lovers".

An edition published by Wood in 1747 for the Castle Society is also recorded although not available for examination. The other libretti of the Castle Society are described later on, in order of date.

Acis and Galatea was given more than once at Hickford's Concert Room in Brewer Street. One performance especially worth recording was that for Miss Oldmixon's benefit in 1749, when the singers were Miss Oldmixon, Signora Galli, John Beard and Reinhold. The conductor was the famous violinist Dubourg, who was also announced to "play a Solo".

Another performance was given (date untraced) at Hickford's room for the Benefit of the Sister of the late Robert Hiller of Westminster Abbey.

A libretto, which it is quite impossible to date accurately, was issued by Cluer Dicey, probably about 1750. The title reads:

> Acis and Galatea. A Serenata Performed at the St. Cæcilian Concert at the Crown Tavern Behind the Royal Exchange. The musick Composed by Mr. Handel. London. Printed by Cluer Dicey in Bow Church Yard. [Price Six-Pence.]

The work is octavo, eleven leaves, paginated 5–21. It is divided into two parts, the first part finishing with the chorus, "Happy we," which is indicated in the text. The second part opens with "A Concerto on the Organ", and an original feature is the description of "I rage, I melt, I burn", as "Recitative accompany'd". The text and Dramatis Personæ follow the generally accepted form—i.e., without "Corydon" or "Chloris". The only known copy is in the Balfour Collection, National Library of Scotland.

MUSIC. Edition, No. 6. [1750 or later.]

In the study of Walsh editions of Handel's works one frequently finds strange copies made up from pages out of several issues, presumably thrown together from existing stock sheets to meet some contemporary demand. These copies are always difficult to date, and it is quite likely that some of them with the Walsh imprint may have been issued by his successors. An example of such an issue of *Acis and Galatea* is known. It consists of the title-page and contents of Edition, No. 4(a), but with thirty-eight pages of music selected from that edition and the later (complete) edition of 1743, in the correct order of the work, but with the paginations of the editions from which they were taken. There is no continuous pagination 1–38. The title-page is a very poor impression, and the issue may have been made quite late. For purposes of listing and reference, it has been placed here as "Edition, No. 6" and is assumed to be not earlier than 1750.

One copy of this made-up issue is recorded as having the words "Favourite Songs in" added in manuscript to the title-page before "Acis and Galatea" and "pr.4" added after the word "Handel".

A benefit performance of *Acis and Galatea* was given for Signora Frasi on April 2, 1753, at the Little Theatre, Haymarket. The work was announced "With a Concerto on the Organ by Mr. Stanley. First Violin, with a Solo, by Sig. Giardini".

February 13, 1754, *Acis and Galatea* was given for the benefit of Signora Galli at the New (or Little) Theatre, Haymarket. The announcement stated that "Between the two Acts will be perform'd by particular Desire, a Solo on the Violoncello by Sig. Lanzetti; an Italian Song by Signora Galli; and a Solo on the Violin by Mr. Hallandall" [i.e., Pieter Hellendaal, the elder].

An undated libretto, which it is difficult to place within a few years, was sold in London in 1939 as: "Evidently the First Edition of the Libretto as originally performed at Canons in 1720 or 1721". The work was acquired by the present writer, but on examination proved to be wrongly described as a "First Edition". It is an octavo, unfortunately without imprint. The title reads:

> Acis and Galatea. A Masque. Set to Music by Mr Handel.

On the verso of the title-page are the Dramatis Personæ, then follow pp. 3–12 of text, which is divided into two parts the first part concluding with the chorus "Happy we", set out in full. The text has a number of variations in words and spelling as compared with the original manuscript, the first printed score (1743) and the libretto for Arne's production in 1732. The most interesting feature about it is, however, the Dramatis Personæ, given as:

> Galatea.
> Damon.
> Acis and Galatea.
> Corydon.
> Polypheme and Acis.

It will be remembered that "Coridon" appeared as a new character in the Rochetti production of 1731, which has been described above. This libretto, however, cannot be considered as belonging to that performance, owing to the inclusion of the chorus "Happy we", and a printed variation in the text ("The Woods the Turtle-Dove", instead of "The Floods") which was made in manuscript in some copies of the first complete score (1743), but occurs in dated libretti from 1747 onwards. Moreover Rochetti's production was announced as a "Pastoral". Here it is described as a "Masque". It has yet to be proved beyond all question that the chorus "Happy we" was not used before 1739 and that Handel had nothing to do with the Rochetti production. From the available evidence it is not unreasonable to date this libretto with the Corydon part as 1750 or much later, and it may be similar to a work in the Bodleian Library, Oxford, with a manuscript note on it—"Theatre Wedn.: July 6th, 1774."

A libretto was issued for a performance at the "Musick Room in Oxford" probably 1754 or later, which is almost an exact copy of the one just described, including Corydon in the Dramatis Personæ.

Fuller details are as follows:

> The Masque of Acis and Galatea. As it is Performed At the Musick Room in Oxford.

The title-page, without imprint is followed by Dramatis Personæ:

> Galatea.
> Damon.
> Acis and Galatea.
> Corydon.
> Polypheme and Acis.

The text (pp. 3–12) is the same as that in the edition previously described, including Corydon's air, "Would you gain the tender creature", pp. 9–12 being paginated and set up almost exactly as in the earlier work. The actual date of this issue cannot be determined. The Music Room in Oxford was opened in 1748, and the earliest recorded performance there of *Acis and Galatea* was in May, 1754, so that the libretto must be dated 1754 or later. Probably it is the same work as that listed later on and dated c. 1769.

The appearance of "Corydon" in such late productions hitherto unrecorded, again raises the question of the first introduction of this character in 1731 and whether Handel was responsible for the change.

Fifteen performances at The Oxford Music Room are recorded by John H. Mee from 1754 onwards as follows: May 13, 1754; June 23, 1755; May 24, 1756; February 21, 1757;

November 28, 1757; June 12, 1758; October 29, 1759; July 1, 1762; May 6, 1765; April 21, 1766; July 2, 1767; June 23, 1769; November 18, 1771; May 10, 1773; June 13, 1782.

No copy of the 1755 Castle Society libretto has been examined, but the recorded details are as follows:

> Acis and Galatea. A Serenata as performed at the Castle Society at Haberdashers' Hall, 1755.

The next libretto to be noticed is dated 1756. (British Museum, 1344.m.33.) It is similar in contents and arrangement to the Castle edition of 1747. (British Museum, 11775.e.3.(1.)) The title-page reads:

> Acis and Galatea. A Serenata. The music by Mr. Handel. London: Printed in the Year MDCCLVI.

It is an octavo of eight leaves paginated 4–7, 9–15.

While this survey does not pretend to list the many provincial performances of *Acis and Galatea*, it is worth noting as pointed out by Reginald Wright in "Musical Opinion", August, 1935, that five performances of the work in Bath were advertised in the seven years from 1756 onwards.

The first performance of *Acis and Galatea* at Cambridge was given on February 26, 1756, as recorded by *The Norwich Mercury*, February 28:

> Cambridge, Feb. 26. On Thursday night the Mask of "Acis and Galatea" was performed at Trinity Coll: Hall before a very numerous audience and was conducted by Dr. Randall, Professor of Music in this University.

Dr. Deutsch (*Cambridge Review*, January 17, April 25, 1942) points out that this was the first and only performance of a Handel work at Cambridge before the composer's death. Besides other Cambridge Senate House performances, mentioned below, Deutsch records one on July 1, 1769, and one on July 2, 1772.

The title-page of another libretto, printed in 1756 reads as follows:

> [The] Words of the Pastoral: or, the Masque of Acis and Galatea. [Ornament.] Printed in the Year MDCCLVI.

It is an octavo of five leaves, paginated 4–9.

The only known copy (in the possession of the writer) has unfortunately been cropped, and the word "The" is assumed to have been cut off. (See similar title, 1745.) The work differs from other issues in one or two respects. It is differently set up in the Trio marked "Andante" (The flocks shall leave the mountains) and in the Chorus (Cease Galatea). The Dramatis Personæ are given as "Galatea, Acis, Damon, Clori, Polypheme. Shepherds and nymphs attending." Clori has Damon's air, "Would you gain the tender creature". The work is divided into two parts, opening with a "Symphony", with the Chorus, "Happy, happy, happy, etc.", at the end of Part I, and no concerto before Part II. The text is generally similar to that of the 1756 edition (B.M.1344.m.33.) except for "Prop of my portly" instead of "God-like steps"; "The Floods the Turtle-Dove" instead of "The Woods", etc. It may have been a provincial issue, specially printed for a particular performance, perhaps in connection with some church choir, in view of the change of "God-like" to "portly" steps.

A libretto (British Museum, 1344.m.34.) of an unidentified performance in 1757 has the following title-page:

> Acis and Galatea. A Serenata. As Perform'd at the New Theatre in the Hay-Market. The Music by Mr. Handel. London: Printed for John Watts, 1757.

It is an octavo of eleven leaves, paginated 6–10, 12–21.

The work is in two parts mainly set up from Watts's edition of 1747 (British Museum 11775.e.3.(1.)), but the notice "A Concerto on the Organ" is omitted. This libretto may have been issued in connection with the performance announced for May 2, 1757, as follows:

> For the Benefit of Mr. Jonathan Snow. At the New Theatre in the Haymarket This Day will be performed a Masque, called Acis and Galatea. By Mr. Handel. With a Solo on the Violin by Mr. Hayes. Concerto on the Hautboy by Mr. Thomas Vincent. Concerto on the

Bassoon by Mr. Miller. Concerto on the Harpsichord by Mr. Snow . . . Printed Books of the Masque—Sixpence each.

Jonathan Snow was probably the composer and one time organist of St. John's, Oxford. He published some Variations for the Harpsichord on a Minuet of Corelli and the Gavotte from Handel's *Ottone*.

Acis and Galatea was frequently in demand as the attraction in some benefit or charity performance, but surely one of the strangest reasons for which it was billed was that given in the announcement of June 9, 1757:

> Ranelagh-House. For the Benefit of the Marine Society, towards cloathing Men and Boys for the Sea to go on Board his Majesty's Ships, This Day will be performed Acis and Galatea. Compos'd by Mr. Handel; the Performance to be conducted by Mr. Stanley, in which he will play a Concerto on the Organ. . . . After the first Act, a Number of fine Boys, cloathed by the Society, will appear on the Walks at Ranelagh, in (sic) their Way to Portsmouth.

On August 13, 1759, Beard chose *Acis and Galatea* for his benefit performance at the Long Room, Hampstead. The cast also included Signora Frasi, Miss Young (presumably Waltz's pupil) and Mr. Champness. The performance included a "Concerto on the Harpsichord by Mr. Stanley and a Solo on the Violin by Mr. Hay."

Acis and Galatea was performed at Bury St. Edmunds in September, 1760, as one item in a Handel festival, no copy of the libretto being available.

The libretto of *Acis and Galatea* was included in "The Words of such Pieces as are most usually performed by the Academy of Ancient Music", first edition 1761, second edition 1768. No copy of the first edition has been available for examination, but the 1768 edition is referred to in detail later on.

An edition of the libretto was published in 1762, with the following title-page:

> Acis and Galatea, A Serenata; As it is Performed at the Theatre-Royal in Covent-Garden. The Musick com-

242

posed by Mr. Handel. [Ornament.] London: Printed
for J. Watts: and sold by B. Dod at the Bible and Key in
Ave-Mary-Lane near Stationers-Hall; and the Book-
sellers of London and Westminster, 1762. [Price One
Shilling.]

The work is a quarto, in three parts, eight leaves, paginated,
4-7, 9-11, 13-15, and contains two new airs, "O do not shepherd"
(p. 5) and "In vain you teach" (p.11), added for a new character "Chloris". This is the first recorded notice of the appearance of this additional character in the English version of *Acis
and Galatea*; although, as already pointed out, a character of
this name or "Clori" appeared in Handel's Italian English
version of 1732, and in editions of the music from 1743 onwards, but with different arias to those mentioned here. The
text of the new airs is given below with the description of the
1764 edition of the work (British Museum, 7897.g.26.(1.))
from which some of the details of the 1762 edition have been
taken, and may be open to correction.

The only performance noted in 1762 was announced for
February 12 as:

> For the Benefit of Mr. Robinson at Hickford's Great
> Room in Brewer street . . . the Pastoral Oratorio of
> Acis and Galatea. Acis, by Mr. Hudson, Galatea, by
> Miss Carter (Mrs. Pooke, late Mrs. Robinson not being
> quite well of a Cold) Polypheme, by Mr. Cox.

Acis and Galatea was given for the benefit of Miss Fromentel
at the Great Room, Dean Street, Soho, on February 4, 1763.

A libretto was advertised (*Public Advertiser*) on March 15,
1763, as "Printed for J. Watts; and sold by B. Dod, at the Bible
and Key in Ave-mary-lane", etc. This issue was for the performance on March 16, 1763, when the work was given at the
Theatre Royal, Covent Garden, with a Concerto on the Organ
by Mr. Stanley and a Solo on the Violin by Mr. Hay.

The title-page of a 1764 libretto (British Museum,
7897.g.26.(1.)) reads:

> Acis and Galatea, A Serenata; As it is Performed at the
> Theatre-Royal in Covent Garden. The Musick com-

posed by Mr. Handel. [Ornament.] London: Printed
for the Administrator of J. Watts; and sold by B. Dod and
Company . . . G. Woodfall . . . and S. Hooper . . .
1764. [Price One Shilling.]

It is a quarto of eight leaves, paginated 4–7, 9–11, 13–15.
The Dramatis Personæ are given as:

> Acis.
> Galatea.
> Polyphemus.
> Damon.
> Chloris.
> Chorus of Nymphs and Shepherds.

The part for Chloris is an addition to Handel's original
English libretto as referred to under the 1762 edition. The
work is in three parts: Part I, finishing with the Chorus "Happy
we" (not given in full) Part II opening with "A Concerto on
the Organ" and finishing with "Love sound th' alarm". The
text generally follows the 1747 Watts edition (British Museum,
11775.e.3.(1.)), but with the following important alterations
and additions: After "Shepherd, what art thou pursuing" is
inserted an Air for Chloris:

> O! do not, Shepherd, thus advising,
>   The Lover's pleasing Pains repress;
> The Lover, Passion justly prizing,
>   Secures what only Life can bless.
>
> With Pride the Lover boasts a Treasure,
>   In ev'ry Care his Heart conceals,
> And Tears, for him, have sweeter Pleasure,
>   Than Mirth in thoughtless Laughter feels.

The next recitative is altered to "And see my Love".
After the air, "Would you gain the tender creature", given
to Damon, is inserted another Air for Chloris:

244

> In vain you teach him Duty,
>   To Beauty,
>   His Love is but Desire.
> He gains, the Fair possessing,
> Not half the Lover's Blessing,
>   Not half so pure his Fire.

The origin of the words and music of these airs is not known, nor why they were introduced. In the Museum copy the two airs have been crossed out in pencil. They were omitted from some editions of the libretto about 1770, but were inserted again in performances from 1783 to 1787, and then appear to have been finally dropped.

Copies of the 1764 edition with the Chloris Airs, exist with "A Song for St. Cecilia's Day" ("From Harmony", 4 pp.) at the end.

For a performance by the Castle Society in 1764 a libretto was issued with title as follows:

> Acis and Galatea. A Serenade as it is performed by the Castle Society at Haberdashers' Hall London. 1764.

On November 13, 1764, a performance was given at the Little Theatre, Haymarket, "for the benefit of the widow and distressed family of Mr. Lambe who was unfortunately killed at the late fire near Wardour-street, Soho". The programme was announced as:

> Masque called Acis and Galatea. Composed by the late Mr. Handel. The principal Vocal Parts by Mr. Vernon, Mr. Champness, Miss Carter and Mrs. Vincent. Between the Acts will be performed a Solo on the Violoncello by Signor Chiri. A Concerto on the Bassoon by Mr. Baumgarten. A Concerto on the Hautboy by Mr. Simpson. And a Solo on the Violin by Mr. Hay, who will lead the Performance. To conclude with the Coronation Anthem.

On February 20, 1766, *Acis and Galatea* was given at Covent Garden with the "Ode written by Mr. Dryden" and a "Concerto on the Organ by Mr. Stanley". The libretto of *Acis and Galatea*, together with the "Ode" was advertised the same day

(Price 1s.) by S. Hooper and G. Woodfall, who listed *Acis and Galatea* again on March 5.

Another performance at Covent Garden, including the "Ode" and "Concerto" by Mr. Stanley, was advertised for March 27, 1767, when S. Hooper also announced another edition of the libretto as "Price One Shilling. *Acis and Galatea* A Serenata", etc.

No copies of the libretti for 1766 and 1767 are available.

Reference has been made to the 1761 and 1768 editions of "The Words of such Pieces as are most usually performed by the Academy of Ancient Music." The version of *Acis and Galatea* given in the 1768 edition (printed by J. Dixwell, London) has the ordinary text and characters, without the additional airs, but with "Consider fond shepherd", given to Cloris.

Another edition of the 1764 version of the libretto (British Museum, 7897.g.26.(1.)) was made in 1768. The title-page reads:

> Acis and Galatea, A Serenata; As it is performed, at the Theatre-Royal in Covent-Garden. Set to Musick by Mr. Handel. London: Printed for the Executors of J. Watts, and sold by T. Lowndes, in Fleet-Street. 1768. [Price One Shilling.]

It is a quarto, eight leaves, paginated 4–7, 9–11, 13–15.

The work is in three parts, and contains the airs for Chloris, and "A Concerto on the Organ" at the opening of Part II. The British Museum has two copies of this libretto, 11630.d.4.(15.) and 162.m.26. In the first of these *Acis and Galatea* is followed by "A Song for St. Cecilia's Day" unpaginated, but apparently intended to be performed after *Acis and Galatea*. In the other Museum copy, the first air for Chloris is marked in pencil "additional Song now omitted", and her second air "additional Song omitted".

A copy of this libretto with the "Song for St. Cecilia's Day" has been wrongly recorded as having "Kings Theatre in Covent Garden" on the title-page.

Another issue similar to the 1768 edition in contents, size and pagination, including the Chloris Airs, but differently set up, with different ornament on p. 15, with and without the *Song for*

St. Cecilia's Day, and undated, was also "Printed for the Executors of J. Watts, and sold by T. Lowndes."

Another issue of the libretto of 1768, in three parts, and with the airs for Chloris may have been published about 1770.

References in catalogues to libretti of this period are confusing, consequently in the absence of copies for examination some general and uncertain statements have been omitted from the descriptions given in this list, some details may need correction, and no doubt a number of issues have escaped notice.

MUSIC. Edition, No. 7. [1768–69.]

Messrs. Randall and Abell succeeded Walsh in 1766 and continued to advertise Walsh works and to issue some of them without alteration and with the Walsh title-pages. *Acis and Galatea* was one of the complete works advertised on the Full Score of *Messiah* in 1767. Abell died in 1768, and William Randall continued the business alone. Some time in 1768–69 he issued an edition of *Acis and Galatea* mentioned in an advertisement in *The Public Advertiser*, April 26, 1769. This advertisement may have referred to stock copies of Walsh issues unaltered in any way, or to Walsh copies modified by the substitution of Randall's title-page. It is quite clear that Randall sold Walsh editions of other Handel works, and one copy at least of *Acis and Galatea* has been examined that appeared to be the 1743 Walsh issue except for a substituted Randall title-page. It is reasonable, however, to suppose that the advertisement of April 26, 1769, referred to a new issue, described here as No. 7, a copy of which is in the possession of the present writer.

It is largely a reprint (with alterations) of Walsh's edition of 1743, with the same title-page (*Acis and Galatea A Mask*, etc.) except for the imprint, which is: "London. Printed for W. Randall. Succesor to the late Mr. Walsh in Catharine Street, Strand."

The work consists of title-page, verso blank, the next leaf containing a new Index (including the recitatives) in double columns, the verso of which is blank, then follow pp. 1–89 (verso blank) of music from the earlier plates, except pp. 8, 15, 40, 41, 64, 74 and 76, which are from newly engraved plates. One interesting addition is on p. 36, where "End of the first

Part" has been added after the conclusion of the chorus "Happy we". The uncertainty as to the reason for the division of the work into two parts has already been mentioned. The division was evidently generally accepted by 1769, even if it was in doubt earlier.

This edition, copies of which are extremely rare, was advertised by Randall in his list of works as "On small paper. 10s. 6d," while he advertised his next issue (No. 8) as "On Imperial paper. 12s. 0d."

MUSIC. Edition, No. 8. [1769.]

On November 4, 1769, Randall advertised in *The Public Advertiser* :

> A new Edition of the following complete Scores of Mr. Handel's Works, printed on Imperial Paper, viz. Samson, Alexander's Feast, Acis and Galatea, &c.

This edition of *Acis and Galatea* was a reprint of Randall's previous issue (Edition, No. 7) but on larger and better paper, and with the well known Houbraken portrait of Handel as frontispiece. The detail of this edition is as follows: Frontispiece, Houbraken. Title-page as in the previous Randall issue, adapted from the 1743 Walsh edition, the verso of title-page blank, then follow Index and pp. 1–89 (verso blank) of music as in Edition, No. 7. The only differences between the two Randall issues are in the size and quality of paper, and the Houbraken frontispiece. The earlier work is approximately of the same size as the Walsh score, similar to other Walsh editions of Handel. The later work is a large folio on thicker paper like that of the majority of Randall's publications. Existing copies show the Houbraken frontispiece in different states, as the plate was worked over from time to time. Some copies therefore may be much later than others.

The titles and abbreviated notices of performances from current advertisements recorded by date that follow, although not complete, show how popular *Acis and Galatea* was, and the names of the singers etc., will probably help to identify some hitherto unplaced libretti.

248

> The Masque of Acis and Galatea as it is performed at the
> Musick Room in Oxford. (1769?)

This is the recorded title of a libretto, no copy of which is available. It may be the same work as that described earlier and dated 1754 or after.

> Acis and Galatea, A Serenata. The Music composed by
> Mr. Handel. [Ornament.] London: Printed for the
> Executors of J. Watts, and sold by T. Lowndes in Fleet-
> Street. [Price One Shilling.] [1770?]

This is a quarto, six leaves, paginated 4–6, 8–12. (British Museum, 1344.n.33.) Although this issue gives "Chloris" in the Dramatis Personæ her airs are omitted from the text, which is a reversion to the 1747 Watts edition, except that it has the recitative "And see, my love" instead of "Lo here, my Love". It is in two parts, with "A Concerto on the Organ". Copies were apparently also issued with *A Song for St. Cecilia's Day.*

A later issue of the preceding, with the same title but differently set up, and with slight variations in the printing of the text, is in the British Museum. (T.657.(14.) It has bound up with it a single unpaginated leaf headed: "Music of Bonduca. Purcell."

This libretto dated [1770?] in the British Museum catalogue, is probably later, and may have been issued in connection with a performance of *Acis and Galatea* with the music in *Bonduca* on February 18, 1780.

March 18, 1772. Theatre Royal, Drury Lane. *Acis and Galatea.* To which will be added an Ode written by Dryden. Music by Handel. End of the First Part a Concerto on the French Horn by Mr. Ponta. End of the 2d Act, a Solo on the Violoncello by Mr. Janson.

A similar performance was given on April 3, 1772, but without the Concerto on the French Horn.

A libretto is recorded with the following title:

> Acis and Galatea as it is performed at Mary-le-bone
> Gardens. Printed in the year, 1773.

No copy is available, but the reference is to one of the issues made in connection with the subscription concerts given at the Marylebone Gardens in May and June, 1773. This series of miscellaneous concerts and entertainments included fireworks and other novelties. Barthelemon led a "Select Band" on subscription evenings. The announcement for the first night of the subscription (May 27) was:

> A Concert. The Vocal Parts by Mr. Bannister, Mrs. Thompson, a young Lady (being her 2d Appearance in public) and Mrs. Barthelemon. Concerto Organ, Mr. Hook. Solo Violin, Mr. Barthelemon. After which will be sung an Entertainment of Music, in a manner entirely new, called Acis and Galatea. The music by Mr. Handel. The principal Vocal Parts by Mr. Reinhold, Mrs. Thompson, a young lady, Mrs. Barthelemon, and a Number of the best Chorus Singers. With new Decorations and Dresses. Horns and Clarinets will perform in the Orchestra after the Concert is over. Admittance Two Shillings and Sixpence. Books of the Performance may be had at the Bar.

Mrs. Barthelemon was formerly Miss Mary Young.

Similar performances took place on May 29, June 3 and 10, but with "Miss Wilde" given in the lists instead of "a young Lady". On June 4 the programme was announced as the "Original Coronation Anthems. Composed by Mr. Handel. *Acis and Galatea* will also be performed". The singers were as before, the concert beginning at half-past six, but the Anthems "punctually at Half past Eight".

Further changes were made in programmes on June 17, 24 and 26, when the principal parts in *Acis and Galatea* were taken by the same singers as previously but "before the Serenata (by particular Desire) the Three Italian Musicians, Blind from their Birth, will perform a Comic Act".

This 1773 series of performances of *Acis and Galatea* is of particular interest in the story of the work and one can imagine that it must have been well received to retain its place in the bills of such miscellaneous entertainments.

Reference has been made previously to a libretto (c. 1754 or later) a copy of which in the Bodleian Library has a manuscript note: "Theatre Wedn.: July 6th, 1774."

A Norwich issue of the libretto in 1774 has the following title:

> Acis and Galatea: An Oratorio. As it is performed at the
> Theatre Royal in Covent Garden. Set to Music by Mr.
> Handel. Norwich: Printed by R. Beatniffe, in the
> Cockey-Lane. 1774. [Price Sixpence.]

It is an octavo of eight leaves, paginated 4–14.

April 5, 1775. Theatre Royal, Drury Lane. *Acis and Galatea*,
composed by Handel, and Dryden's Ode. End of First Part,
a Concerto on the Hautboy by Mr. Vincent. End of the
Second Part, a Concerto on the Violin by Mr. Barthelemon.

On June 29, 1775, a performance of *Acis and Galatea* was
given at the Cambridge Senate House, for the benefit of Addenbrooke's Hospital.

A libretto was published at Oxford, c. 1775, with the title:

> The Masque of Acis and Galatea. As it is Performed.
> At the Theatre in Oxford.

It is a quarto, paginated 3–12.

A rare provincial issue of the work is recorded (W. Reeves,
Cat. 36/1912) as:

> Acis and Galatea. Word Book of the Masque. 16 pp.,
> 8vo. Salisbury. Collins & Johnson, on the Canal, about
> 1760.

The date is probably 1775 or after.

Selections from *Acis and Galatea* frequently appeared in programmes of the "Concerts of Ancient Music", London,
(1776–1848), but it is unnecessary to give details here.

February 23, 1776. Theatre Royal, Drury Lane. *Acis and
Galatea* with an Ode by Dryden, music by Handel. With a
Concerto on the Organ by Mr. Stanley.

March 8, 1776. Theatre Royal, Drury Lane. *Acis and Galatea*
with an Ode by Dryden, music by Handel. Principal vocal
parts by Miss Linley, Miss M. Linley, Miss Draper, Mr. Norris
and Mr. Reinhold. End of the First Part, a Concerto on the
Organ by Mr. Stanley. End of the Second Part, a Concerto
on the Violin by Mr. Linley, Jun.

February 28, 1777. Theatre Royal, Drury Lane. *Acis and Galatea* with Dryden's Ode, music by Handel. Principal vocal parts by Miss Linley, Miss M. Linley, Miss Draper, Mr. Norris, Mr. Champness and Mr. Edwards. End of the First Part, a Concerto on the Organ by Mr. Stanley. End of the Second Part, a Concerto on the Violin by Mr. Linley, Jun.

March 14, 1777. Theatre Royal, Drury Lane. *Acis and Galatea* and the Coronation Anthems. Principal vocal parts by Miss Linley, Miss M. Linley, Miss Draper, Mr. Norris, Mr. Champness and Mr. Edwards. End of the First Part, a Concerto on the Organ by Mr. Stanley. End of the Second Part, a Concerto on the Violin by Mr. Linley, Jun.

March 19, 1777. Theatre Royal, Covent Garden. An Oratorio, *Acis and Galatea*, music by Handel. In Act I a Song by Mrs. Farrell, new composed by Dr. Arne. With a Solo on the Violoncello by Mr. Cervetto and a Concerto on the Violin by Mr. Lamotte. After which will be a Miscellaneous Concert. Song, Mr. Saville (composed by Dr. Arnold). Song, Mr. Reinhold (composed by Signor Giordani). Song, Mrs. Farrel (composed by Dr. Arne). Song Mr. Tenducci; Song, Miss Harrop. With a Violin Obligato, accompanied by Mr. Lamotte. The music entirely new composed by Signor Sacchini. To conclude with, The Coronation Anthem, "My Heart is inditing, etc."

March 21, 1777. Theatre Royal, Covent Garden. An Oratorio, *Acis and Galatea*, music by Handel. In Act I a Song by Mrs. Farrell, new composed by Dr. Arne. With a Solo on the Violoncello by Mr. Cervetto and a Concerto on the Violin by Mr. Lamotte. After which will be a Miscellaneous Concert. Song, Mr. Saville. Song, Miss Storace. Song, Mr. Reinhold (composed by Signor Giordani). Song, Mrs. Farrel (composed by Dr. Arne). Song, Mr. Tenducci. Song, Miss Harrop. With a Violin Obligato accompanied by Mr. Lamotte. The music entirely new composed by Signor Sacchini. To conclude with the Coronation Anthem "Zodoch [*sic*] the Priest".

March 6, 1778. Two performances were given on the same day: Theatre Royal, Drury Lane. *Acis and Galatea* with Dryden's Ode. Principal vocal parts by Miss Linley, Miss M. Linley, Mrs. Farrell, Miss Draper, Mr. Norris and Mr. Webster. The First Violin by Mr. Linley, Jun. End of the First Part, a Concerto on the Organ by Mr. Stanley. End of the Second

Part, a Concerto on the Violin. As there are very few Songs in *Acis and Galatea* that can be adapted for Mrs. Farrell's voice, she will sing a Cantata between the Acts.

The prices for this performance were Pit, 5s. First Gallery, 3s. 6d. Second Gallery, 2s.

The prices for the other performance given at the Theatre Royal, Covent Garden, on the same day, were Boxes, 10s. 6d. Pit, 4s. First Gallery, 3s. and the other advertised particulars were: *Acis and Galatea*, composed by Handel. Principal vocal parts by Mr. Vernon, Mr. Meredith, Mrs. Wrighten and Mrs. Weichsel. First Violin Mr. Baumgerten [*sic*]. End of the First Part, a Concerto on the German Flute by Mr. Florio. Part the Third, a Concerto on the Piano Forte by Miss Weichsel, Concerto on the Hautboy by Mons. Le Brun, Concerto on the Violin by Master Weichsel. After which will be performed a select Collection of Sacred Canons, by the most eminent ancient and modern Composers. To conclude with the celebrated Canon of "Non nobis Domine".

Interesting features of these announcements of March 6, 1778, are the naming of the "First Violin", (which was sometimes done previously), the Concerto on the "Piano Forte" and the Canon "Non nobis Domine" which was doubtless the one usually attributed to William Byrd.

April 3, 1778. Theatre Royal, Covent Garden. *Acis and Galatea*, music by Handel. Principal vocal parts by Mr. Vernon, Mr. Meredith, Mrs. Wrighten and Mrs. Weichsel. First Violin Mr. Baumgerten. End of the First Part a Concerto on the Violin by Master Weichsel. Part the Third, Miscellaneous. Concerto on the German Flute, Mr. Florio. A favourite Hunting Song by Mrs. Wrighten. A Duetto for the Violin and Tenor by Master Weichsel and Mr. Stamitz. A favourite Song by Mrs. Weichsel. To conclude with a Concerto on the Piano Forte by Miss Weichsel.

For a performance at Newcastle, a libretto was published with title:

> Acis and Galatea, a Serenata. As it will be performed at the Assembly Rooms, in Newcastle, on Thursday evening the 8th of October, 1778. Conducted by Mr. Hawdon. The Music composed by Mr. Handel. Newcastle: Printed in the Year MDCCLXXVIII. [Price Six-Pence.]

It is a quarto of six leaves, with the names of the singers given with the text, and including the words of the Coronation Anthem, "Zadock the Priest" and between the Acts, "An Organ Concerto, by Mr. Hawdon."

February 26, 1779. Theatre Royal Drury Lane. *Acis and Galatea*, composed by Handel. Principal vocal parts by Miss M. Linley, Miss Draper, Miss Wright (being her third appearance in public), Mrs. Kennedy (late Mrs. Farrell), Mr. Norris and Mr. Webster. First Violin Mr. Richards. End of the First Part a Cantata by Mrs. Kennedy. End of the Second Part a Solo on the Violoncello by Mr. Cervetto. The Third Part will consist of Songs, Chorusses etc., selected from the Works of the late Henry Purcell.

March 3, 1779. A similar performance to that mentioned on February 26 except for the changes: "End of the First Part, a Concerto on the Organ by Mr. Stanley. End of the Second Part a Song by Mrs. Kennedy."

March 19, 1779. Theatre Royal, Hay Market. At Play-House Prices. *Acis and Galatea*. Vocal parts by Mr. Vernon, Mr. Champness, Mrs. Wrighten and Mrs. Barthelemon. End of Act I a Trumpet Concerto, Mr. Serjeant. End of *Acis and Galatea* a Concerto on the Violin by Mr. Barthelemon. To which will be added Victory, an Ode, inscribed to Admiral Keppel. Music principally composed by Mr. Barthelemon, with Grand Chorusses.

December 10, 1779:

> For the Benefit of a Family in great Distress. At Free-Masons Hall in Great Queen Street . . . Acis and Galatea, an Oratorio By the late Mr. Handel. Principal Vocal Parts by Mess. Vernon and Champness, Mrs. Wrighten and Mrs. Weichsel. To conclude with Handel's Grand Coronation Anthem . . . The Orchestra (in which will be upwards of a Hundred of the most capital Performers) will be led by Mr. Stamitz, who with Master Weichsel, will play a Duet on the Tenor and Violin. After which will be a Ball &c.

Rarely in these early records do we get any indication of the size of the orchestra, and the reference above is therefore of particular interest.

February 18, 1780. Theatre Royal, Drury Lane. *Acis and Galatea*. To which will be added the music in *Bonduca*, etc., by the late Henry Purcell. Principal vocal parts by Miss M. Linley, Miss Draper, Mrs. Wrighten, Mr. Norris and Mr. Webster. First Violin by Mr. Richards. End of the First Part, a Concerto on the Organ by Mr. Stanley. End of the Second Part, a Concerto on the Violin by Mr. Cramer, etc.

A libretto that may have been issued for this performance has been referred to earlier (c. 1770).

March 3, 1780. Theatre Royal, Drury Lane. A similar announcement to that of February 18, 1780, but with a Concerto on the Violin by Mr. Cramer at the end of the First Part, and a Concerto on the Organ by Mr. Stanley at the end of the Second Part.

A libretto was issued with title as follows:

> Acis and Galatea. A Serenata. As Performed at the Theatre Royal, Drury-Lane. The Music by Handel. [Ornament.] London, Printed for J. Barker, near the Pit Door, Russel-Court, Drury-Lane. [Price Six-Pence.] Where may be had all Oratorios, Plays, &c.

It is an octavo, eight leaves, paginated 4–7, 9–15, followed by a single leaf with the text of the "Coronation Anthem. Composed by Mr. Handel." (British Museum, 11775.e.2.(2.)) [1781?] The text is almost exactly the same as the 1747 Watts edition, in two parts, except that it has "And see, my love" instead of "Lo here, my love". "Chloris" does not appear in the characters or text and there is no mention of a Concerto for the Organ. The Dramatis Personæ are given as "Acis, Galatea, Polypheme, Polyphemus, Damon, Nymphs, Shepherds, etc." From pencilled notes on the British Museum copy, the cast at some performance c. 1785 included Mr. Dignum (Acis), Mr. Reinhold (Polyphemus), Mrs. Crouch (Galatea), Miss George (Damon).

Another libretto has title as follows:

> Acis and Galatea, A Serenata; As it is performed at the Theatre-Royal in Drury-Lane. Set to Musick by Mr.

Handel. With the after-pieces, St. Cecilia's Day, Music of Bonduca, and Coronation Anthems. London: Printed by Assignment from the Heirs of Messrs. Tonson and Watts, for T. & W. Lowndes . . . MDCCLXXXIII. [Price Six-Pence.]

It is an octavo, twelve leaves, *Acis and Galatea*, paginated 4–8, 10–12, 14–16, the four following leaves with the text of the other works unpaginated. (The King's Music Library, R.M.5.d.19.(2.)) The text is practically as the 1764 edition. (British Museum, 7897.g.26.(1.)) The Dramatis Personæ include "Chloris". The work is in three parts, with the Airs for Chloris (the first slightly altered), and "A Concerto on the Organ at the opening of Part II. Part I finishes with the Chorus "Happy we", Part II with "Love sound th' alarm".

Charles Bannister announced on April 19, 1783, particulars of his benefit performance to be given at the New Theatre Royal, Covent Garden, on April 28, as "A Tragedy, Alexander the Great . . . After which will be performed (for the first time) *A Serenata called Acis and Galatea*, etc. The bill was subsequently changed to *The Beggar's Opera* and *The Flitch of Bacon*.

March 24, 1784. Theatre Royal, Drury Lane. *Acis and Galatea*. An Oratorio, music by Mr. Handel. To which will be added the Music in *Bonduca*. Composed by the late Mr. Henry Purcell. Principal vocal parts by Miss George, Mrs. Kennedy, Mr. Norris, and Mr. Reinhold. First Violin, Mr. Richards. End of the First Part, a Concerto on the Hautboy, by Mr. Parke.

July 1st, 1785. Senate House, Cambridge. For the Benefit of Addenbrooke's Hospital, *Acis and Galatea*. Principal vocal parts by Miss Harwood, Miss Abrams, Mr. Reinhold, Mr. Knyvett and Mr. Harrison. Principal instrumental by Messrs. Cramer, Cervetto, Mich. (i.e., Richard) Sharp, Gariboldi, etc. Assisted by a numerous and capital Band, to increase the effect of which, the Double Drums, made for the Commemoration of Handel, will be employed.

A libretto was issued for this performance by T. Hodson (or Hodson and Whynne).

Another libretto has title as follows:

256

> Acis and Galatea, A Serenata: As it is performed at the Theatre-Royal in Drury-Lane. Set to Music by Mr. Handel. [Ornament.] London: Printed for J. Bell . . . 1787. Price one shilling., &c.

It is an octavo, ten leaves, paginated 4–8, 10–16, 18, 19, with text similar to that of the 1783 edition (R.M.5.d.19.(2.)) including the "Chloris" airs, but in two parts, without the "Concerto on the Organ" At the end is "Part III, Miscellaneous", including instrumental and vocal items, concluding with the "Coronation Anthem", the singers named being Mrs Crouch, Miss George, Mr Dignum, Mr Reinhold and Madame Mara. A Violin Concerto was played by Mr. Shaw. This libretto was issued in connection with performances on March 7 and 9, 1787. (British Museum, 1344.m.35.)

MUSIC. Elizabeth Randall, Wright and Preston Editions

After the death of William Randall the publisher, probably early in January, 1776, the business was carried on by Elizabeth Randall his widow, who continued to stock and advertise the works issued by her predecessors, including

> Acis and Galatea compleat, with Chorusses, printed on imperial Paper 12s. 0d. On small Paper 10s. 6d. Songs only 4s. 0d.

These were presumably the Randall or Walsh editions which have already been described, as no copies have been traced with Elizabeth Randall in the imprint as publisher. Wright and Wilkinson succeeded Elizabeth Randall probably early in 1783, at the old address 13 Catharine Street, Strand, an address made famous in music publishing by the earlier Walsh and his partners and successors for over one hundred years. Wright & Wilkinson, afterwards Wright & Co. or H. Wright continued to advertise the earlier Handel works and added to them a number of large scores with the Houbraken portrait in keeping with the William Randall series. No copy of *Acis and Galatea* from Randall's plates with Wright's imprint is available, but such copies were probably issued perhaps with minor alterations.

On February, 10, 1787, Wright advertised (*The World*) complete scores of Handel's works "chiefly new editions; and it can be reasonably assumed that a new edition of *Acis and Galatea* was included in the new editions. No copy of this edition is available for examination, but from the re-issue of it by Preston and other sources the details can be reconstructed. The title-page, adapted from that used by Wright for *Joseph*, *Theodora*, etc., was presumably as follows:

> Acis and Galatea An Oratorio in Score, Composed by Mr. Handel London, Printed for H: Wright... (Successor to Mr: Walsh) in Catharine Street, in the Strand. Of whom may be had the following Oratorios in Score, complete with Chorusses. Messiah, etc.

Although the music was from entirely new plates, it was based on Randall's edition in contents, style and layout, and consisted of Houbraken frontispiece, title-page, verso blank, probably an index leaf, and with the music on pp. 1–89, followed by a blank page. Presumably Randall's plates were so worn or damaged that a re-engraving of the whole work except the title-page was necessary. One number at least of this edition was sold separately by Wright: (pp. 64–70) the trio, "The Flocks shall leave the Mountains", with Wright's imprint on p. 64 and "Price 1s."

In 1803 or a little later Wright went out of business and soon afterwards Thomas Preston, then of 97, Strand, acquired the existing stock of Wright's plates, and issued a number of re-prints and other editions of Handel's works, amongst them *Acis and Galatea*. Although this was after 1800, available details are given here as the volume was a re-issue of the new Wright edition, and included the Houbraken portrait, from a very much worked plate. The title-page was adapted from the Wright issue and is as follows:

> Acis and Galatea An Oratorio in Score, Composed by Mr. Handel Price £1 .. 1 .. 0. London. Printed & Sold by Preston, at his Wholesale Warehouses, 97 Strand. Of whom may be had the following Oratorios in Score, complete with Chorusses. Messiah, etc.

The work was paginated 1–89 similarly to the earlier issues. The plates of Preston's issue were sold in December, 1849, at the sale of Coventry and Hollier's stock, and were acquired by J. Alfred Novello, who in 1850 issued another reprint of *Acis and Galatea* from them, with the title-page altered to give a Walsh imprint, to support Novello's statement that the work was from the "Original Plates engraved by Mr. Walsh, and which were corrected by Mr. Handel himself". This was quite inaccurate, as the title-page and contents were from the Wright-Preston plates, although Novello did use some early Walsh plates in *Messiah*, *Judas Maccabæus* and the *Coronation Anthem* which he advertised at the same time, together with the *Dettingen Te Deum*, which was also from Wright or Preston plates, not Walsh. In Novello's reprint of *Acis and Galatea* each item in the work is numbered, which was not so in the earlier editions.

BLAND'S EDITION

About 1780–81 John Bland issued an edition of *Acis and Galatea* with the following title:

> The Overture and Songs in the Oratorio of Acis and Galatea, for the Harpsichord or Piano-Forte. (Price Three Shillings.) London: Printed for J. Bland, No. 45, Holborn, etc.

It was a folio, presumably made up from the Overture and a number of the *Songs* previously published separately, each number being headed with the title and the imprint, "Printed for J. Bland No. 45 Holborn", etc. John Bland, who was in business c. 1776–95, claimed to be the first music printer to publish singly the works of Handel and other celebrated composers.

HARRISON'S EDITIONS

The earliest issue of *Acis and Galatea* that was not a reprint or re-issue of Walsh or Randall's editions has been generally considered to be that of Dr. Arnold, published in 1788 as part of his collected edition of Handel's works (1787–97). It is clear, however, that besides the John Bland edition a little known but important edition published in 1784 by Harrison & Co. (James

Harrison) of 18, Paternoster Row, preceded the Arnold and was the first real rival issue to those of Walsh and Randall.

It was advertised by Harrison in March, 1784, (*Public Advertiser*) as "*Acis and Galatea*, with Dryden's Ode on St. Cecilia's Day, the Choruses in Score", and was issued as parts 8–11 of *The New Musical Magazine*, at 1s. 6d. a part, and the whole work for 6s., as against the Randall editions at 10s. 6d. and 12s.[1]

The complete volume, an oblong folio, has title-page as follows:

> Acis and Galatea, A Masque. Composed by M^r: Handel, For the Voice, Harpsichord, and Violin. London: Printed for Harrison & Co., N°. 18, Paternoster Row.

The *Acis and Galatea* portion of the work consists of title-page, verso blank, + blank, verso pp. 4–47, verso blank. *Dryden's Ode on St. Cecilia's Day* follows, without title-page, and consisting of blank, verso pp. 2–25, verso blank. The whole volume is numbered throughout at the bottom of the pages as parts 8–11, except on pp. 33 and 34 of *Acis and Galatea*. The Bass is figured. "Would you gain the tender creature" is given to Damon, "Consider fond shepherd" to Clori, and the chorus "Happy we" concludes the first part of *Acis and Galatea*.

A second issue (c. 1785) was made of the two works together as above, with a few differences in *Acis and Galatea*. This slightly later volume has p. 20 entirely re-engraved in five-lined staves instead of four-lined; extra figurings in places (pp. 25, 34 etc.); "T. S." [i.e., Tasto Solo] added to p. 34; "Chorus" added to p. 36, and the part number "9" added to pp. 33 and 34. The symphonies, appearing in small notes in the first issue, are omitted in some cases from the second.

With the various works of *The New Musical Magazine*, Harrison gave "valuable Letter-Press". This appears to refer to the libretto of the particular work. A number of these libretti are in the British Museum, catalogued separately, and not identified as belonging to the Harrison series. The details of the *Acis and Galatea* libretto are as follows:

Acis and Galatea. A Serenata.

---

[1] Fuller reference to Harrison's publication of Handel's works and to Arnold's association with Harrison is made in Chapter III.

It is an octavo, two leaves, paginated 2, 3, two columns of text on each page. (British Museum, 11770.g.2.(36.))   It has the Watts 1747 text generally, is in two parts, but with "And see, my love", instead of "Lo here, my love", and with "A Concerto on the Organ" at the beginning of Part II. Chloris is in the list of characters, but there is no part for her in the text. At the end is *A Song for St. Cecilia's Day.*

In 1786–87, Harrison & Co. issued another work in weekly parts at 1s. 6d. a part, entitled, *The Songs of Handel,* etc. The series consisted of the Overture and Songs of various oratorios, etc., each work with a separate title-page and pagination, the pages numbered at the bottom with the serial number of the part (1*, 2*, etc.). *Messiah* was the first work of the series, and it was prefaced by the general title to the first volume:

> Harrison's Edition, Corrected by D^r. Arnold.   The Songs of Handel.   Volume the First.   Containing all the Overtures, Airs, Duetts, &c. in The Messiah, Judas Maccabæus, Acis and Galatea . . .   For the Voice, Harpsichord, and Violin.   London: Printed for Harrison and C^o. N°. 18, Paternoster Row.   Published as the Act directs, May 27, 1786.

Acis and Galatea was issued as parts 6 and 7 of the series, the title-page reading:

> Harrisons Edition, Corrected by D^r: Arnold. The Overture and Songs in Acis and Galatea, A Masque. For the Voice, Harpsichord, and Violin.   Composed by M^r. Handel. London: Printed for Harrison & Co. N°. 18, Paternoster Row.

The volume is an oblong folio similar in style and size to the vocal scores of Harrison's *New Musical Magazine,* but it contains only the Overture, Songs, etc., with figured Bass. It consists of title-page, verso blank + blank + 4–27, verso blank + "Contents" page, verso blank, and with the serial numbers 6*, 7* at the bottom of the pages.

Harrison & Co., afterwards Harrison, Cluse & Co., also published *The Piano-Forte Magazine* [1797–1802], and in Volume 6 of that work issued an edition of *Acis and Galatea,* with the following title-page:

> The Overture, Songs, Duett, and Trio, in Acis & Galatea, a Masque. Composed by, G. F. Handel. London: Printed for Harrison, Cluse, & Cº. 78, Fleet Street.

The work is octavo in Pianoforte Score, with unfigured Bass, containing twenty-three numbers including the Overture. It is paginated 4–43, with title-page and "Dramatis Personæ" and "Contents" leaf, the characters being given as "Acis, Polypheme, Damon, Galatea", but "Cloris" is given "Consider fond shepherd" in the body of the work. It is divided into two parts on the "Contents" leaf, but it does not contain the chorus "Happy we". The bottom of the pages bear the numbers 88, 89, which indicate the serial parts of *The Piano-Forte Magazine*, and enable the work to be dated approximately c. 1798–99.

ARNOLD'S EDITION

The general details usually given about Arnold's collected issue of Handel's works are very often contradictory and inaccurate, but the series as a whole is not of concern at the moment only the volume of *Acis and Galatea*. This was issued in 1788, with title-page reading as follows:

> Acis and Galatea A Serenata Composed for the Duke of Chandois in the year 1720 By G. F. Handel.

The work is large folio and consists of title-page, verso blank, pages 3–102 of music, contents leaf page 103, verso blank.

The complete set of Handel's works was issued in parts, each part being numbered at the bottom of the pages. The enumeration in *Acis and Galatea* is 28, 29 and 30. The contents of the work are the same as in Randall, but differently laid out and engraved and with different figurings to the Bass. It is divided into two parts at the end of the Chorus "Happy we". Clori is given as the character instead of Damon for the number "Consider fond shepherd".

As Arnold advertised from time to time different editions of his collected series of Handel's works, some variations may be found in the later issues of *Acis and Galatea* belonging to the series.

An undated libretto (c. 1792) in the British Museum (1344.m.31) has title as follows:

> Theatre Royal, Drury-Lane. Fifth Night. Part I. A Grand Selection of Sacred Music. Part II. and III. The Favourite Serenata of Acis and Galatea. [Ornament.] London. Printed by C. Lowndes . . . (Price Six-Pence.)

The text is practically that of the 1747 Watts issue, in two parts. It is an octavo of nine leaves, paginated 4–6, 8–18, without the Chloris airs, and the singers were Mrs. Crouch, Mrs. Bland, Miss Leake, Kelly, Dignum, Meredith and Master Welsh. The characters are not given.

A performance in 1792 is recorded in the libretto (British Museum, 11777.b.7.(5.)):

> Acis and Galatea, A Masque and A Miscellaneous Act. As performed at The New Theatre, In Durham, On Thursday October the 17th, 1792. Printed by L. Pennington, Bookseller.

It is an octavo of eight leaves, paginated 2, 4, 6–10, 12. The text is practically the same as the Watts edition of 1747, in two parts, with no part for Chloris, and no Organ Concerto.

Corydon, the new character who first appeared in the cast in 1731, and in the preceding survey is last recorded in 1754 or may be 1769, remained as a memory as late as 1799, when the name appeared in the list of Dramatis Personæ in the two volume edition of Handel's libretti published by Heptinstall, London, although there is no part for Corydon in the text.

EDITIONS FOR FLUTE

Besides the vocal editions of *Acis and Galatea*, Walsh put out an edition for the Flute only, as he did in the case of a number of his operas.

The title-page reads:

> Acis and Galatea for a Flute containing the Songs and Symphonys Curiously Transpos'd and fitted to the Flute in a Compleat manner The whole fairly Engraven &

carefully Corected London Printed for & Sold by I:
Walsh Servant to his Majesty at the Harp & Hoboy in
Catherine Street in yᵉ Strand. & Inᵒ. & Ioseph Hare at
the Viol & Flute in Cornhill near the Royal Exchange.

The work issued in 1724 or early 1725 is an oblong octavo
volume, and consists of title-page, "A Table of the Song Tunes",
etc., and twenty-nine leaves of music, all printed on one side of
the paper only, paginated 1–24 at top outer corners and 25–29
at the top centres. The contents are ten named numbers from
Acis and Galatea, followed by ten opera airs, four from *Ottone*
(Handel), one from *Erminia* (G.B. Bononcini) and five from
Floridante (Handel).

There is no indication on the title-page of the inclusion of the
opera airs, and Walsh must have put them in just to make up
an average size volume, in keeping with the twenty-four or so
similar volumes of opera airs for the flute which he issued, and
not concerning himself with accuracy in the title-page.

Walsh also advertised in *The Daily Advertiser* on April 6, 1744,
*Handel's favourite Airs in Acis and Galatea, etc. set for a German
Flute and Bass*. This work was issued as Part III. of Vol. V.
of the first edition of the collection, *Sonatas, or Chamber Aires,
for a German Flute, Violin, or Harpsichord*, etc. Besides six
numbers from *Acis and Galatea*, the part contains five from
Esther (including "Tua bellezza", an additional song), and an
"Air by Mr. Handel in the Sacred Oratorio", i.e., "He was
despised" from *Messiah*.

EDITIONS OF THE OVERTURE

The Overture to *Acis and Galatea* was first published in the
collection "Six Overtures for Violins in all their Parts . . . the
2ᵈ Collection", by John Walsh and John and Joseph Hare,
about 1725.

The Harpsichord edition first appeared in 1730 in the
collection *Six Overtures fitted to the Harpsicord or Spinnet . . .
The Fourth Collection . . . Printed for and sold by I: Walsh . . .
and may be had of I: Hare, &c.*

Walsh and his successors also published many later editions
of these collections of Handel's "Overtures".

It has not been considered necessary to record in this review details of the numerous single sheet issues of separate items from *Acis and Galatea*, or of the excerpts that appeared in song books or in harpsichord and other instrumental collections of the eighteenth century, of which there were many.

Other details in the story of *Acis and Galatea* may be contained in sources not examined by, or available to, the present writer, but the account as it stands is a fairly comprehensive survey of the early performances, together with the particulars of the issues of the music and text, and much new matter.

A writer in 1740, referred to *Acis and Galatea* as an English work "which in every respect charms, to this day persons of all ranks and capacities". It is sufficient to add, that time has not robbed *Acis and Galatea* of its freshness; and admirers of Handel justly consider it as one of the most perfect expressions of his genius.

VIII

THE EARLIEST EDITIONS
OF THE *WATER MUSIC*

THE
EARLIEST
EDITIONS
OF THE
WATER MUSIC

The various attempts that have been made to discover the facts behind the popular story of the origin of the *Water Music* are known to all students of Handel's life; and consequently they are only referred to briefly here as an introduction to the almost equally perplexing problem of the publication of the music.

It is quite certain that royal water parties on the Thames were common enough during the eighteenth century. Records exist of a number not mentioned in the biographies of the composer, but only one seems without question to have been associated with Handel's music; that which took place on July 17, 1717. It is mentioned by various writers, but documented by Streatfeild and corroborated by the Friedrich Bonet report, discovered a few years ago, as described by Professor Wolfgang Michael in the *Zeitschrift für Musikwissenschaft*, August–September, 1922, and made accessible to English readers by Newman Flower.

This authenticated event, however, does not rule out the possibility that Handel may have provided the music for earlier or later water processions. We have no contemporary record of what the music actually included on the occasion of July, 1717. Bonet's report gives the players as fifty, and the instruments as "des trompettes, des cors de chasse, des haut bois, des bassons, des flutes allemandes, des flutes françaises à bec, des violons et des basses, mais sans voix".

Streatfeild's opinion seems to be sound. He says, "It is quite possible that the *Water Music* as we now know it was not all written for the same occasion. Its twenty-five numbers may very well represent Handel's share in numerous water-parties". The same writer, however, continues with an inaccuracy: "It should be remembered that the *Water Music* was not published until 1740."

In the following attempt to bring together hitherto unknown details of the publication of what has always been one of Handel's most popular instrumental works, it will be seen that what we know of the performance in 1717 is by no means the whole story. Even if the work was first produced then, it may have been much shorter in form than in the later versions of the Barrett Lennard manuscript copy (Fitzwilliam Museum), and the *Händel-Gesellschaft* edition. No advertisement of the publication of the work during the years 1715–17 has been traced.

The mysteries of production and publication would probably be solved if the autograph manuscript of the work could be traced. Handel must have been a fairly methodical person or he would not have left behind in one collection the original manuscripts of the great majority of his compositions, that are now in the King's Music Library, British Museum. Most of the missing works or portions of them are known in other collections in England and abroad, but the autograph of the *Water Music* seems in the main to be irrecoverably lost. One small portion in two movements is in the Manuscript Department of the British Museum. (Add. MSS. 30310.) Chrysander printed these two movements in Vol. 47 of the *Händel-Gesellschaft* edition as a "Concerto. F major". His remarks on the work are as follows: "This short concerto in two movements must have been written as early as about 1715. It properly belongs to this place (Vol. 47) because both of the movements were used in the Water Music. The autograph has been in the British Museum since 1877. In the printed catalogue of manuscripts acquired from 1876 to 1881 . . . this piece is described, not as a predecessor, but falsely as 'selections from the Water Music'. The name *Concerto* is chosen by me as the most suitable. In the autograph there is no title at all; and we can only gather from it that the music was written as an independent work."

To identify this Concerto see Letters I,J,K, of the Thematic catalogue, in which each movement of the *Water Music*, whether part of a set of movements or not, is given a separate letter or number.

In the Catalogue of Manuscript Music in the British Museum (Vol. III, 1909) the "Concerto" is described as follows:

> "Add. 30310. ff. 52–62. Paper; about 1715. Oblong folio . . . Two movements, the first unnamed, the second "Alla Hornpipe" for horns, oboes, bassoons and strings, in score by Handel. *Autograph* . . . The above date is deduced from the fact that the whole appears (arranged for different instruments) in the "Water Music", which was written in 1715 or 1716."

Among the Handel manuscripts in the Fitzwilliam Museum, Cambridge, is the fine collection of early copies, generally said to have been made by J. C. Smith, and formerly in the possession of H. Barrett Lennard. This collection includes a full score of the *Water Music*, undated, but doubtless made during Handel's lifetime and with his authority. It does not appear to have been known to Chrysander, but may have been used by Arnold, although there is no evidence to this effect. It consists of movements in the following order: Thematic catalogue, 1, 2, 3, A, B, C, D, E, 4, 5, 6, 7, 8, 9, 10, 11, F, G, I, J, K, 12, 13, L, M, A new number, N, O, P, Q, R, S, T, U, 14, 15, 16, 17, 18, 19, 20, 21. The contents and order are the same as in the Walsh harpsichord edition published c. 1743, with the exception of the new number between M and N, which does not appear to exist elsewhere. It is in two movements, very similar to passages in L and M, which precede it in the manuscript, but there is no evidence that the new movements were intended as alternatives to or variants of L and M.

It is impossible to give here the detail of the instrumentation of the numbers in the manuscript, which does not differ very substantially from the Arnold edition. It should be carefully studied in any attempt to reconstruct accurately the *Water Music* as

THEMATIC CATALOGUE OF THE FIRST EDITIONS FOR ORCHESTRA AND FOR THE HARPSICHORD

NOTE. *Each movement whether part of a set of movements or not, is given, for reference purposes, a separate letter (A-U) or number (1-21). Movements which occur in both editions are only indicated in the harpsichord catalogue by the respective letters of the edition for orchestra.*

Repeats are omitted from the catalogue, except the special note attached to "N", which is apparently intended in the original edition to apply to "O" as well. Some obvious mistakes in the original editions have been corrected.

INSTRUMENTAL PARTS

VIOLINO E HAUTBOY PRIMO

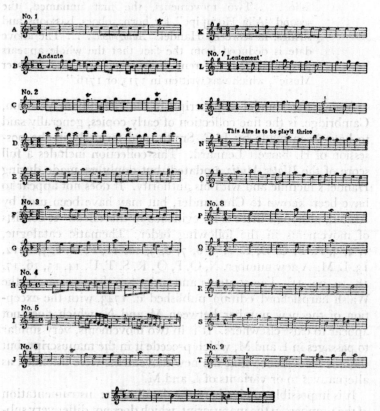

Note: The numbers 1-9, given above, occur in the first edition.

HARPSICHORD EDITION

a whole, since it is probably the earliest authority for the major part of the work. Obviously, Arnold made changes in the order of the pieces for some reason best known to himself. One point of interest is that the manuscript corroborates in part Arnold's use of "Flauti piccoli", which Chrysander criticizes but adopts. Bonet's list of instruments given above includes "des flutes françaises à bec", identified by Professor Michael as "Flauti piccoli", Rockstro mentions a piccolo, but that seems to be a misreading of "Flauto piccolo".

Neither the Barrett Lennard manuscript nor the harpsichord printed edition (which is the most complete of the Walsh editions) contain the item H, which fortunately occurs, however, in the Walsh instrumental parts, c. 1733.

One constantly perplexing difficulty encountered in dealing with early editions of Handel's works is the existence of a considerable number of miscellaneous collections of marches, minuets, pieces, and songs, issued by the publisher John Walsh and his contemporaries and containing various Handel items. It is impossible, in many cases to distinguish original publications from arrangements of works, or from excerpts taken out of works already in existence. Early in the story of the *Water Music* this problem is encountered. Movements issued in the larger editions of the work had appeared previously in other publications, and it is not known whether they were made popular by the *Water Music* and then used elsewhere, or were published as separate works of Handel and incorporated in the *Water Music* when the composer put it together for performance or publication.

Among the many interesting issues of Walsh is *The Lady's Banquet*, which appeared in six books from about 1704–35. This work contains lessons for the harpsichord or spinet selected from short movements of various composers. The first edition of the third book was advertised in *The Post Boy*, November 29–December 1, 1720, and contains two numbers used in the *Water Music* which may be the earliest issue of any part of the work. The first number (Thematic catalogue, Nos. 12 and 13) is described as "A Trumpet Minuet by Mr Hendell" and it is given in the Barrett Lennard manuscript for trumpets and violins the first time, for horns and oboes the second time, and for complete orchestra the third time.

The second item in *The Lady's Banquet* is entitled "A Minuet for the French Horn by Mr Hendell" and is given for horns, oboes, bassoons, strings, etc. in the Barrett Lennard manuscript. (Thematic catalogue, Nos. 6 and 7.)

No reference is made in *The Lady's Banquet* in either case to the *Water Music*, and as these numbers do not appear in Walsh's first edition of the orchestral parts of the work issued about 1733, but occur in the harpsichord edition c. 1743, they may not have been used in the earliest performances.

The second item from *The Lady's Banquet* must have been a very popular melody as it was used as a song tune to different sets of words as mentioned below, and described in these instances as "A Trumpet Minuet". It also appeared in

> The New Country Dancing Master 3^d. Book, being a choice Collection of Country Dances... The Tunes Airy and pleasant for the Violin or Hoboy, and most of them within the compass of the Flute. Price 2s. 6d. London. Printed for and sold by I. Walsh... and Ioseph Hare, &c.

This work was issued December 21, 1728, and the "Trumpet Minuet" is on p. 130, with a second pagination (10) indicating that it had previously appeared in some earlier collection.

On April 19, 1729, Walsh advertised a work which has the following title-page:

> A General Collection of Minuets made for the Balls at Court The Operas and Masquerades Consisting of Sixty in Number Compos'd by Mr. Handel. To which is added Twelve celebrated Marches made on several occasions by the same Author. All curiously fitted for the German Flute or Violin Fairly Engraven and carefully corected. Price 1s. 6d. London. Printed for & sold by I. Walsh in Catherine street in the Strand. Ios: Hare in Cornhill, and I: Young in St. Paul's Churchyard.

Many of the numbers have the operas indicated from which they were taken. Three unnamed items, however, Nos. 20, 28 and 33 appear in the Walsh harpsichord edition of the *Water Music*. Nos. 28 and 33 are respectively the "French Horn"

Minuet and the "Trumpet" Minuet as given in *The Lady's Banquet* mentioned above. No. 20 has not been traced in an earlier form, except as the Song "Cloe when I view thee smiling", referred to later on, and which may be dated c. 1725. The Minuet No. 20 is on page 18 of the harpsichord edition. (Thematic catalogue, Nos. 14 and 15.)

Among the volumes of contemporary manuscript copies in the King's Music Library is a volume from the Aylesford Collection (R.M.18.b.8.) the exact date of which is unknown, but it is certainly eighteenth century. This volume contains miscellaneous compositions for the harpsichord including the three numbers not hitherto identified, from *A General Collection of Minuets* mentioned above. The "Trumpet Minuet" (Thematic catalogue, Nos. 12 and 13) also appears as a "French Horn Minuet" in a manuscript collection of harpsichord lessons made in 1735 by John Barker. (British Museum. Add. MSS. 31467.)

The three minuets must have been very popular as they occur again in a late publication of Walsh's entitled: *Handel's Favourite Minuets from his Operas and Oratorios with those made for the Balls at Court, for the Harpsicord, German Flute, Violin or Guitar*, the earliest advertisement of which appears to be that in *The Public Advertiser*, December 15, 1762, but the work may have been issued before then. This collection also includes under the title "Minuet" two other movements from the *Water Music* (Thematic catalogue, P and Q) which appeared in Walsh's first edition of the orchestral parts.

Handel's popular instrumental pieces were frequently used as song tunes during the composer's life time, in many cases probably without his permission. They appeared in single sheet form as a rule without any publisher's name, and also in the song books of the period. The three minuets referred to above went through a number of issues as songs about 1720–30. The first (Thematic catalogue, Nos. 14 and 15) appeared in sheet form as "A Song to a Favourite Minuet of M^r. Handell's" and as "A New Song   A Minuet by M^r. Handell. The Words by Mr. P——s" (Phillips). It also occurs in the following collections: *The Merry Musician*, Vol. III. (Walsh 1730), *The Musical Miscellany*, Vol. V. (Watts, 1731), *The British Musical Miscellany, Vol. IV.* (Walsh, 1735), and *Calliope*, Vol. I. (Simpson,

PLATE
NO. 13

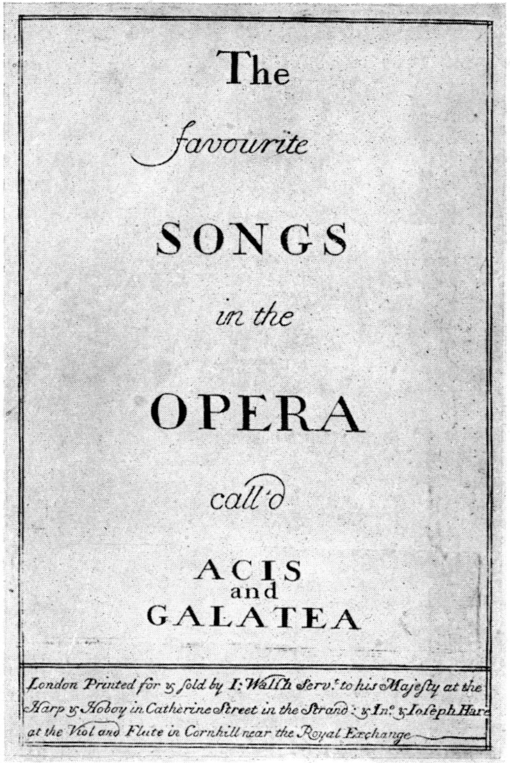
The
favourite
SONGS
in the
OPERA
call'd
ACIS
and
GALATEA
London Printed for & sold by I: Walsh Serv.t to his Majesty at the Harp & Hoboy in Catherine Street in the Strand: & Jn.o & Joseph Hare at the Viol and Flute in Cornhill near the Royal Exchange

TITLE-PAGE OF THE FIRST EDITION OF THE SONGS IN "ACIS AND GALATEA," 1722

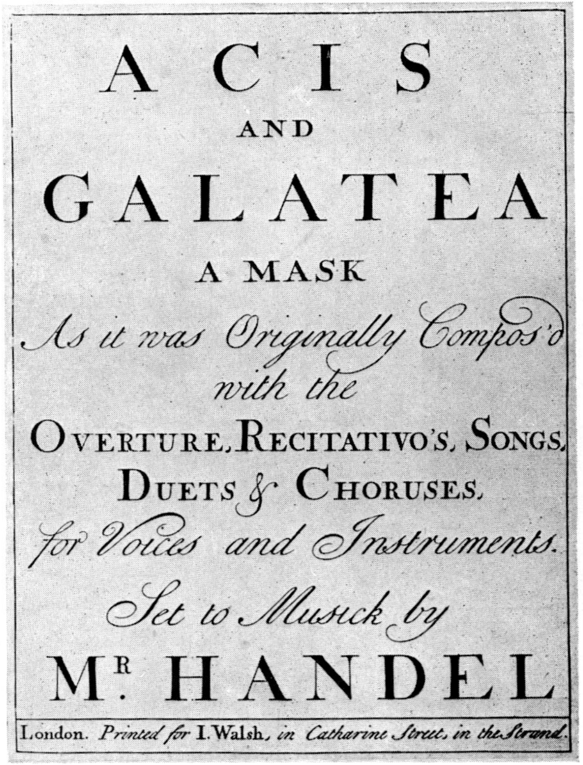
ACIS
AND
GALATEA
A MASK
As it was Originally Compos'd
with the
OVERTURE, RECITATIVO'S, SONGS,
DUETS & CHORUSES,
for Voices and Instruments.
Set to Musick by
MR. HANDEL
London. Printed for I. Walsh, in Catharine Street, in the Strand.

TITLE-PAGE OF THE FIRST COMPLETE EDITION OF "ACIS AND GALATEA," 1743

From copies in the possession of Wm. C. Smith

HANDEL'S
Celebrated WATER MUSICK
Compleat.
Set for the HARPSICORD.
To which is added,
Two favourite MINUETS,
with Variations for the Harpsicord.
By GEMINIANI.

London. Printed for I. Walsh in Catharine Street in the Strand.

Just Publish'd Compos'd by Mr Handel.

Forty two Overtures from all the Operas for the Harpsicord.
12 Organ Concerto's.
Sets of Lessons and Fugues for ye Harpsicord, with Banquet, a Collection of Dance Tunes in 8 Books for the Harpsicord.
Sonatas or Chamber Aires from all his Operas, for a German Flute or Harpsicord in 4 Vol:
12 Solos for a German Flute or Harpsicord.
L'Allegro il Penseroso in Score.
Alexander's Feast, and Dryden's Song.
Oratorios of Saul, Esther, Athalia, and Deborah.
Acis and Galatea, a Serenade.
Four Coronation Anthems.
The Queens Funeral Anthem.
The Te Deum and Jubilate.

Select Aires or Sonatas in 4 Parts for a German Flute and 2 Violins and a Bass.
12 Sonatas or Trios for 2 German Flutes &c/Bass.
The choice Songs from the late Operas for German Flutes, and French Horns in 2 Parts, 3d Coll:
12 Grand Concerto's for Violins &c. in 7 Parts.
6 Concerto's for Violins and for the Harpsicord or Organ. Opera 3d.
6 Concerto's for Violins Opera 6th.
The Celebrated Concerto in Alexander's Feast, w/ five other Concerto's in 8 Parts.
The Water Musick for French Horns in 7 Parts.
42 Overtures for Violin in 8 Parts.
20 Opera's compleat, Printed in Score.
Apollo's Feast 6 Vol: containing the Favourite Songs and Overtures in Score from all the Operas.

TITLE-PAGE OF THE FIRST COMPLETE EDITION OF THE "WATER MUSIC," FOR HARPSICHORD, c. 1743

The Celebrated
WATER MUSICK
in Seven Parts
viz.
Two FRENCH HORNS
Two VIOLINS or HOBOYS
a TENOR
and a Thorough Bass for the
HARPSICORD
or
BASS VIOLIN
Compos'd by
Mr. Handel.

Note The rest of the Works of this Author may be had where this are sold.

London. Printed for and Sold by I. Walsh Musick Printer & Instrument maker to his Majesty at the Harp & Hoboy in Catharine street in the strand. N°489

TITLE-PAGE OF THE FIRST EDITION OF THE INSTRUMENTAL PARTS OF THE "WATER MUSIC," c. 1732-3

From copies in the possession of Wm. C. Smith.

1739). The words in each case are the same and quite characteristic of the time:

> Cloe when I view thee smiling,
> Joys celestial round me move,
> Pleasing visions, care beguiling
> Guard my state and crown my love.
> To behold thee gaily shining
> Is a pleasure past defining
> Every feature charms my sight.
> But, O Heav'ns! when I'm caressing,
> Thrilling raptures never ceasing
> Fill my soul with soft delight.
>
> Oh! thou lovely dearest creature!
> Sweet enslaver of my heart,
> Beauteous master-piece of nature,
> Cause of all my joy and smart.
> In thy arms enfolded lay me,
> To dissolving bliss convey me
> Softly sooth my soul to rest;
> Gently, kindly, oh my treasure!
> Bless me, let me dye with pleasure,
> On thy panting snowy breast.

The number which appeared in *The Lady's Banquet* as "A Minuet for the French Horn" (Thematic catalogue, Nos. 6 and 7) was issued in several editions in sheet form (1720–30) as "A Song the words by Mr Kirkland set to a Trumpet Minuet":

> Phillis the lovely, the charming, the fair,
> Pitty your Strephon who loves too dispair!
> Pitty dear nymph a poor languishing swain,
> And doome not the hopes of a lover in vain.
>
> Cupid direct her and make her inclin'd,
> (Tell her) her Strephon will ever be kind.
> Tell her he languishes tell her he dyes
> And waits the Phisician that dwells in her eyes.

Crowns are but trifles to Phillis's charms,
Cupid convey her secure to my arms.
Then may blesst Strephon for ever remain,
Tho' fixt in a cottage a happy young swain.

Another arrangement of the same tune appeared in various editions and collections: *The British Musical Miscellany*, Vol. V. (Walsh, 1736) etc., as a "Song to Mr. Hendel's Trumpet Minuet" with six verses commencing: "Thyrsis afflicted with love and despair".

The same tune slightly altered was used in 1729 in *Polly* the second part of the *Beggar's Opera*, with the words "Abroad after misses most husbands will roam". *Polly* also included a number "Cheer up my lads", which was an adaptation of the two movements of the "Trumpet Minuet" from *The Lady's Banquet*. (Thematic catalogue, Nos. 12 and 13.) This minuet was previously popular as a song, "The Soldier's Call to the War, set to the French Horn Minuet," and was issued in a number of anonymous editions.

The Overture to the *Water Music* did not appear in connection with the other numbers of the work until the harpsichord edition c. 1743, but some years before that it must have been popular as an instrumental item, the orchestral parts being issued c. 1725 in a folio publication with the following title-page:

Six Overtures for Violins in all their Parts as they were perform'd at the King's Theatre in the Operas of Thesus Amadis Pastor Fido The Pastoral The Water Musick Julius Caesar the 3ᵈ. Collection. In the 1ˢᵗ. and 2ᵈ. Collection is contain'd the Overtures in Floridant. Flavius. Otho. Radamistus. Muzio Scævola. Acis & Galatea. Astartus. Crœsus. Camilla. Hydaspes. Thomyris and Rinaldo. N.B. there may be had where these are sold all the Operas in Italian and English that have been printed in England. London. Printed for and sold by I: Walsh Servant to his Majesty at the Harp & Hoboy in Catherine street in the Strand. and Ino. & Ioseph Hare at the Viol & Flute in Cornhill near the Royal Exchange.

This set of overtures was one of eleven collections issued by Walsh and John and Joseph Hare. or Walsh alone, from 1723 to 1758, and went through a number of editions. Complete sets of parts of any of these are not common, but even imperfect sets of the first issues are of the utmost rarity. It is only necessary to give here the details of the editions containing the *Water Music* Overture, which preceded the publication of the more or less complete work for a group of instruments or for the harpsichord. There is a little uncertainty as to how many parts there were to the *Water Music* in the first edition of the Third Collection of Overtures. The complete list appears to have been seven: Hautboy Solo, Violino Primo, Violino Secondo, Violino Primo Ripieno (issued in the Hautboy Secondo part of the set) Tenor, Bassoon e Violoncello, and Basso. "The Six Overtures for Violins," etc., were re-issued c. 1727, with the same title-page as the first edition, except for the substitution of *Admetus* for *The Pastoral*.

Another edition of the "Six Overtures", etc., was issued c. 1730, with a newly engraved title-page, which reads the same as that of the preceding edition down to and including "3ᵈ. Collection". After that it continues:

> N.B. Where these are sold may be had all Mr. Handel's Overtures in 7 parts also Apollo's Feast in 2 Volumes . . . London. Printed for and sold by I : Walsh . . . and Ioseph Hare, etc.

A Fourth Collection of Handel's Overtures was issued in April, 1727, and early in 1728 Walsh and Hare substituted *Elpidia*, by L. Vinci, etc., for *Rinaldo*, Handel's only work in the First Collection, which was then re-published as a collection of overtures by various composers. Handel's collections numbers two to four were then re-issued as numbers one to three, the *Water Music* Overture being in the Second Collection. From time to time these three sets were advertised as "18 Overtures of Mr. Handell's made into Concertos for Violins in Seven Parts". In December, 1730, Walsh and Hare re-published them together with a Fourth Collection consisting of *Parthenope* and other new numbers, advertising them as "Twenty-four Overtures for Violins etc., in Eight Parts". The order of the various items was changed, and the series paginated throughout, the *Water Music* appearing on page 21. In this issue the various overtures are not numbered. The instrumental parts of the *Water Music* Overture were apparently the same as in the earlier editions, but with the Violino Primo Ripieno in the Violino Terza part of the series.

Another issue c. 1734, "XXIV Overtures in Seven Parts" by Walsh alone, advertised as "a new edition", has an additional part "Violino Secondo Ripieno" for the *Water Music*. The twenty-four were issued again c. 1739 as "XXIV Overtures for Violins, etc., in Eight Parts", with "2ᵈ. Edition" on the title-page, and in this edition, and probably the previous one as well, the Overtures were numbered throughout, the *Water Music* being No. XVIII.

Walsh continued to put out further collections of Handel's "Overtures for Violins", etc., until he had published eleven separate collections, and editions of twenty-four, sixty and sixty-six. The available details of these various issues for instruments, and similar sets for the harpsichord mentioned later on, are so incomplete, and the existing copies of them differ so much one from another, that the information given here must be considered still open to amendment. The original plates subsequently passed in turn into the hands of Randall, Wright and Preston, who all went on printing from them, with modifications.

About 1760 Walsh issued "Handel's Overtures . . . for Violins in four Parts", which were only impressions from the plates of the collections in seven or eight parts.

Before leaving for the moment the question of the *Water Music* Overture, it is as well to point out that in Walsh's first edition of "Six Overtures for Violins . . . 3ᵈ. Collection" c. 1725, all of the parts except the "Tenor" contain not only the two movements of the Overture, but also the movement "Adagio e Staccato", which follows the Overture in the Walsh harpsichord edition. (Thematic catalogue, No. 3.) In the later editions by Walsh, "XXIV Overtures", etc., and "Handel's Overtures from all his Operas and Oratorios", etc., this extra number "Adagio e Staccato" was omitted, the two preceding movements being repeated, not the first only as in the first edition.

The British Museum set of parts of the Third Collection (not all of the first edition) has the "Aire" (Thematic catalogue, No. 4) added in a contemporary manuscript hand to all of the parts except the "Tenor", thus showing that the performances of the *Water Music* Overture varied from time to time.

Walsh and Joseph Hare, or Walsh alone, issued various sets of Handel's "Overtures fitted to the Harpsichord or Spinnet", which went through editions in sets and as collected series of twenty-four, sixty or sixty-six, similar to those of the instrumental parts. The Fourth Collection, issued by Walsh and Hare probably at the end of 1730, contains *Parthenope, Lotharius, Acis and Galatea, Pastor Fido, The Water Musick* and *Rinaldo*.

The first four collections of overtures were brought together in a different order and re-issued by Walsh and Hare, or Walsh alone, with the general title "XXIV Overtures fitted to the Harpsicord or Spinnet", etc. in one or two editions from 1730 onwards, the *Water Music* appearing as No. XVIII. It is paginated 64–66 at the top (the new serial pagination of the series) with the original pagination 23–25 of the Fourth Collection at the bottom.

On May 12, 1733, *The Country Journal* and also *Fog's Weekly Journal* had a most interesting advertisement:

> New Musick, this Day Published A Choice Sett of Aires, call'd Handel's Water Piece, composed in Parts for Variety of Instruments. Neatly engraven and carefully corrected and never before printed. Price 1s. 6d. . . . London: Printed for and sold by Daniel Wright next the Sun Tavern the corner of Brook-street, Holbourn.

No copy of this work, which may have preceded Walsh's edition of the instrumental parts of the *Water Music*, has been traced by the present writer. Daniel Wright, the elder, was publishing from about 1709 to 1734, and issued a number of works in imitation of editions by Walsh. It is impossible here to enter into the question of the extent to which music publishers of the period pirated each other's works. On the superficial evidence they all seemed at times more or less unscrupulous. Daniel Wright, the elder, the one with whom we are concerned, was described by Hawkins as "a man who never printed anything he did not steal", but Hawkins is not always to be relied on. It is a pity that Wright's edition of the *Water Piece* is not available for examination.

In December, 1726, Walsh and Joseph Hare put out an extremely rare work:

> Forest (or Forrest) Harmony, or the Musick of the French Horn, as it is perform'd in the Field, Park, Forest or Chace; with the proper Notes, Terms and Characters made use of in Field-Hunting. To which is added the choicest Hunting Songs, etc.

No copy of this First Book of a set is available for examination so that we do not know whether it contained Handel items. Book II, issued in June, 1733, is of importance in the history of the *Water Music*. A copy, probably incomplete, is in the British Museum (b.4.), and the title-page is as follows:

> Forrest Harmony, Book the Second: Being a Collection of the most Celebrated Aires, Minuets, and Marches; Together with several Curious Pieces out of the Water Musick, made on purpose for two French Horns, By the Greatest Masters. N.B. These Aires may be play'd on two German Flutes, two Trumpets, or two Violins &c. Price 2s. 6d. London. Printed for and Sold by Iohn Walsh, Musick-Printer, and Instrument-maker to his Majesty, at the Harp & Hoboy, in Catherine Street, in the Strand. No. 460.

The work is oblong octavo, and the Museum copy contains fifty-one pieces, but from contemporary evidence, it should have sixty or sixty-eight. Among the fifty-one pieces are three from the *Water Music*:

No. XXXVI marked "Presto", consists of two movements. (Thematic catalogue, N and O.)

No. XXXVII headed "Water Musick", consists of two movements. (Thematic catalogue, C and D.)

No. XXXIX headed "The Water Musick", is one movement. (Thematic catalogue, I.)

There may have been other extracts on the pages missing from the British Museum copy. Third and fourth volumes of *Forrest Harmony* were issued in 1736 and 1744 respectively. The third was "By the best masters" and the fourth by "Antonio Bennegger".

The title-page of Walsh's first edition of the instrumental parts of the *Water Music*, an extremely rare work, is as follows:

> The Celebrated Water Musick in Seven Parts viz. Two French Horns Two Violins or Hoboys a Tenor and a Thorough Bass for the Harpsicord or Bass Violin Compos'd by Mr: Handel. Note. The rest of the Works of this Author may be had where these are Sold. London. Printed for and Sold by I: Walsh Musick Printer & Instrument maker to his Majesty at the Harp & Hoboy in Catherine Street in the Strand. No. 489.

(See Plate No. 14.)

The work is folio, and extremely well engraved. The parts are Corno Primo, Corno Secondo, Violino e Hautboy Primo, Violino e Hautboy Secondo, Alto Viola, Violoncello e Cembalo, and Bassoon.

The date of issue is a matter of uncertainty. It has been placed as early as 1731, but the first advertisement traced in the contemporary journals is that of December 7, 1734, but it appeared earlier, as it was advertised on the Walsh edition of Handel's "VI Sonates à deux Violons . . . Second ouvrage", issued in 1733, and on the Fifth Collection of Handel's "Six Overtures For Violins", etc., advertised June 22, 1734. The Walsh serial number places it about 1733, and from all the existing evidence it is fairly safe to assume that the approximate date is 1732 or 1733, but it is uncertain whether it preceded the edition advertised by Wright, May 12, 1733. The use of the word "celebrated" is a testimony to the popularity of the work.

Walsh's issue of the instrumental parts was anything but complete as we know the work to-day, although the issue may have represented a form in which the work existed and was played at the time. It did not include the Overture, but contained nine numbered pieces, or groups of pieces, containing twenty-one movements in all. (Thematic catalogue, A-U.) Speaking of this Walsh issue, Chrysander says in Vol. 47 of the *Händel-Gesellschaft* edition: "Walsh printed only nine of the twenty pieces of which this work consists, in ten divisions. . . . What his seven instruments give is also incomplete with regard to the number of instruments. The small value of this publication is still further diminished when the musical contents of the several parts are tested. The violins and hautboys are combined in the same part, but when they part company the hautboys always have too little given them. The trumpets are not mentioned by Walsh, but some of the notes belonging to them are put into the horn parts; is is unintelligible how any rational mode of playing was possible under these circumstances. The two horns are given by him in C Major, but the fifth movement (Thematic catalogue, I) has over the first horn the presscription in German 'D Horn' and over the second, in German and English 'D Horns'. This publication of Walsh is perhaps the least reliable of all the instrumental works which that energetic but unconscientious publisher put forth in parts. Thus the original parts of Handel's score are not to be gathered from it."

Walsh issued, probably about 1750, a later edition of the parts, mainly from the original plates, but with a new title-page:

> The Celebrated Water Musick in Seven Parts viz. Two French Horns Two Violins or Hoboys a Tenor and a Thorough Bass for the Harpsicord or Violoncello Compos'd by M^r. Handel. Note. All the Works of this Author may be had where these are Sold. London. Printed for I. Walsh, in Catharine Street in the Strand.

It is a plain title-page without line border to each part. There were two issues at least of both the first and second editions of the parts.

The most complete issue of the *Water Music*, made by Walsh, was a very nicely engraved edition for the harpsichord. Although it lacked the movement which fortunately appeared as No. 4 in the instrumental parts (Thematic catalogue, H), it can be regarded as an authentic issue. The title-page reads as follows:

> Handel's Celebrated Water Musick Compleat. Set for the Harpsicord. To which is added, Two favourite Minuets, with Variations for the Harpsicord, By Geminiani. London. Printed for I. Walsh in Catharine Street in the Strand. Just Publish'd, Compos'd by M^r. Handel. Forty two Overtures from all the Operas for Harpsicord, etc..

(See Plate No. 14.)

The work is folio, paginated throughout 2–27 at the top outer corners, with additional pagination 64–66 at the top centre, and 23–25 at the bottom centre, of the pages of the Overture. This number is headed "XVIII Overture in the Water Musick". This heading of the overture and the paginations 64–66 and 23–25 are from the item as it appeared in the collection of "XXIV Overtures fitted to the Harpsicord".

The Geminiani Minuets occupy pp. 20–27, and the inclusion of them in the work is interesting in view of the well-known story about Geminiani's part in the reconciliation of Handel and George the First, in 1715.

The exact date of the first issue of the harpsichord edition is not quite certain. It has been placed by some authorities as early as 1740, but that date seems to be open to question. The earliest advertisement traced is that of February 26, 1743 (*London Daily Post*), and from other contemporary evidence this was probably about the time of publication.

In the harpsichord edition the order of pieces as given in the instrumental parts is followed, but with the new movements inserted. As already pointed out, the harpsichord edition contains the same movements (with one exception) and in the same order as in the Barrett Lennard manuscript at the Fitzwilliam Museum. The references to the Thematic Catalogue have already been given in connection with the description of the manuscript and are therefore not repeated here.

A second edition of *Handel's Celebrated Water Musick Compleat. Set for the Harpsicord*, etc., was put out by Walsh probably between 1750 and 1760. The title-page and contents are the same as in the first edition, but copies exist on rather larger paper. The pagination is the same except for the two Geminiani Minuets, which are paginated 28–35 at the top and have the original pagination 20–27 transferred to the bottom of the pages. The new pagination to the Geminiani Minuets is probably from an unidentified issue of Geminiani's works by Walsh, perhaps copied from *Pieces de Clavecin Tirees des differens Ouvrages de Mr. F. Geminiani... Londres... J. Johnson... 1743*. In this Johnson edition the two minuets which appeared with the *Water Music* have the pagination 28–35 and are engraved similarly to Walsh's publication. In a Walsh catalogue, c. 1748, he advertised "Geminiani's Lessons" which may have been the work that he copied from Johnson. The two Geminiani Minuets were also issued without publisher or place as "Menuetti con variazioni Composti per il Cembalo da F. Geminiani". This work, paginated 1–8, is finely engraved, similarly to the numbers as they appeared at the end of the Walsh harpsichord edition of the *Water Music*.

Another issue of the *Water Music* for the harpsichord was made by Walsh (or Randall) probably between the years 1760–65 (or c. 1770) with the same title-page as that of previous issues. The contents and pagination are the same as in the second edition, but the first and third pages of the overture, including the title at the commencement of the item have been re-engraved, the word "Overture" being in Roman capitals, not italics. These plates had already appeared in this form in a Walsh (or Randall) collected edition of "Handel's Overtures, from all his Operas and Oratorios", sixty-six in number, issued about 1760–65 (or c. 1770); an earlier edition having appeared probably towards the end of 1758, with the *Water Music* Overture engraved as in the first and second editions of the complete work for harpsichord.

John Simpson, a publisher who was in business from about 1734 onwards, advertised *Handel's Water Musick for the Harpsichord, 6d.* at the back of *The Delightful Pocket Companion* [1745?], *Calliope* [1746], and other works. No copy has been traced.

A Walsh publication of 1758 has the following title: "Warlike Music . . . Being a Choice Collection of Marches and Trumpet Tunes for a German Flute, Violin or Harpsicord. By Mr. Handel, St. Martini," &c. It is in four books, and includes in Book II a movement (Thematic catalogue, letter I) from the *Water Music*. The collection must not be confused with a much earlier work of Walsh entitled *Musica Bellicosa*, which was sometimes advertised as *Warlike Musick*.

It is impossible to give particulars here of the many tutors, etc., published from 1750 onwards, that contain extracts from the *Water Music*, or to record other early editions of portions of the work issued after Handel's death.

To complete this review, details must be given of the first score of the work issued by Arnold in his monumental edition of

Handel's works 1787–97, of which it formed part of sections 23 and 24, and has the following title:

> The Celebrated Water Musick In Score Composed in the Year 1716 By G. F. Handel.

It is a large folio, paginated 3–53. The work is given in full score, with varying instrumentation to the different movements, ranging from four Strings to the full complement of Trombe, Corni, Oboi, Fagotti and Strings, with figured Bass, and with occasional use of Traversi and Flauti Piccoli, to the latter of which reference has already been made.

The contents include all the movements in the editions of the instrumental parts, and for the harpsichord, in the following order (Thematic catalogue) 1, 2, 3, A, B, C, D, E, 4, 5, (4 and 5 repeated, different instruments) 6, 7, 8, 9, 6, 7, 10, 11, F, G, H, I, J, K, P, Q, R, S, T, U, L, M, N, O, 14, 15, 16, 17, 18, 19, 20, 21, 12, 13. The order of movements is apparently Arnold's own. His edition is the only early printed model which we have of the whole work, and has been accepted as such by Chrysander in Vol. 47 of the *Händel-Gesellschaft* edition, to which the reader is referred for a fuller discussion of the subject.

The authority for Arnold's instrumentation is not known. He probably had access to the Barrett Lennard copy (which in this respect, as already pointed out, does not differ very substantially from Arnold's edition), or other manuscripts may have been available in his day that have since disappeared.

If the earlier history of the performances and issues of Handel's ever popular suite is vague and uncertain, it is quite clear, as the contemporary papers testify, that from about 1734 onwards, public performances were not uncommon. To-day, the *Water Music* in one form or another is more popular than ever, and although this imperfect sketch does not pretend to tell the whole story of its publication, the bibliographical details provided should enable students and collectors to identify copies of the various editions, and to learn something about the growth and development of the work.

INDEX

This index includes all personal names and short titles of works, with references in some cases to excerpts from them. The Handel items are given as a rule without his name. For complete titles of the various editions of *Acis and Galatea, Messiah,* and the *Water Music,* and details of the performances, the respective chapters should be consulted. It has not been considered necessary to include under Handel a detailed index of Chapter II but only a brief outline with references also to biographical material elsewhere in the text. As all statements taken from other sources are fully documented a bibliography has not been provided and the authorities quoted are not included in the index.

Barret and Wamsley, 232
Barrow, singer, 190
Barthelemon, F. H., 250, 251, 254
Barthelemon, Mrs., F. H., 250, 254
Bartleman, James, 132
Bartolozzi, Francesco, 100
Bass Songs, 78–80, 86, 91
Bath, Performances of *Acis and Galatea* at, 240
Batson's Coffee-house, 62
Baumgarten, bassoonist, 245
Baumgarten (Baumgerten), K. F., 253
Bayly, Miss, singer, 193
Beard, John, 151, 158, 186, 228, 242
Beatniffe, R., 251
Beechey, Sir William (Beechy, Sir H.), 114, 140
Beggar's Opera, The, 202, 256, 278
Behold a Virgin (*Messiah*), 78, 88
Bel labbro formato (*Ottone*), 178
Bell, J., 257
Belshazzar, 70, 149, 150, 157–160
Bencraft, actor, 192
Bennegger, Antonio, 282
Bennet, Charles, 182
Berenice, 39, 126
Berselli, Matteo, 47
Bertolli (Bertoli), Francesca, 166, 167, 178, 219
Bickham's *Musical Entertainer*, 129
Bingley, Lord, 45
Binitz, von, 24
Birchall, Robert, 94
Bland and Weller, 94
Bland, A., 94
Bland, John, 94, 95, 259
Bland, Maria Theresa, 263
Bonduca, H. Purcell, 249, 255, 256
Bonet, Friedrich, 269
Bononcini, G. B., 13, 14, 46, 159, 264
Boschi, Francesca (Vanini), 28
Boschi, Giuseppe, 28, 33, 182
Boy, The, 186, 228
Boyce, William, 189, 190
Breitkopf, Johann Gottlob Immanuel, 102
Brerewood, Th., Junior, 210
Brett, singer, 189, 190
Britannia, T. A. Arne, 185
Britannia, J. F. Lampe, 173, 174
British Musical Miscellany, The, 276, 278
Broschi, Riccardo, 182
Brown, Lady, 104, 148, 155
Brown, Abraham, 234
Burlington, Juliana, Countess of, 32, 43
Burlington, Richard, Earl of, 32, 42–46
Burney, Charles, 132, 133, 148
Burney, E. F., 98
Bury St. Edmunds, Performance of *Acis and Galatea* at, 242

But lo! (*Messiah*), 72
But who may abide (*Messiah*), 71, 72, 99
Button and Whittaker, 94
Buxtehude, Dieterich, 18
Byrd, William, 253

Cadell, T., 138
Caffarelli (Gaetano Majorano), 187
Caio Fabrizio. Pasticcio, Recitatives by Handel, 178, 179, 183
Caio Fabrizio, J. A. Hasse, 183
Caldwall (Caldwal), James, 139
Calliope, 276, 286
Cambridge, Performances of *Acis and Galatea* at, 240, 251, 256
Camilla, M. A. Bononcini, 278
Campioli (Antonio Gualandi), 219
Cannons (Canons), Edgware, 43, 44, 197–202, 213, 238
Cantatas, 26
Carestini (Carestino), Giovanni, 169, 178, 179, 181, 183, 186
Carey, Henry, 173, 188, 212
Caro vieni (*Poro*), 210
Caroline, Queen, 42, 51, 52, 179, 180, 201
Caroline Elizabeth, Princess, 51, 52, 201
Carrioli, Angelo (Giovanni Carestini), 181
Carter, Miss, 243, 245
Carter, Mrs., 210, 211
Carteret, family of, 18
Carteret, John. *See* Granville, Earl
Castle, Paternoster Row, The, 235
Castle Society, London, 235, 236, 240, 245
Cato. Opera, composer unidentified, 174
Caulfield, John, 38, 69
Cease, zealots, cease to blame these heavenly lays. Poem on Messiah, 107
Celeste, Signora, 178
Cervetto, James, 252, 254, 256
Champness, singer, 242, 245, 252, 254
Chandos, James Brydges, 1st Duke of, 42, 44, 46, 141, 197–202, 208, 213, 214, 219, 235, 262
Charitable Musical Society, Dublin, The, 231
Charke, actor, 176
Cheer up my lads (*Water Music*), 278
Chiri, Signor, 245
Chloris (*Acis and Galatea*). *See* Clori
Choice of Hercules, The, 192
Christchurch, Dublin, 231
Church Music, 199
Cibber, Susannah Maria, 151, 152, 157, 167, 172, 173, 212, 213
Cipriani, C. B., 100
Clark (Clarke), M. W., 132
Clayton, Thomas, 190

Music", 41, 42, 269, 270; association with the Earl of Burlington, 42–47; visits Germany (1716–17), 44; association with the Duke of Chandos (1718–20), 42–44, 46, 197–202, 208, 209; Royal Academy of Music (1719–28), 45–49, 200, 201; visit to Dresden (1719), 46, 47; settles at Brook Street, 49, 50, 165; music-master to the daughters of George II, 51, 52, 201; composer of music for the Chapel Royal, 52, 53; The second Royal Academy (1728–33), 56, 61; goes to the Continent to obtain singers and visits his mother at Halle (1729), 53; Oxford (1733), 54, 55, 176, 186, 216, 220–222; Italian operas (1733–38), 55–61, 131, 166, 167, 175, 177–182; Ireland (1741–42), 62, 82, 83, 230; Oratorios (1743–59), 61–64, 83–86, 103–105, 145–161; letters in the press, "Messiah", etc., 105–108, 152–157; stays with Harris family (1745), 159, 160

Handel, Karl, 12

Happy we (Acis and Galatea), 223, 227, 228, 230, 231, 233, 236–239, 241, 244, 248, 256, 260, 262

Hare (Simpson and Hare), 232

Hare, John, 48, 49, 204, 205, 207, 209, 264, 278

Hare, Joseph, 48, 49, 204, 207–209, 220, 264, 275, 278, 279, 281, 282

Harmonious Blacksmith, The, 198

Harris, family of, Salisbury, 160

Harrison and Co. (James Harrison, Harrison, Cluse & Co.), *Acis and Galatea*, 96, 259–262; *Messiah*, 95–99, 101; *Handel's Songs*, 98, 261; *Rapin's History of England*, 137, 138

Harrison, Samuel, 256

Harrop, Sarah, 252

Harwood, Miss, singer, 256

Hasse, J. A., 182, 183

Hauck, Friedrich Ludwig (I. M.), 171, 192

Hawdon, Matthias, 253, 254

Hay (Hayes), violinist, 241–243, 245

Haym, Nicolò Francesco, 43

Haymarket Theatre (Little, New, Theatre Royal), 54, 147, 172–176, 188, 189, 191–193, 212–214, 237, 241, 245, 254

Haymarket Theatre, Opera House. *See* Opera House

He was despised (rejected) (Messiah), 72, 74, 78, 84, 87, 90, 264

Heads of the most illustrious persons of Great Britain. Engraven by George Vertue, Mr. Houbraken, etc., 125, 129, 137

Heath (James?), engraver, 98

Heaton, Isaac, 92

Heidegger, John James, 32, 34, 35, 43, 45, 46, 53, 54, 56, 187

Hellendaal (Hallandall), Pieter, 238

Hendel, non può mia musa, 28

Henslowe, Cecilia Maria, 192

Heptinstall, T., 263

Hercules, 149, 150–152, 156, 157, 160

Hereford Choral Society, 102

Hickes, family of, Leyton, 189

Hickford's (Great) Room, Brewer Street, 159, 175, 199, 236, 243

Hill, Aaron, 31–33

Hiller, Johann Adam, 102

Hiller, Robert, 236

Hillier, Miss, 188

Hodson, T. (Francis?), 256

Hoey, James, 235

Hogarth, William, 127, 128

Homer, 203

Hook, James, 250

Hooper, S., 244, 246

Hopkins, (Francis?), 232

Hopkinson, Cecil, 102

Houbraken, Jacob, 90, 92, 93, 113–142, 248, 257, 258

How beautiful (Messiah), 96

Howard, Samuel, 89, 91

Howkins, Rev., 92

Hudson, Robert, 243

Hudson, Thomas, 100, 113, 139, 141

Hughes, John, 203, 211

Humphreys, Samuel, 175

Hurdis, Rev. Dr., 92

Hydaspes, F. Mancini, 278

Imeneo, 83

Impara ingrata (Atalanta), 170, 186

In vain you teach him duty (Acis and Galatea), 243, 245

Incledon, Charles, 102

Interlude, An, J. E. Galliard, 188

International Inventions Exhibition, London, 1885, 170

Island Princess, The, Daniel Purcell, 188

Israel in Egypt, 170, 187

Jacobs, of Sandwich, 140

Janson, violoncellist, 249

Jennens, Charles, 41, 60, 139

Jephtha, 70

Johann Adolf, Duke of Saxe-Weissenfels, 10, 12

Johann Wilhelm, Elector Palatine, 29, 30, 40

Johnson, John, 232, 285, 286

Jones, singer, 219